T0322388

KEIR STARMER

A LIFE OF CONTRASTS

NIGEL CAWTHORNE

GIBSON SQUARE

Do as adversaries do in law
Strive mightily, but eat and drink as friends

The Taming of the Shrew, Act I, sc. 2
William Shakespeare

The publishers would like to thank the 2020 and 2021 interns for their
spirited help with reading, conducting research and interviews.

This first edition published in the UK in 2021 by Gibson Square.

ISBN: 9781783341924
email: rights@gibsonsquare.com
website: gibsonsquare.com

Papers used by Gibson Square are natural, recyclable products made from wood grown in sustainable forests; inks used are vegetable based. Manufacturing conforms to ISO 14001, and is accredited to FSC and PEFC chain of custody schemes. Colour-printing is through a certified CarbonNeutral® company that offsets its CO2 emissions.

CONTENTS

Vanity Projects

I should start by admitting that this book, the first biography of Keir Starmer, is somewhat driven by a personal interest in the man. Starmer is the MP of Holborn and St Pancras in which Bloomsbury, where I live, is located. I also do most of my work in the British Library on Euston Road, also in his constituency. In truth, I feel a bit of connection. As children we also went to the same school, Reigate Grammar School, though not at the same time. I did not know him back then, any more than I knew David Walliams, another former pupil—they both arrived years after I had left.

Back when I attended Reigate the school was state funded. I went on to study physics at University College, London. Starmer went on to do law at Leeds and an advanced degree at Oxford.

However, as 'Guido Fawkes' gleefully pointed out on order-order.com, RGS became a fee-paying school around the time Starmer was there.

In 2021, it charged upwards of £19,740 per year. With 1057 pupils, the school was doing very well with average grades of 3 As, and, of the 5000 secondary or so schools in Britain, it is ranked in the top 50 of Britain's 400 plus independent schools.

In addition, the school could also count on the Leader of the Opposition's warm support as Ambassador for the RGS Foundation in 2016, even though the Labour 2021 Manifesto calls this type of school 'the Conservatives' grammar schools vanity project'.

These fees are curious to consider. Today, a millennial with Starmer's Surrey background no longer has the automatic educational access that propelled the Leader of the Labour Party himself through his career and dropped him in Parliament running for Prime Minister. They form a considerable threshold, notwithstanding Reigate's head master being the son of a seventies glam rock-star. Over their GCSEs and Sixth Form a millennial going to RGS will need at least £138,180. Yet funds for bursaries 'are limited' RGS tells the parents of prospective pupils.

For our parents—my mother was recently widowed and the Starmers had their own worries—there were no additional financial concerns after the eleven plus. Though not a cinch, free access was still taken for granted. But a millennial in need of financial support will have to compete every year for a limited number of bursaries that may or may not cover the whole of the outlay in a school where they are the odd one out in many ways. Furthermore, those considered in need of financial assistance in 2021 are families with up to 'a total gross annual income of £85,000'. That is almost twice Britain's median income in 2020.

I very much doubt that either of our parents could have afforded to send us to RGS these days. If that millennial, possessed with the same eleven plus results as Starmer, didn't get a bursary and was from a household with Britain's median disposable income in 2020 of £29,000, their family would be left with £10,000.

Here the RGS Foundation stepped in and administered 'Changing Lives' scholarships through its 1675 Bursary Fund and one of its other initiatives was the Henry Smith Club dinner. In 2020, the donation of £1675 a year for seven years by ten club members would support a child through school with the school chipping in the balance of £2990 going forward (in the programme's first year, 2013, the formula was seven members' annual donation for one school year of one child).

In January 2017, Starmer himself was one member who fondly spoke of his memories to the Smith Club's 60 members in the East India Room at the 'splendid' East India Club. The club's president was Sir Peter Gershon, chairman of both Tate & Lyle and National Grid, who was a pupil at the school from 1958 to 1965. At that time, his parents did not have to pay any fees either and Reigate fell well within the ideal of founder Henry Smith's to create a 'free school for the poor children of the Reigate area'. Things have changed somewhat since then.

Starmer is not responsible for the fact that state funding for secondary schooling like ours was cut in the past. But it looks as if his time—and mine—was the last gasp of effortless social mobility.

Many American believe in their youth that they can become President of the United States if they apply themselves. In the UK, through Heath, Wilson, Callaghan, Thatcher, Major ran a similar vector in the twentieth century.

When I was in school, you didn't have to tell us that we were getting a very good education. In turn, we studied for it, with Starmer maybe bunking off a bit less than I did. At our school, only dances and trips needed to be paid for. And, certainly, those pupils whose parents could afford them felt exclusive.

Today, RGS's entire existence and not merely its range of extra-curricular activities is predicated on pupils who can afford her fees. No doubt that comes with its own feeling. This maybe how things go and the school is now a passport to 'world-class universities, medical school, top-10 ranked universities, Oxbridge, and elite Russell Group courses' where the eleven plus was previously good enough.

Starmer undoubtedly profited from Reigate and it set him confidently on course for his career successes. Yet—while he was lucky to be on the right side when the axe felled schools like ours—what do things look like for the Starmers of today, female and male, who also would like to become a political leader?

I write this biography in a world where the UK has suffered the highest impact on its population of Corona in Europe if not the world. Despite the first Corona lockdown, however, RGS's 2020 class headed off 'to life-changing opportunities with some of the very best results in the country, yet again!', the school's website congratulated them.

One wishes today's Reigate's pupils the best of luck as much as one can't begrudge Starmer his early stroke of luck. But what of the other pupils with aptitude in the over 4000 or so state schools in Britain not so fortunate to be well buffeted from the circumstances into which they are born? I am not sure how his and my millennial self are doing.

While baby-boomers by and large couldn't stand Starmer's predecessor Jeremy Corbyn as a 1970s throwback, the sixty seven year old was considered cool enough by Glastonbury revellers for a jubilant billing at its world-famous Pyramid Stage. He pulled in hundreds of thousands hanging on to his words and wearing the T-shirt as a Glastonbury thumbs-up. It was a political first that even Corbyn's close Parliamentary collaborator Tony Benn had never pulled off with his yearly stage homilies at the festival's Left Field since 2002.

It is unlikely that Keir Starmer will ever follow in either men's unelectable wellies if only because he himself has said, 'The idea that all politicians must now be entertainers I think is interesting, but not right'. Although Starmer once more nimbly defended Glastonbury's Chief Druid, he seemed to be quashing that hope for the Festival's bookers.

Yet Tony Blair swept into office having rolled an air of competence, guitar-playing and Cool Britannia into one nationwide personal brand. Starmer will also have to give the next generation at least some hope of progress that is more than a power point presentation of 'read-outs' if he wants to lead Labour to power.

If one looks at the 24 prime ministers since 1900, 13 were privately educated (7 of them at Eton) and 9 at selective-entrance state schools (8 of them grammar schools), which tells a story. Of the 12 prime ministers since Starmer's birth in 1962, 7 prime ministers attended state schools with selective-entrance and 5 independent schools (4 were at Eton). Comprehensive schools have yet to make an entry despite the first one being founded in 1946.

Labour leaders seem at risk of a 'learn Tory lead Labour' problem when it comes to education. Tony Blair was privately educated, (Fettes—2021, upwards from £121,770). While Jeremy Corbyn attended a 'vanity' grammar school similar to Reigate, director of strategy Seumas Milne went to one of the 'great nine' public schools (Winchester) as in fact did Starmer's left-wing guru Tony Benn (Westminster).

The fact that even Corbyn's 2019 Labour election manifesto finally dropped the party's opposition to selective tests after half a century—he voted against in the past—is still not the same as a fair secondary education for younger generations.

In 2019, Starmer himself said, 'In most walks of life, people are judged by who they are. Politics is different... people do, understand-ably, want to know who you are and what you come from, but it does feel odd.' Disarmingly off-guard, he didn't sugar-coat it when he admitted, 'I don't like it.' While one sympathises with Starmer's irritation, being a politician is hardly just another job—his parents would agree. They told him to study law.

Starmer's ambivalent response to politics brings to mind the self-deprecating words of a US senator after being voted out of office, 'I was the best candidate, but they disagreed—the bastards.'

Henry Smith, born like Starmer in Wandsworth and ostensibly a self-made professional, had the vision thing in 1675, but in 2021 there seems to be some doubt whether Starmer QC does, too. One of the things this biography aims to do is uncover brand Starmer.

It may be unfair that a conservative Etonian politician—whose secondary education weighs in at a value of over £900,000 for him and two brothers, plus a relatively modest £60,000 for his sister—merely has a political case to answer about education and not a personal one. Yet if Johnson were to abolish independent schools tomorrow, few could or would accuse him of unfairly depriving the young who are currently growing up in similar circumstances to his.

For a politician whose platform is 'change lives for the better' but whose own advancement—like Corbyn's—was the result of equitable state support, it looks and feels different. Is it merely a case of optics that the country's top jobs, including that of Leader of the Opposition, are held by a selectively educated few?

One doesn't begrudge the good fortune whereby anyone young with aptitude whatever their background, receives an appropriate education, whether private or public. Starmer's parents chose a grammar school education for him with the eleven plus, exams for which he worked very hard. Though Labour through and through, they had every opportunity to put their son in a school advocated by their party as better, which they firmly declined to do as will become clear below.

As to what is a good education, the Labour Manifesto 2021 says, 'The world's most successful education systems use more continuous assessment, which avoids "teaching for the test".' It might be true, though his parents' opting for such a method set their bright working-class son on a path of success, as it did with 8 other prime ministers. After a further quarter of a century of Labour leaders since Tony Blair, a case is starting to present itself of good education unequally provided rather than half a century of Labour losing a class-struggle to a 1970s Pink Floyd-style tune.

In the twenty-first century, the vector has changed. Three prime ministers were privately educated and only two went through state schools, and that balance will—depending on the Puritanical grade of the scalpel—at best add O-levels to the grammar-school tally at the next General Election.

Is there a new caste of mandarins that leads the country as it did in the nineteenth century when the government of Great Britain was the domain of the 'great nine' and of its nineteen prime ministers nine were Etonians?

1. The Starmers

There was a certain hope pinned to Keir Starmer, who rose from rookie MP to leader of the Labour Party to potential Prime Minister in just five-years. Not a professional politician though, he was unlike the modern variety who moved directly from university to Westminster, such as David Cameron and Nick Clegg. He had a distinguished career in the law along the way. As a young barrister he took on human rights cases, fighting against the state and big corporations, and only went into politics to fight cuts to the NHS and social care system inflicted by austerity. But he had also been Director of Public Prosecutions, which earned him a knighthood as he cornered the Tory stomping ground of Law and Order.

As someone who was not very well known, apart from being the only Labour politician journalists liked to refer to with the honorific Sir, he almost seemed too good to be true. He was a left-wing Tony Blair with right-wing credentials. Certainly, after five long years of Jeremy Corbyn leading the Labour Party from an obscure rear committee room stocked with grand ideas, one of Starmer's main attributes was that he was not another Corbyn full of untested hot-house ideas. In that sense, his election shared a lot with that of Joe Biden in the USA, whose key qual-ification was that he was not Donald Trump. Like Biden, Starmer just about managed to rope in more than fifty per cent.

Enough to win the Labour leadership election, it did raise the question who is Keir Starmer and what kind of leader—if not Prime Minister—can we expect?

Despite his elite schooling, Starmer is the first leader of the Labour Party with a genuinely working-class background since Neil Kinnock. While Starmer's predecessor, Jeremy Corbyn, was seen as a dangerous Marxist among the likes of Tony Benn, Michael Foot, Che Guevara and even Karl Marx himself, he was also irredeemably middle class. But Starmer, though dismissed as a Blairite centrist by members of Momentum—the militant rump of Labour's Corbynistas—is indeed from the left of the party. A Conservative cabinet minister described

Starmer as 'a Trot, yes, but a professional.'

Born on 2 September 1962 in the inner London borough of Southwark, Keir was brought up in the countryside near Oxted, in the depths of blue Surrey. He was the second born after his sister Anna. It's a commuter town with mock-Tudor houses and stucco fronts. In 2011, the *Daily Telegraph* listed Oxted as the twentieth richest town in Britain. Compared with Southwark, one of London's most deprived areas in the sixties, whose local socialists and communists were once a target for Oswald Mosley's blackshirts, respectability rather than poverty marked out the area.

23 Tanhouse Road, Broadham Green, near Oxted

However, his parents did not take the 7.15 to London Victoria every morning. His father, Rod, was a toolmaker who worked in the light industry sprinkled around East Surrey's stock broker belt and serving Gatwick Airport which opened in 1958. He worked in a factory every day from 8am to 5pm before coming home for his tea and going out to work again for a thirteen-hour work week. Starmer's own hours as a barrister were not too different.

Starmer's mother, Jo, short for Josephine Anne, was a nurse until she became too ill to work. They got married in Surrey in 1960 and were often hard-up.

Keir's childhood was spent in a ramshackle, pebble-dashed semi-detached with his two sisters and brother Nick. It was located in Broadham Green, on 23 Tanhouse Road, in the middle of a strip of some twenty Edwardian style houses on a country lane wedged in by fields just outside Oxted. It was a 'bit like a building site, never quite finished,' he said. According to a schoolfriend, it was a 'very joyful and very intense house'. There was no lock on ideas and you had to say what was on your mind, 'everyone had to make their points of view known'. His parents would continue to live at the family home until they died three years apart.

There was a clear absurdity and joy to the lives of the Starmers, who, unusually, kept donkeys in their garden. The Starmers were animal lovers and ran a sanctuary for donkeys who were otherwise on their way to the abattoir or some grisly fate in Spain. As each of the children left home, Starmer joked, a new donkey moved in to replace them. They also looked after rescue great danes.

As the second of four children, there was a certain pressure on Keir to grow-up quick, a pressure exacerbated by his mother's illness. His mother struggled with Still's, a rare and incurable condition which caused painful swelling of joints and organs that would have prevented Jo from having children if medication to suppress its chronic symptoms had not been discovered in the 1960s.

As a child, Keir spent long devastating nights in the hospital by her side. 'She is very ill and has been very ill for over fifty years,' he said when first standing for election in 2015. 'She's been on steroids for fifty years to deal with the disease. There have been huge and very damaging side-effects. She's been in and out of high-dependency units for as long as I can remember. It was something we grew up with. I certainly have seen the NHS from the inside for decades. 'By the time Keir would become an MP, she had been unable to speak for five years and died two weeks before his election.

His father, though a 'complicated man', was deeply committed to his mother and spent long nights away from the house in the hospital. 'He was a difficult man… he kept himself to himself, he didn't particularly like to socialise,' says Starmer, 'but he had this utter devotion and commitment to my mum… on the many occasions she was in the hospital he would stay with her the whole time, he wouldn't leave the hospital, he would sleep on any chair or whatever was available.'

Channelling his anxieties into something practical, his 'dad knew exactly the symptoms of everything that might possibly go wrong with my mum. He knew exactly what drugs or combination of drugs or injection would be needed. He stopped drinking completely just in case he ever needed to get to the hospital with her.' Applying his toolmaking skills, he modified her wheelchair after she needed one later in life so that they could continue walks in the Lake District on their holidays.

In 1975-76, Jo had a serious relapse. 'I remember one occasion when I was about thirteen or fourteen, my dad phoning me from the hospital and saying, 'I don't think your mum's going to make it. Will you tell the others?' That was tough.' Even as a young-teenager, Starmer was seeing expectations for leadership thrust upon him.

Nonetheless, Rod himself remained somewhat of a closed book to his son: 'I don't often talk about my dad', Starmer told the BBC's Desert Island Disks listeners. He was 'a dad who was obviously sort of somewhat cut off from his children', said Helena Kennedy QC who supervised Starmer's pupillage as barrister.

Starmer himself said, 'we didn't have discussions around the kitchen table. We didn't have guests very often to the house. And just because my dad was working most of the time, he didn't particularly want to socialise. And he wasn't a man for debating. His view was the view. And that was it. Again that made life difficult. Made me much more prepared, I suppose, as I grew up to countenance other views. But most of what, particularly my dad thought was not up for grabs for discussion.'

During Starmer's 2020 leadership campaign there was a furious wide-ranging debate by opponents whether Jo and Rod were sufficiently working class for their son to measure up in a Labour leadership fracas on the subject of parents. Contended Angela Rayner had told a local paper her mother 'can't read nor write, and my father hardly ever worked due to health issues, so there was precious little money and certainly no reading material in our house when I was growing up', and she had as a 16-year-old single mum been given a Manchester council flat with son Ryan, as school for her had meant larking about with friends rather than learning. In contrast, Starmer's family hailed from the rural working class which was always more genteel in appearance as they laboured in closer proximity to and supervision under the rich, as well as having, in England, nature as an ally when things got tough.

Born in 1934. Rod himself hailed from modest country-hunting stock and both his father Herbert—Rod was his youngest son—and grandfather Gus lived nearby in nearby Godstone, a twenty minute bicycle ride from their (great-)grand son Keir's home in Tanhouse Road. Broadham Green was a good place to return to for him from Wandsworth, London, when Jo and he had Anna, their first child, followed by Keir, named after Labour's first leader Keir Hardie.

Gus, Keir's great-grandfather, was still alive when Keir first went to school. Borne in 1882 in Horncastle, Lincolnshire, Gus was the oldest of eight sons to George, a Lincolnshire game keeper from a family of game keepers and beaters on large estates. George moved to Gateforth, Yorkshire, and Gus was briefly a game watcher under his father before moving to Liverpool, where he married his wife Katherine. Their son Herbert was born in 1905 in Liverpool, whereupon a year later the family moved again further south where the jobs were and Gus became game keeper at Marden Park, Caterham. The estate had just been purchased by stockbroker Walpole Greenwell, created baronet of the place shortly thereafter, and the estate, too, was but a twenty minute cycle ride from Tanhouse Road until junctions 5 and 6 of the M25 were built in 1979 when Keir was seventeen.

Gus was well-respected by the Greenwells and seemed to have been good at his job. His father George seemed to have moved in with him, as he died in Surrey, and Gus's third son Reggie, Starmer's uncle, would work for the family, too, and was employed as their land agent from 1937 to 1979.

Both Gus and Katherine, Keir's great-grandfather and great-grandmother, lived in Godstone when they both died in 1974 when Keir was twelve. Used to living off the forest, what would they have thought of their great-grandson Keir becoming, of all things, a vegetarian? 'I gave up as a matter of principle years ago on the basis that eating meat wasn't the right thing for the body and the planet', said Starmer. In an outside shed, Gus's orchard 'larder' previously contained the bucket that served as the family's toilet. But later he kept his saw horse and hung freshly killed game for the pot. There, in the 1950s, he also kept his hunting retrievers named after minerals, 'Rock, Stone, Grit etc.', and would shoot them when they were too old to hunt. Apart from retrievers for the Greenwells' hunt, Gus also bred pheasants for their friends and family shoots on the estate behind Marden's football pitch. His day job consisted of killing magpies, jays, owls, hawks, falcons, badgers, moles, rabbits and 'practically everything that walked, ran or flew' to protect their eggs from predators, except foxes as that would have been grounds for dismissal by the family.

Gus's long life occasionally bumped against the fixed lanes of the rural lower classes. After being invalided during the First World War, he was for a while the estate carter, fetching coal for 'the big house', fencing, as well as hurdles, before being employed again as game keeper. Later during the Second World War, as a sixty-year-old, he was in the Surrey Home Guard and passed his countryside knowledge on to one of his grandsons, Keir's uncle, on how to hand-kill rabbits after making rabbit squeals with your mouth, dispatch downed pheasants, shoot pigeons, as well as beating for a shoot or hunt in the park grounds.

Keir's grandfather, Gus's oldest son—also a bicycle ride away during Keir's youth and adolescence—seemed slightly less class-bound, though he never moved far away from Oxted, and was bookish. Surrounded by pets, he and his four siblings grew up in the four-room cottage whose plumbing, apart from the outside bucket loo, consisted of a 20-gallon rainwater barrel for drinking and cleaning. Even though the title was not in the peerage, the estate of the freshly minted baronet was still run along feudal lines—though Lady Greenwell demanded in vain that the porter's wife curtsey for her. During shooting days, the family of six were expected to give their cottage and table over to lunch to the guests of the Greenwells. Sir Walpole, the first baronet, had a reputation as a 'pig', but his son Sir Bernard was well-liked when he inherited the title. He tipped generously for personal services rendered, and the parents of a new-born could expect £2 and the second Lady Greenwell made a coat for the baby.

Even though Herbert went to a rural primary school, Woldingham School, in the 1910-20s, everything was as it ever was before the Second World War. When Keir's father Rod was born on Christmas morning, 1934, Sir Bernard gave Herbert 50 shillings (£2.50) to his delight.

It is not difficult to understand what it meant when Starmer was knighted by Prince Charles in 2014 and Rod wrote with hyperbole, 'at the Investiture at Buckingham Palace we were the proudest parents there; Keir was treated like a Lord and we were looked after like a Lords Mum and Dad'. Rod wrote these words in the newsletter of the Barn Theatre, Oxted, of which Ronnie Corbett was a patron in 2000, and they were in 2005 when the Duke of Kent visited. Neither of their families and ancestors had witnessed anything like what they were experiencing.

Keir's grandfather Herbert Starmer nonetheless reflected Britain's gently broadening franchise of education to the countryside when he was a boy. Apart learning how to read and write, there was recitation, composition, geography, history, and singing, and Herbert was school friends with Doris Parsons, who became his wife. Her aunt was one of the two teachers in their school and they looked after some 25-30 children each. Though the Herbert and Doris missed Surrey's free school meals from 1914, there was medical care, too, as from 1907, eleven years before the Spanish 'flu, preventative public-health inspections for weight, height, cleanliness, nits, lice and signs of infectious diseases such as whooping cough, scarlet fever, measles and diphtheria.

Like Keir's mother's family, the Bakers, the Parsons were locals. In his retirement, Herbert was a member of the Bourne Society, a vibrant local history association of Godstone and Caterham founded in the 1950s around the time when rationing ended. Herbert himself contributed the recollections of his youth to its magazine, but without any negative judgement or condemnation of others regarding his own station in life or that of his parents beyond nostalgia. In 1991, when Keir was in his first year at Leeds university, Herbert died, followed ten years later, a year before Starmer took silk, by his grandmother Doris.

If Jessica Mitford is to be believed, it was not uncommon for a game keeper's son like Rod to become a socialist. Like his father and grandfather, however, Rod had no further aspirations apart from having strong Labour views and the freedom to express them.

In 1997, Rod was briefly one of the directors of the non-profit Donkey Breed Society, devoted to driving, showing, championship shows, ploughing, religious activities, donkey awards and trekking. It didn't last long and he resigned 3 years later when he was 66. His utter passion in retirement, apart from looking after Jo, was the Southern Counties Cycling Union (1898) and the one-man Surrey Ravens Cycling Club. He didn't participate in the races, but organised, marshalled, and promoted time relays until his death in December 2018, aged 83. Ten years earlier his devotion was recognised when he was cited as one of the 'old-boys' dotted around Britain whose tireless work kept the sport alive.

Starmer's earliest memory was not of his mother but of his father and helping clean their first car, a Ford Cortina—a model first launched in Britain in the month of Keir's birth a few years earlier. Jo was to receive her first cortisone shots around this time that would keep her mobile and would allow the family to expand to four children. 'It was just incredible to have a car and I was very excited about having a car and I just remember doing that with my dad', Starmer recalled.

Despite their complicated relationship, Keir was another one of Rod's passions. Helena Kennedy QC recalled meeting Rod, then 68, at the party thrown to celebrate Starmer's appointment as QC in April 2002. 'I spoke at the event about Keir's commitment to the most disadvantaged who came before the courts. His work on death penalty cases and asylum for refugees, on gay rights and anti-racism. His work with me on battered women. His mum was there in a wheelchair and she was beaming, and his father had his arm round her and they said how proud they felt. But then Keir's dad sobbed and sobbed. Life had not always been easy, but here was their son trying to get justice for people.'

Gus, Katherine, Herbert and Doris all bobbed up and down with Britain in general and Surrey in particular. But, though Rod was clearly not adverse to change with an independent streak, it was Jo who was cut from a different cloth.

2. Collapse

Young Keir's primary school was the now defunct Merle Common First School situated a forty minute walk south from their home in Merle Common, a hamlet like Broadham Green on a country road outside of Oxted. Di Cooper, senior nurse at Musgrove Park Hospital, was in the same class and remembered him well as 'quite a serious child'. Her family kept donkeys, too, and got one from the Starmers to look after. She remembered visiting the house at Tanhouse Road, Broadham Green, just outside of Oxted, where the 'family lived very modestly'. The progress of Still's disease had by that time already deformed Jo's hands, Di recalled.

A force of nature, Jo hardly let her illness get in the way. Some twenty five years later, she still dominated her illness when one of Starmer's colleagues visited her. 'She was ruddy-cheeked and packed with energy', he said. It was only when she handed him a cup of tea that it became clear how disease had ravaged her body.

As in many rural families, Jo had a strong connection to the church and its local networks and received help from friends once it became necessary. Apart from Still's, one of her four children had a disability.

With a church friend from the left, while Keir still lived at home, she was also studying at Open University. Jo was slightly younger than Rod and theirs was one of the first generations in Britain to benefit from universal free secondary education from the age of eleven to at least fifteen.

Jo and Rod's free education was first introduced through the 1944 Education Act—judged by some 'one of the finest pieces of twentieth century legislation'—by Winston Churchill's education minister Rab Butler (Marlborough, an independent school founded in 1843 to educate the sons of Anglican clergy). The act provided for an aptitude test at the age of eleven to direct pupils with an aptitude for studying at university, such as teenage Jo, to a secondary education at Britain's grammar schools. The act also raised the compulsory school-leaving age to fifteen. These were seismic changes. Reigate Grammar School, for example, cost £4 per trimester in 1943, the year before the Act was passed. It was the kind of outlay that few beyond the middle class could afford—a boarding school was in a stratospheric, unimaginable category of its own. The Act wiped away all these fees.

Yet Jo and Rod, born in 1934 and 1939 respectively, were unlucky. Jo in particular, as she wanted to go to university which required grammar school before the Open University was founded. Within a short period of time, the Act became a victim of its own success as there were not enough grammar-school places to keep up with the increased number of pupils who sat for the eleven plus. Thus, the exam became the means to severely limit the number of pupils who got through rather than a general aptitude test broadening the number of young people receiving a grammar school education.

With war-rationing ending as late as 1954 in Britain, Clement Attlee's Labour government did not allocate sufficient funds to build enough grammar schools to keep up with the pace of demand for places generated by the 1944 Act. Nor did the Conservatives over thirteen years of government after him. Left to their own devices, grammar schools returned to pre-1944 attitudes as the increasingly difficult eleven-plus self-selected towards the middle classes and this proved to be the beginning of the carping at the schools. Their free access and claim on state funds was no longer easily parried as a reward for bright children hailing from all backgrounds in lieu of unity in the face of all the hardships endured during the war.

In 1951, a year after Jo's eleven plus, a further restriction on the booming number of pupils was introduced just before Winston Churchill returned to power. The newly styled O-levels acted as a fifteen plus entry exam in all but name to two further years of A-levels. As the age of compulsory education was only raised to sixteen in 1973 by Margaret Thatcher as education secretary, this second 'funnel' with a certificate, the GCE, never became as controversial as the eleven plus.

Both gifted and a hard-worker to the bone, Keir, however, rose to meet the expectations of his parents and passed the eleven-plus exam in 1974. He finally took the prize enshrined in the 1944 Act that had escaped Jo and Rod in 1945 and 1950 respectively.

Talking about his parents, Starmer said that they were at pains to treat the achievements of all four children equally so as not to accord their oldest son a special position in relation to his siblings. In 2020, one of them worked in the construction industry after studying mechanical engineering at Redhill Technical College and another was a social-care worker after working for a time in the NHS like Jo herself.

But his progress as the first one to sit the exam successfully and claim its opportunities was important to them. There was always Jo and Rod's— as it turned out—prophetic reminder that good fortune could not be taken for granted. Starmer would say in 2014, for example, that one of his two sisters was on a zero-hours contract.

As Jo took life with both hands, there was a certain pressure on their children not to squander their privilege: 'My parents didn't have the opportunities they would have liked, but they didn't complain about that because they thought they were part of a society where the next generation would have those opportunities', said Starmer.

About his mother Starmer spoke at times with uncharacteristic intimacy and unguarded warmth. He once recalled how around the age of seven he watched how the disease suddenly overwhelmed her and she collapsed at the Merle Common First School along the gutter on the other side of the road.

On BBC Desert Island Discs, he emphatically acknowledged that his commitment and work-ethic were inspired by his mother's own persistent fight against her disease. 'She's been a massive fighter all her life,' he said. 'She managed to walk and work for many years.' Eventually, though, she had to have her leg amputated and his father had to give up work to become her full-time carer.' Though ultimately confined to a wheelchair and unable to eat or, eventually, speak and sleep properly, she remained stoical.

'She wouldn't have moaned. If you'd asked her how she was, she'd say "fine, how are you?"', he said. Even so, the circumstances affected everyone. 'When you're in a family with someone who has got something really seriously wrong with them, a serious illness, you don't feel you can complain. You don't emote. You don't have tantrums. You have to make life better for other people so you learn to close off your own needs and emotions', observed Kennedy QC, Starmer's pupil master. The Starmer siblings knew what a world of difference their behaviour and contribution made to their parents who were battling it out with the disease.

And just as Starmer's parents shaped his dedication to success so too did they shape his politics. Talking of them, Starmer recalled: 'We didn't have much money, and they were *Guardian*-reading, Labour-leaning parents. That inevitably created an atmosphere where my thinking developed.'

With the intense atmosphere at home and at work, as well as four young children, Rod's favourite piece of music was Beethoven's pastoral sixth symphony rather than the pulsating *sturm-und-drang* of Beethoven's ninth and last symphony. In an invitingly Freudian synthesis of his youth, Starmer himself would pick the ninth's 'Ode to Joy' movement for its 'incredible noise' as a favourite piece of a music at a 2019 Desert Island Disc fundraiser in his constituency.

On BBC Desert Island Discs, Starmer also chose Jo's favourite piece of music: Jim Reeves's song 'Welcome to My World', a hit in 1963. It was released in the UK just before the time when he knew she started the steroids that allowed her to stay mobile and have children in defiance of the disease. The only US country singer to become popular in the UK at the time, Reeves's ballads resisted even the onslaught of the Beatles and were British chart successes for decades after his death in a plane crash in 1964.

Starmer remembered listening to the song together while his mother made jam sandwiches after school. As a child they attended church services together, which for his mother was an important social event. He joked that the Pineapple—a 'very dog-friendly' pub serving Thai and gluten-free food off the Kentish Town Road in his constituency—was his equivalent. Many of Starmer's other BBC Desert Island Discs choices were songs reminiscent from the time when US music offered rays of optimism and he was at his Merle Common primary school:

'The Israelites' (1969), Desmond Dekker's reggae song; and

'Bridge over Troubled Water' (1970), Simon and Garfunkel's folk rock.

3. The Right School for Keir

In the year Keir successfully passed his eleven plus exam, politics in Britain were hardly placid. Britain joined the common market and Reigate Grammar School was still publicly-funded by Surrey Council, but Britain's economy was teetering. On 1 January 1974, pummelled by the oil crisis, Ted Heath introduced restrictions that severely limited commercial use of Britain's coal-powered electricity to 3 days following miner's strikes over demands of a pay rise of 35 per cent as against a government-recommended 27.5 per cent, the then going rate of inflation. The month before, Heath had closed pubs and shut down TV broadcasts after 10:30pm in an attempt to flatten the country's electricity curve in the evening and prevent the country running out of fuel.

Reigate Grammar School was the education Keir's Labour-supporting parents most desired for him. They worked hard and so, they assumed, would their children. While there was broad criticism in the 1960s how grammar schools should improve, many children passed the eleven plus. In 1970, the exam still directed close to 800,000 pupils to 1400 selective-entrance schools, almost 1 in 4 of all pupils in secondary education in England and Wales.

The four Starmer siblings neatly reflected this 1970 split, with Keir passing the eleven plus and receiving his place at the grammar school and the other three going elsewhere. The nearest secondary school to the Starmers was Oxted School, a mixed comprehensive. It was a twelve minute cycle ride from their home in Tanhouse road and Keir's brother attended it from 1976. Had Starmer been born even a few years after 1962, the statistical chance that the eleven plus would direct him to a selective school would have precipitously dropped to 1 in 25. In 1973, when he sat the exam, the odds had already halved to 1 in 8.

Within his September 1974 grammar-school cohort, Starmer was part of a further elite. Reigate, as a 'voluntary' school, was part of a select group of 232 state schools, together with another category: 179 hybrid-independent ones receiving 'direct grants', so called as they were funded by the central government rather than local authorities. Typically, these

411 schools were ones that had existed for centuries and the rigid state-grammar school mould didn't apply to them fully. Most of the 'voluntary' schools were religious institutions, but Reigate was part of 22 'voluntary-controlled' county schools, which meant that although they hadn't been founded by the local authority they had to follow the national syllabus (it meant, for example, that pupils were prohibited from taking both physics and English) because they were fully state-funded. Together, this subgroup of 411 state-funded 'historical schools' dwarfed the 276 exclusively fee-paying independent and boarding schools that had previously generated the class of administrators required in the colonies.

Behind the buzz of state-school classrooms like Keir's, a Byzantine set of rules and funding sources covered the outgoings of these 411 hybrid institutions and, importantly, who owned what. But in practice they were run as an harmonious marriage between an independent school and a state grammar school because staffing and curriculum responsibilities were shared between the local education authority and independent board of governors. Despite the appreciable amount of funding that these schools received, parliament would lumped this sizable subset together with the 276 independent schools rather than the state grammar schools in its yearly statistical pea-soup on Britain's education.

Keir's Reigate Grammar School was a typical example. Founded in 1675, the same century as Charterhouse, the youngest of Britain's 'great nine' public schools, it started out as a school for the deserving poor funded by a property developer with no family who made his money in London. Jeremy Corbyn's grammar school, Adam's Grammar School in Newport, was similarly funded in 1656 by an unmarried merchant who made his fortune in London, and a 'voluntary' school at the time.

When Keir was twelve and began his first year at the school in 1974, still no fees were payable and Surrey County Council still funded Reigate under Butler's 1944 Education Act and ran it together with the Reigate's governors as a state boys-only school.

But the catalyst to end selective entry in the state system had already been introduced by Labour's elite. Three years after Starmer's birth, Anthony Crosland, the Labour Education Secretary in Harold Wilson's first government sent round a pithy confidential circular with a triage of the order in which the three subtypes of grammar schools were going to be terminated. Rare for a mid-ranking politician, he was famous outside of Britain and in his obituary, the *New York Times* said that he 'could have been cast as Lord Bellamy' in Upstairs Downstairs, the equivalent of Lord Grantham in the TV series that was the global Downton Abbey phenomenon of the 1970s. An avid book writer and fierce opponent of the eleven plus exam, he came from a Plymouth Brethren background and was educated at Highgate School (2021—£151,500). Originally privately funded in 1565, it was one of the 276 exclusively fee-paying schools in 1965. Crosland told his wife in confidence, 'If it's the last thing I do, I'm going to destroy every f**king grammar school in England. And Wales and Northern Ireland.'

Like Jo and Rod, grammar-school educated Labour Prime Minister Harold Wilson himself, however, strongly believed in the quality of schools that selected on the basis of the eleven plus exam (of which privately-educated Tony Benn, too, was a fierce opponent— Westminster: 2021, upward from £172,854). Wilson protected grammar schools as best he could, though less because he was utterly wedded to them and more because he wanted a credible alternative before ditching them. Like Jo and Rod, he wanted to maintain the drawbridge to social mobility and a school type that was the state-system's jewel in the crown rivalling if not beating public schools. Wilson had attended Royds Hall Grammar School in Huddersfield, which had already turned comprehensive in 1963. Although he remained loyal to the school in its reincarnation, he seemed otherwise to have been underwhelmed by what he saw. Wilson's Sixth-form school, Wirral Grammar School for Boys, of which he was also a loyal alumnus, in contrast continued to exist as a selective state school by virtue of only doing A-levels. But Crosland was the greater strategist and the slow rumble of what he had set in motion in 1965 would inexorably reap grammar schools over the next decades, come Labour or Conservative governments.

In truth, despite the loud rhetoric, during Starmer's adolescence the demise of schools with selective entry was less a question of ideology and more of a question of money in Britain, at the time the sick man of Europe plagued by massive inflation, hammered by strikes and, at times, not enough fuel in the country to keep industry going fulltime. For local authorities who funded selective schools, the move to comprehensives was not a hard one, even for Tory-dominated ones. Slashing grammar schools and lumping them together in large comprehensives made secondary schooling in their catchment area cheaper to run.

This was a broad-based pendulum swinging back. In the nineteenth century a political consensus on greater state investment had created Britain's state system of education that, through a patch-work of rules and regulations, had raised literacy from half of the population since the Civil War to virtually 100 per cent in 1900. It was followed by investment in secondary education with a time lag of up to half a century when Butler provided free education of both to all in 1944, including Jo and Rod. Up until the Act this national expenditure on Brits at the beginning of their lives was as uncontroversial as the gargantuan costs of Corona measures from 2020 that benefited the segment of Britain's population reaching the end of their life.

This was not a distant abstraction at the 23 Tanhouse household. Keir's parents had lived through it on front row seats. When Rod was eleven, Butler's act had just received the royal assent and the fees for his first year in secondary education disappeared by Parliamentary magic. Though a nurse in the NHS, Jo always wanted to go to university and had she successfully passed her eleven plus in 1950 it would have got her a free place at the high table of secondary education: a grammar school. The two of them did not need to be reminded that free education was compensation for national wartime unity. Jo saw with her very own eyes, as much Rod—a skilled toolmaker rather than a manual labourer—that over fifteen years this elite reward of their youths was being taken away by Labour and Conservative governments and not replaced.

When Margaret Thatcher was appointed as Conservative Education Secretary in 1970, she broadly held the same opinion as Harold Wilson, Jo and Rod, about the eleven plus. Even so, what Crosland had set in motion outsmarted her, too. By the time Ted Heath lost the elections four years later, in 1974, the number of grammar school pupils had plummeted by half. When Keir was eleven and Wilson came back in power on 4 March 1974, only 400,000 pupils attended 800 state-funded selective schools whereas 2,5 million students flocked to 2500 comprehensives. Jo and Rod decidedly did not agree with what was happening in Westminster. Their son—gifted to the extent that the other 1 in 4 children in England and Wales who passed the eleven plus were—would do best by being challenged in school with others who were gifted and being challenged, prevented from larking about with pals during class time on a low-grade diet.

Under Wilson Britain's economy stabilised. The Brentwood Cross Centre opened as the country's first shopping mall and the Brotherhood of Man conquered the Eurovision song contest as well as no 1 chart positions around the world with earworm 'Save Your Kisses for Me'. Only China seemed to be in trouble with Tiananmen Square.

But the short reprieve for Jo and Rod didn't last. Wilson unexpectedly resigned on 5 April, two years after his fourth election victory.

Wilson's replacement was James Callaghan (Portsmouth Northern Grammar School, closed to become part of a comprehensive the year before in 1975). He lacked Wilson's commitment to selective schooling and his newly-appointed education minister Shirley Williams (St Paul's, funded from a 1512 bequest by John Colet, unmarried Dean of St Paul's Cathedral: 2021 cost—£181,209) promptly instructed all local authorities to submit plans for schooling without an eleven plus in November that year.

4. Tanhouse Road

For Jo and Rod there was a highly stressful edge to reading about all this educational turbulence reported in the *Guardian* and elsewhere. Would Reigate would remain public and free? If not, how would they ever afford keeping Keir at the school? Labour through and through, they did not think that a comprehensive was a fairer school for Keir and did what it took to keep him at the school. If they had said in September 1973 that they wanted Keir to have the education they themselves were promised if you won the eleven plus prize, and that this was, in a kind of way, their and their child's right—irrespective of the circumstances of their parents—it would have been hard to disagree with them.

This was by no means the only anxiety they had to deal with at this time. There was the full blast of Still's disease on Jo. It was during Keir's first few years at Reigate that his mother was having one of her most serious relapses and his father didn't think she would make it and rang Keir to tell the others. Determined, she pulled through in the end with her children, who all shared in their parent's agony.

Yet even under Wilson, the axe began falling closer and closer to Keir's classroom, raising the pressure at 23 Tanhouse Road. The subset of grammar schools funded through the government's 'direct grant' system had almost immediately been told their financial support was being terminated, as set out in Crosland's 1965 memo. On 30 July 1975, Wilson's education minister Reg Prentice (Whitgift, an independent boarding school first funded by the Archbishop of Canterbury in 1596: 2021—£138,180) gave its 179 schools a stark choice: join the state system—which 51 mostly Catholic ones did—or return to independence; the choice of the remainder, with the closure of some. The end of the direct grant from central government mirrored the demise of the locally-funded grammar schools. In 1981, the year of Keir's graduation, there were 170,000 pupils left at local grammar schools in England and Wales left of the original 800,000, and the special group of 35,000 at 'voluntary' schools had shrunk to a third of what it was in his first year at Reigate.

This must have been nail-biting for Jo and Rod after the joy of Wilson's re-election had faded. Already during Keir's first year at Reigate, in the same 1974 circular that terminated the direct grant, Labour also dealt a body blow to the school when Prentice issued a notice warning 'voluntary-aided' schools like RGS that they 'cannot expect to continue to receive the substantial financial aid which their schools enjoy through being maintained by the local education authority'. Without an Act of parliament this was no more than a paper tiger, but the writing was on the wall. It was a race against time whether they would be able to keep Keir at the school.

It was another stroke of bad fortune for Jo and Rod that in Tory-blue Surrey the anti-eleven plus movement had been set in motion under Margaret Thatcher as Education Minister. She had made the exam a political issue and polarised parents across Britain into pro- and anti-groups regardless of their political colour. In Surrey, in particular, there was a very vocal and effective group founded in 1970 called Surrey's Stop the Eleven Plus (STEP) chipping away at schools like Reigate. The group organised meetings, petitions, car-stickers, surgery visits, and demonstrations with bus-loads of pupils at county hall. Even in this reliably conservative county—the 1973 local elections returned almost 70 per cent the seats to the Tories, one of their worst results, ever—this had an effect on Surrey's educational policies.

In 1972, the year before Keir sat his eleven plus and when Margaret Thatcher was in the middle of her term as Education Secretary, the county was busily creating comprehensives and closing grammar schools. Oxted School, the comprehensive for local children 10 minutes from 23 Tanhouse Road, was a good example. It had been founded as a grammar school in 1923, segregated for boys and girls. But in 1972, Surrey, with the approval of Margaret Thatcher, terminated the entrance exams to 22 of the county's state schools and reorganised all of them in the same year as comprehensives, including Oxted.

Labour peer Charles (Lord) Garnsworthy (Wellington School: 2021—from £112,980) discussed Oxted County School that year in the House of Lords and pointed that it was the solidly Tory-led Surrey council that had decided to repurpose all 22 and that this was not a Labour concoction. Garnsworthy's reason for touching on Oxted grammar school in his speech concerned Thatcher's refusal to wave through conversion of just one of the 22 Surrey schools that Surrey was refounding as comprehensives—a grammar school for girls. In 1978, the school Thatcher's refusal had 'saved' would be closed anyway by newly elected Surrey county council: the Conservatives won 68 council seats this time, with 2 going to Labour. This 1977 result was up from 46 and 12 respectively in 1973.

Even though he had got in just in time, the tide finally lapped at Keir's school at the end of his first year when Surrey County Council and Reigate's school governors appeared at logger heads. In May 1975, Surrey council announced that its plans for comprehensive education had been approved by Thatcher's successor, Labour's Reg Prentice. From September 1975, selection for all secondary schools in Reigate, Britain's sixteenth richest town, and its less-fashionable neighbour Redhill, would cease.

It didn't take long for the parents of Reigate's boys at the school like Keir to be up in arms about the decisions Surrey council had publicly announced, and the school's governors took action throughout 1975. In particularly, they followed closely what was happening in Twickenham at a voluntary-aided secondary school Hampton Grammar School (founded in 1557 by a rich eponymous London brewer). As only the second voluntary-aided school in the country it had closed and reopened as a fee paying Hampton School on 1 September 1975 (2021—£148,890) further to Prentice's pressure on voluntary schools.

The *Times* reported that Hampton headmaster and governors had put together a very considerable £157,000 from its richer parents and controlled a fairly considerable £60,000 a year from its historical endowment anyway. Upon reopening as a private school, it had success-fully started with about the same number of fee-paying pupils (810) as it had state-funded ones in the year before.

The sparring between Surrey county and Keir's school continued. As a voluntary-controlled institution, Reigate's governors had the largest set of powers within its quaint corner of Britain's education, given their influence over hiring staff and the like. But as a 'voluntary-controlled' county school—as opposed to an 'voluntary-aided' institution such as Hampton—the buildings' deeds were held by the local authority and the school didn't have its own foundation income like Hampton. Still, the governors rather than Surrey did have the upper hand in the headmaster's day-to-day running, setting the dates of school terms and holidays, and the daily schedule for the school's pupils, and, crucially, determining the rules of admission and whether this would happen through the eleven plus, or not.

Surrey county funded all of Keir's school's running costs, buildings, equipment and furniture as required by Butler's 1944 Act but did have the decisive influence that comes with ownership and paying the bills. The refusal of the governors to drop the eleven plus exam in Keir's second year meant that the county could now appeal to the Education Minister that the county stop its financial aid to the school under a 'cease to maintain' order and force the governors' hand.

Keir still had three years to go to complete his O-levels. How were Jo and Rod going to afford these fees?

5. Scraping Through

All the uncertainty inevitably ran deep chills down the spines of all parents who were not well off. They received a school notice that from September 1976—Keir's second year at the school—the grammar school would become an independent fee paying school like Hampton School. There was a difference. Hampton School intentionally dropped the word 'Grammar' from its name to signal clearly its novel private status to parents as it drew in 810 boys in the first year of complete independence. Reigate held on to the word in a seamless connection with the past, appealing to the goodwill of parents with boys in the school and in Surrey at large.

It galvanised the dreaded question in the minds of Jo and Rod where they would get the money from to continue Keir at the school, as it did for those other parents who couldn't afford the new fees either.

Again the saga reached the House of Lords where the school was used on 7 October 1976 as an illustration by Labour whip Phyllis, Baroness Stedman (Peterborough County Grammar School for Girls, closed to become a comprehensive in 1976 after which it closed in 1982), of the government's 'sympathetic hearing' of the concerns of parents like the ones of Reigate. Surrey County, she reassured the Lords, 'are paying the fees of existing pupils on their O-level courses, now aged 12 to 15, and of those pupils who had already entered the Sixth form before the school ceased to be maintained'. The pressure of the parents had worked and it must have brought relief at 23 Tanhouse Road that the state would continue to pay for Keir's education after it had gone independent.

Yet that was it. Surrey county 'refused to pay for the pupils aged 16 who wished to stay on for further sixth form work', Stedman said. Jo and Rod would still have to start paying fees for Keir's Sixth form. It was money they just didn't have.

Reigate's parents of pupils doing their O-levels like Keir remained up in arms and thought the government should pick up payment for their boys' Reigate's Sixth-form as well. Indignantly, they directly appealed to

Labour Education Secretary Shirley Williams arguing that Surrey county was acting unreasonably and asking her to force the council to pay for their children's fees.

Williams, however, wrote flatly back to Reigate's parents that she saw 'no need to intervene; there is nothing wrong with a break in a child's education at 16, provided they have been through their O-level courses and provided that, if they have started their A-level courses, they are allowed to finish them.'

Baroness Stedman recited this in the Autumn of 1976 in the House of Lords and the issue dragged on after Reigate became a fee paying school in September, during which month Williams was appointed by Callaghan on the 10th. Before Williams' pushback against the parents' demands Reigate's parent's request had been dealt with by Wilson's newly appointed education minister Fred Mulley (Warwick School, an independent boarding school founded by Aethelflaed, daughter of Alfred the Great, in 914, 2021—upwards from £97,440).

Keir could stay, for now. He was spared the humiliating experience of, after having completed two years at Reigate, being sent down together with the other boys whose parents couldn't afford to pay RGS's newly-introduced fees and having to move from year nine to O-levels at a comprehensive—Surrey had closed all local grammar schools by now—in the area such as nearby Oxted School.

But what about his Sixth-form? Jo and Rod were determined to continue Keir at Reigate despite its 1976 privatisation. The school had the same name and it was now once again exclusive and independent as they as children had always known it before 1944, once again sealed off with towering fees.mj

The financial roller-coaster ride for the Labour-supporting Starmers now moved to his A-levels. Jo and Rod's rising anxiety was, now where? Keir had enrolled just in time at Reigate and, once again saved by the bell, was now benefiting for another three years from Surrey, due to its generosity in applying further state funds to him from the Conservative and affluent county. Keir would at least have his grammar-school O-levels like Harold Wilson at Royds Hall Grammar School in Huddersfield. But how could Jo and Rod afford Reigate's Sixth Form fees that neither Surrey nor Williams were minded to pay for? Where would be Keir's Wirral Grammar School for Boys—the school to which Wilson had moved to do his Sixth-form?

Philanthropy was not high on the list of priorities of new independents. Focused on financial survival now that state funding was cut off, voluntary state schools that became independent were decidedly parsimonious, giving a cold shoulder to pupils whose parents couldn't afford to pay. Reigate was now swept up in the exclusive maelstrom that affected Britain's richer regions, pockets where parents could afford independent fees. Of the 232 'aided' schools, nine were like Hampton and Reigate in a position to go private and did: Emanuel School, Godolphin and Latymer School, Colfe's Grammar School, Batley Grammar School, Royal Grammar School Guildford, William Perkins's School, Wolverhampton Grammar School, Kirkham Grammar School Preston, King Edward VI Grammar School Southampton.

It would, paradoxically, lead to an enormous boost of funds into these new public schools. In 1975, the year before Reigate, Hampton school had not only started with 810 fee-paying pupils without any problem, but also money to spare. With its new funds and release from government oversight, Hampton ploughed money into a Sixth-form common room, a large library, a music department, science and language laboratories and squash courts. It was a case of survival of the fittest. They were now in direct competition with the 276 exclusively fee-paying schools and the additional 119 independent schools that had lost their direct grants from the central government after 1974.

Though a charity, it did mean that in its first years Hampton School spared little money on bursaries for boys with no purchasing power. Hampton offered 14 bursaries in total, and each one covered half of the £620 fees on average, the *Times* reported in 1975. Thus, Hampton set aside £4095 of its £502,110 in 1975 fees income, or 0.8 per cent. This £4095 amounted to a 7 per cent share of the additional annual income of £60,000 the school received in 1975 from four centuries of endowments to what had started out in 1557 as a 'free scoole'. Having been free for a long period during the 20th century, in 2021 Hampton had 50 free places out of a total of 1243.

In 1981, sixteen years after Crosland's corrosive 1965 circular the net result was that there were some 160 schools with access through eleven plus entrance exams left of an original 1700, while the number of exclusively fee-paying schools had almost doubled to at least 406, mainly situated in the richest parts of England and Wales. The number of comprehensives stood at 3398 taking in 93 per cent of pupils, including Keir's siblings, most of them in the poorer parts of England and Wales. This had rocked up from a mere 8 per cent at Keir's birth in 1962. As with his mother Jo, a few years difference in Keir's birthdate made an enormous difference. Though he was lucky in the way that she was not—in 1950, when she was eleven, the exam he passed had slammed the emergency brakes on broad access to grammar schools.

Though the first comprehensives dated back to at least 1946, and despite the lion share it took of England and Wales's young talent from 1970, in 2021, the non-selective and much advanced school by local labour and conservatives authorities—the latter more often than not in areas where they had a clear majority of local councillors—had yet to produce a prime minister after being in existence for 75 years. Two Scottish primary schools had managed to do that as David Lloyd George and Ramsay MacDonald both attended small parish schools. In fact, in 1975 the grammar school in Glasgow that had educated two prime ministers also joined Britain's fee-paying schools (2021—£84,336). Corbyn's 'voluntary' grammar school in Newport lasted until the 1980s, when the school's catchment area had become affluent enough and it also finally made the leap RGS had made and it was rechristened as fee-paying Haberdasher's Adams. The parents of a 2021 Corbyn needed £85,008 to launch their child on the same path as the former Labour Leader.

No matter what privately-educated Labour populists said about educating Britain's social classes who couldn't afford private schools, or the Surrey Conservative apparatchiks did, working-class Jo and Rod were not going to let the prize that had been dangled in front of their own eyes as teenagers slip through their fingers for Keir.

6. Keir's History Boys

While Keir was doing his O-levels at Reigate and Surrey continued to pay the fees for another three years, the Starmers certainly couldn't be accused of being narrow-minded or inverted snobs who only valued countryside or working-class culture. They specifically wanted him to have a different education from the one they had themselves, common to their working-class background.

Jo may have liked more popular tunes against Rod's love of classical music, but when Keir turned out to have an aptitude for music as well as studying they expected him to develop both equally. Even if he was on track to become the first Starmer to go to university, there was no need to hot-house their children, nor to protect Keir from a curriculum tailored to his needs. They worked hard and took it for granted that in his spare time their second child would apply himself too.

Thus Keir played the recorder, flute, piano and learned the violin with classmate Quentin Cook, aka DJ and musician Fatboy Slim who would enter the *Guinness Book of Records* with the most number of hits under different names. In some ways similar to law, music is a fascinating mix of rigidity and creativity. Clear patterns, scales and arpeggios to follow, but the opportunity to reorder them, flatten a note or change the tempo to create a different sound.

Starmer even became an exhibitioner at the Guildhall School of Music on Saturdays until the age of 18. It required a routine of practising his scales at home, though deep down if it had been up to him he would have skived off to play football instead as an adolescent, dreaming of becoming a professional. From Oxted there were direct trains to Victoria and London, taking about an hour each way. With a mother who fought Still's every inch of the way, it would have been very selfish to resist his parents. His teenage room, however, was plastered with posters of footballers and Blondie's rock lead Debbie Harry, and instead he played football twice week where on the pitch he recalled he was 'the sort of driving force of midfield'.

Keir was lucky here, too, to enjoy the new school's freedom outside the state system. RGS's 1976 reincarnation as an independent school meant that it, too, invested in music teaching as a rising number of fee-paying parents 'expected their children to learn an instrument'. In 1978, when Keir was sixteen and in year eleven, the last year Surrey paid for his place at the independent, the diminutive, vivacious and formidable Deirdre Hicks (Cheltenham Ladies College) was appointed by RGS to teach woodwind instruments. The following year the music department was headed by Oxford organ scholar (later Professor) Bob Marsh who, as RGS's director of music, appointed the very well-connected Rosemary Few to teach piano and clarinet and began the musical-theatre performances at the school in which David Walliams would debut only a few years later as Queen Henrietta Maria in an opera by Richard Rodney Bennett.

Keir was one of Hicks's first flute students and she coached him for a performance as soloist of the Suite No. 2 in B Minor by J.S. Bach in St Martin's Church in nearby Dorking. Though its level of difficulty is mostly intermediate, it contains the popular 'Badinerie' which required quite advanced musical skills to perform well. He acquitted himself 'expertly' in the words of Marsh.

Did yet another career choice beckon? Starmer recalled, however, 'I realised at the age of 17-18 that the other people at the Guildhall were hugely talented, whereas I just practised hard.'

Either way, he couldn't have made his parents happier. While Rod may have been inscrutable at home and even appeared difficult to his son and brooked no argument, he did not hide his pride in Keir at work. One of Rod's fellow tool-workers, a Marxist rather than a Labour supporter, recalled from their days together in the factory, 'I remember the joy on the proud father's face at Keir's birth, and for every one of his many educational and legal successes.'

Did all this application make Starmer a dull boy? Although now he may appear on television as a polished, jacket and tie-wearing moderate, and, like a Ford Cortina, totally reliable, technically quite good but a little boring, his school friends at the time begged to differ. The almost obsessive focus that he shared with his father when it came to school work and musical practice—coming through as somewhat wooden seriousness today—none of it was visible in his school days.

He was gregarious, personable and deeply passionate like his mother.

Years later Starmer described his school days as both 'challenge and laughter'. It was the latter part that his school friends saw in the musician and unfulfilled footballer. Though near the top of his class, he was not by any means the clever class swot. One friend, Andrew Cooper, recalling their school years, said, 'He was very popular. He was often the one at the centre of the crowd telling the jokes.'

As a young man on the brink of puberty, Starmer did not hesitate to debate loudly with his more Conservative-leaning classmates, grabbing with both hands the freedom to contradict and discuss that he had outside of 23 Tanhouse Road. At Reigate, another one of his close school friends was Andrew Sullivan, today a conservative columnist in the US. Like Wilson, Thatcher, Jo and Rod, Sullivan was passionate about grammar schools, so much so that he roused heated opposition among his school peers—even if everyone was aware that the opportunities Reigate was giving them came free of charge to their parents.

Sullivan was the one who, by his own admission, was ridiculed as 'the clever swot'. As a contemporary of the year above noted, in a large group of quite quick boys there were always those 'in a standard deviation beyond the rest of us. And Andrew was one of those, if not in the same league as the boy who learnt all the logarithm tables, just for the fun of it.'

Though both were similar in physical stature, Keir, from rural Broadham Green, was described by Sullivan as a 'bruiser, with a Bay City Rollers haircut, a fat tie, an unbuttoned collar and an air of real roughness.' The culture in the 1970s was tougher than it was in 2021, replete with teenage 'feet-staring box-room' rebels as a contemporary put it. 'Our class was known for being full of "hard lads",' Sullivan said. At the end of their O-levels 'one of our collective band of brothers burnt our then prefab classroom to the ground in a final act of defiance'.

Sullivan deeply loved the school and has since said that Reigate Grammar School gave him 'the superb education my parents could not have afforded'.

Though their politics were vastly different their friendship was shaped by a love of tit-for-tat argument, and intellectual challenge. Already Keir was not one to form friendships on the basis of political congruence but rather on the basis of a willingness to discuss. In East Surrey, where there was not much unemployment, this was less controversial than it might be in a place with swathes of urban deprivation such as inner-city Liverpool.

Looking back, Starmer said that, though they shared a similar rural background and had parents with little money, 'We fought over everything, Andrew and I. Politics, religion. You name it.'

Sullivan became an unrepentant Thatcherite after she took over as Tory leader in 1975, while Starmer was, in the words of another school friend, 'left, left, left.' The pair would begin their debates on the bus from Godstone travelling to the extremely affluent Reigate area from their corners of Surrey, Sullivan from East-Grinstead, and they did not end until they returned home on the bus at the end of the day.

The bitter economic problems of the country at the time was reflected in their furious debates. 'It was the political 1970s as well—the era of Thatcher and the Anti-Nazi League, and a polarisation that tore the country apart,' said Sullivan. 'I was on the hard Thatcherite right and a Catholic'. Of Starmer he said, 'my main sparring partner in my class also got on the 410 bus every morning, a little after I did, and he was just as passionate as I was—but very left-wing… he was a wild man, not the carefully controlled person you see today.'

And already Starmer had his penchant as MP for cornering the Prime Minister with irrefutable evidence and a need for air-tight argument (even if about decorating the grace-and-favour apartment in No 11). 'We spent almost every minute of the bus trip yelling at each other about politics,' said Sullivan. 'He'd bring books to lecture me; he scoured every piece of news to prove me wrong; heck, he even showed up at Christian Union meetings—he was an atheist, I recall—to take my arguments apart. And the feeling was mutual.'

Starmer must have found Sullivan infuriatingly slippery like Johnson, given that Johnson was far less of a workaholic than Sullivan or he himself. A bus-rage contemporary of theirs, one year above, recalled what Starmer was up against with Sullivan. He 'was impossible to beat in an argument. And I'm talking aged 11 and 12'. He recalled pre-Thatcher debates with Sullivan 'about Heath and Wilson, electricity black-outs, and entry into the Common Market. He was persistent, quick-witted, and so stubbornly right wing I can remember at least three occasions when my head exploded.'

The arguments on the bus gave the future Director of Public Prosecutions also his first brush with the law. 'Some mornings, the police showed up to complain about the general rabble on the 410 bus,' Sullivan recalled. 'And I'm pretty sure we made life a living hell for some teachers, their weaknesses immediately detected by the male teenage mind and then mercilessly exploited. All for a laugh, of course. And the laughs made us one.'

The two adversaries were necessarily close though. In morning assembly they were lined up in strict alphabetical order and Sullivan was directly behind Starmer for seven years.

While 'Keir was rowdy, laddish, wild,' another classmate recalled, Sullivan had his eye firmly on Oxbridge. 'Apart from publishing scurrilous tracts and refusing to be a prefect,' Sullivan said he was a good boy. He attended the Christian Union. Although today famously gay, he was not out then though while in February 1978, Tom Robinson's 'Glad to Be Gay' was practically the school anthem, one of their Reigate contemporaries said, who also recalled that the school 'remains the gayest place I've been outside of Heaven nightclub', the London club opened in December 1979 by Jeremy Norman, chairman of Burke's Peerage. Another pupil 'was flamboyantly gay and once paraded through the grounds in a green satin dress and full makeup', said another classmate, while a high-camp though not necessarily gay row of pupils demanded to know in English class, 'Hamlet, he's queer isn't he, Sir?'

Other members of Starmer's close gang were Andrew Cooper, later Baron Cooper of Windrush, Director of Strategy for the David Cameron-Nick Clegg public-school tandem of 2010-2016 and Paul Vickers, RAF pilot and later defence correspondent for the BBC and *Private Eye*. 'He was very charismatic and humorous. And he was very popular,' said Cooper of Starmer. 'In the queue for the bus, he would be the person leading the conversation and telling the jokes.'

Sullivan compared Reigate Grammar to the school portrayed in

Alan Bennett's The History Boys (2004) and set in the 1980s. 'We were all quite clever—but, because this was a state school, we also had a real mix of backgrounds—at least as far as Surrey went,' he said.

Last year at RGS, Sixth-form, The Duke of Edinburgh's Award Float,
Lord Mayor's Show November 1980

The group shared a mordant quick-witted sense of humour, old jokes and private nicknames. 'We too had a charismatic and somewhat strange history teacher who lived in a converted cricket pavilion,' said Sullivan. 'Our ears too were full of the Vapors, the Jam and New Order; each morning we would compete to see who could remember the most Monty Python jokes.'

7. Reigate's Ballance

Yet it would be a mistake to think that the close pack of Keir's 'history boys' cramming for Britain's best universities were anywhere near the school's mainstream. As in The History Boys, teaching staff's looked up to the 276 public schools, with its teachers clad in billowing gowns and effortless Oxbridge access.

At Reigate, rugby was Headmaster Howard Ballance's dominant obsession, followed at some distance by cricket, hockey, basketball and the army. Starmer, who managed to play football twice religiously from the age of ten despite his hectic schedule, was decidedly in the unfashionable sports set, apart from his pop haircut. Football at the school was a sixties novelty and a contemporary of Keir's said about those who played 'it, 'you know, if this had been a football school, we'd have been the main men'.

'It was always about rugby', conceded Sullivan, but the year he and Starmer arrived 'we sent more children from modest backgrounds to Oxbridge than any other state school in the country'.

In actual fact, Sullivan's memory regarding modest backgrounds only lightly skimmed the surface of what the boys saw and what was happening behind the scenes at Reigate. Starmer, Sullivan, Cooper and 'less-famous names', in the words of Sullivan, were being deployed in a set of chess moves by adults that were quite different from Bennett's play.

The central character in Keir's History Boys' drama was Headmaster Ballance, who was a unique and brilliant character and somewhat of a chancer. Without him Reigate's grammar school would have fallen on its sword in 1974 and vanished, amalgamated into a co-ed comprehensive like Wilson's O-level Royds Hall Grammar School. But also, if Ballance had succeeded the way he had mapped it out in detail, it would have meant Starmer, Cooper, Sullivan and Vickers ending up outside the school gates and all four would have gone to local comprehensives or Catholic school in the case of Sullivan. They had no idea that this was the case, nor did their parents.

Before his appointment at Reigate, Ballance—a grammar-school boy from Birmingham, where he was a keen rugby and hockey player, who thereafter read history at Magdalen College, Oxford—was Headmaster at Alderman Newton's Boys' School in Leicester. He moved to Reigate just in the nick of time. Leicester, whose city council flip-flopped between Conservative and Labour control, decided that the school would turn comprehensive, which it did in 1969, the year after Ballance moved on to Reigate Grammar School in Tory-blue Surrey.

Ballance was quite unlike Headmaster 'Felix' in Bennett's The History Boys. By coincidence, Alan Bennett was born on 9 May in the same year as Starmer's father, 1934—and five years before Jo. He got into one of Leeds's four grammar schools, Leeds Modern School, and was there from 1946-1951 after sitting his eleven plus successfully in 1945. Unlike Jo, however, he was there right at the beginning of Butler's educational reform. A butcher's son, he was exactly the pupil the 1944 Act had in mind when it abolished school-fees within the year of its royal assent. Leeds as a city had ample educational capacity with at least four grammar schools to absorb more pupils whereas the secondary education available in a rural district such as East Surrey had more conservative educational reserves.

Unlike Keir's Headmaster Ballance, Bennett's real-life headmaster 'Felix' would have taken it for granted in 1946 that state-grammar schools were fixtures in Britain's educational system, even if the number of hopefuls were growing by leaps and bounds and something had to be done to stem the influx. By the time Bennett went on to study history at Oxford in 1951, entry exams to the Leeds Modern School had grown two days as opposed to one day in his time in order to allocate the by now scarce places in relation to the number of people who sat for it. Schools with eleven plus access were themselves, however, part of the immutable order of education in Britain.

Ballance both foresaw what was coming and spotted a great opportunity when he was appointed at Reigate in 1968, tweedy with a mop of regimented hair. He understood perfectly well that the debate about comprehensives was purely about money. When he first started out as a teacher, he had taught at three independent schools. Yet for his own career advancement to headmaster he had left independent education and joined the state system that had originally schooled him. Ballance was ambitious and knew from first-hand experience the principles of private education, where he worked first, and the state system where he made his promotions. He saw that Reigate Grammar School had the barebones of an independent school with its long history and location in an area with a plentiful supply of well-heeled families.

Howard Ballance 1968

What he intended to do with the school, he shared with very few others behind closed doors in 1968. He had been an artillery captain during the Second World War and was trained by the army to keep need-to-know marching orders close to his chest. In fact, he used to keeping his teachers standing in his presence and praised or castigated them seated from behind his desk like an army officer.

On 23rd May 1971, four years before Surrey council's announcement regarding the end of selective education in Reigate and Redhill, he made his first charge to close the doors to free students such as Keir, Sullivan and Cooper and welcome fee-paying pupils. That day, Education Secretary Margaret Thatcher was sent a letter that informed her of the grammar school's 'discontinuance' as a 'voluntary' school. Reigate Grammar School, she was told, was to close its free doors in summer 1973 to reopen to fee paying pupils 'on the new basis that September'.

As in the alternative-history theme of The History Boys, Reigate's 1971 letter raised the question what would have happened to the future boys from rural Broadham Green and East-Grinstead without their self-possessed reliance on the school? It would have changed history. Keir,

Sullivan, Cooper and Vickers might have taken the eleven plus but there would have been no grammar school to go to.

Ballance, a practical man used to logistics, had lined up all ducks for a seamless exit of RGS from the state system and to continue it wholly-funded through fees as a private enterprise from September 1973. His master stroke would even have beaten Hampton School by two years with his dauntless front to Thatcher.

The letter by the chairman of the governors, a local Justice of the Peace and chartered surveyor, even contained a bold outright bargain to Thatcher for the premises as 'provisional financial arrangements have been made with the Crusader Insurance Company'. This local Reigate life insurance company was to buy 'the existing school properties, buildings and equipment, not already vested in the Foundation'. Its portfolio already included one of Reigate's schools as Crusader owned The Priory, the stately pile at the heart of Reigate village, which it rented out since 1948 to Surrey council as the premises for the county's comprehensive middle school for pupils age 8 to 12.

How then did this very capable, driven army officer, teacher and Magdalen alumnus come to fail in 1971, and how was it that Margaret Thatcher saved Keir, Sullivan, Cooper and Vickers' futures from Ballance's campaign?

8. Rescued by Margaret Thatcher

None of Reigate's parents were aware of what was going on behind the scenes, nor the boys themselves. Not even the teachers knew. At the time of the letter Keir was 8 and in year, and in the summer of 1973 when Ballance planned to end of the school's free education, Keir was with all his might getting ready to sit his eleven plus which Jo and Rod deeply hoped would get him into Reigate. If the school had not been free, he would have to go to one of the comprehensives in the area such as nearby Oxted School. And so would, Andrew Sullivan, whose parents couldn't afford private fees either. Even Andrew Cooper, who sat his eleven plus a year earlier than Keir, would have missed getting into Reigate for free. Crusader's hardnosed involvement, the confrontational tone of the letter to Thatcher, and the commercial last of Ballance's campaign required solid financial underpinnings like Hampton School, which had received no state funding and collected fees from all boys.

Fortunately for Keir, Sullivan, Cooper and the further band of history boys who had to rely on the county paying for their fees, Ballance's 1971 swashbuckling ambush of Margaret Thatcher was ballsy rather than well-conceived. It may even have caused some rolling of eyes among civil servants at the department. The letter claimed a right that neither existed in the letter nor spirit of the law. Rab Butler's provisions of the 1944 Education Act were at least as elegantly crafted as Anthony Crosland's time bomb under selective education. Once a school had opted in 'voluntarily' as a maintained school, there was no way back. Not for the school at any rate. In fact, the local authority could not withdraw from this marriage either. Even the Secretary of State could not unilaterally change such a union, except by having Parliament repeal the Act.

Thatcher's department sat on the letter for two years until June 1973—the summer when Keir was diligently preparing for his eleven plus in September to gain his much hoped-for place at Reigate and two months before Ballance intended to start charging fees—before they sent their response. During this lull created by Margaret Thatcher, Keir, Sullivan, Cooper, and Vickers floated into the school after their exams, as East Surrey boys had for three decades since 1944.

Whitehall's tardy response followed a 'windfall' £20 million for Thatcher in the 1973 Spring budget that allowed her to invite each local authority in Britain 'to submit its one most urgent project' in rationalising local schooling. She approved 51 of 113 school proposals from around the country, though not Surrey County's 'one most urgent' request to replace Reigate Grammar School with Reigate College: the county wanted to open a co-ed Sixth-form school only for pupils, like Harold Wilson's Wirral Grammar School for Boys. Only after having given Surrey the thumbs-down on its application for a share in the windfall funds, the department finally wrote to the school itself.

In nebulous, vote-saving, but nonetheless damning jargon, Reigate's chairman was informed by the department that his letter was 'inappropriate'. He was politely instructed to talk to the county council's education authority, who were sent a copy of Thatcher's response. This was a legal point. With the 1971 letter Ballance had put the department on notice that there was disagreement between the school and the local authority and the marriage had ended. Under these circumstances, the Education Secretary could permit the county to stop funding a school of 'voluntary' plumage—though only Surrey County Council could set this in motion through an official petition.

It was now game on for Reigate. But Ballance had pluckily been preparing for this fight well in advance. From his first day at the school in 1968, he began transforming everything with a view to creating an independent school like the ones where he had first worked as a young teacher. He needed a school with a great reputation in order to get Reigate's parents to start paying fees and wean them off expecting a right to something that had been free until then. Jo and Rod knew this all right, but Ballance needed parents who could afford fees to be in no doubt about the exceptional educational quality over and above the state system that Reigate was offering. Unlike his predecessor Headmaster Howard, Ballance didn't try to make the school invisible and float on unseen below the county's radar but started beating the school's drum loudly wherever he could in order to promote it continuously.

'Hardly a week went by without the *Surrey Mirror* featuring a photo of a Grammar School boy publicising his latest achievement', was one teacher's testimony of Ballance as the new broom at the school. The steady stream of news may even have galvanised Jo and Rod's desire that Keir go to Reigate.

In a military, pragmatic fashion, Ballance also reorganised pupils according to class through virtual public-school style houses 'resembling the sorting hat in Harry Potter' as one contemporary of Starmer's history boys described it. As in boarding schools, 'The posh Reigate kids were always put in the same house, along with the kids of what we'd now call "pushy parents", keen for their kids to be in the house that won everything ("Doods"). The village kids, the waifs and strays, the handful of single-parent kids were shuffled off into the losers' house ("Underhill"). Redhill kids were congregated somewhere else and so on', he recalled. There was a mathematical symmetry as to fee-paying potential: yes, no, some of it. He had ample experience on which he could draw, at his last independent school, King's Worcester, Ballance was Housemaster.

Howard Ballance at King's Worcester

It affected Keir too. Thus, in his third year, September 1976, the first year of independence, Sullivan, Cook and Vickers were in 3KU, Kinnersley and Underhill, the house for village kids (or 'losers' according to some of the students' point of view, or 'hard lads' in Sullivan's), while Keir and Cooper were in its classroom next door. They had a school reputation as a result of Ballance's sorting hat, and then there was the fact that they were gathered in the temporary prefab classroom. But rather than feel singled-out or picked on (though one of them clearly had other ideas when he set fire to their teaching shed after their GCEs), they got on famously among themselves. 'When our class was going to be broken up in the third year, we protested so loudly that the headmaster decided to keep us together, despite our reputation', recalled Sullivan. He wrote the petition for this, which was signed by all of 3KU.

Without knowing it, the history boys had also signed up to Ballance's sustained branding campaign. Although they were quite surprised that he agreed, there was no loss for the headmaster in keeping 3KU and its hard elements contained in one place, separated from the second year of fee-paying pupils who were being admitted to the school grounds, and while elsewhere the school continued redressing itself in a more commercial Brideshead Revisited style appropriate to a private school, and he continued pushing for better exam results, better amenities, and more rugby. Sullivan called the boys the 'collective band of brothers', and no doubt he was not the only one who saw it that way. There was an advantage in putting the school's history boys on autopilot.

Ballance was a shrewd judge of character and tolerated extraordinary lapses in discipline and eccentricities at the school as long as the pupil was brilliant enough. One of them, the school's top English, languages and art student from the year below the history boys, the last year to be admitted for free, missed every single morning assembly because he preferred to go for a walk on his own and built the colosseum from library books without repercussions. Another time when he happened to arrive on time for assembly because his watch was fast, he got a rapturous applause from all the boys. Not even the pupil's swearing on 'an industrial scale' phased Ballance, who was rewarded for his patience when the boy won a national essay prize.

9. Latin and Reigate College

The news that the free school was in peril first became public knowledge in 1975, Keir's first year. Jo and Rod and Reigate's other parents and its boys knew for certain that the school's existence was in the balance and things were looking desperate.

Behind the scenes Surrey had been busy since 1973. Margaret Thatcher might not have allocated windfall funds to replace Reigate, but the election of Wilson in February 1974 gave Surrey a new opportunity to get rid of Ballance who had gone over their heads to Whitehall. The county proposed to reorganise as comprehensives the four secondary schools in Reigate and Redhill that were under its immediate control, unlike Reigate. The two church schools had their own governors, like Reigate, but these deferred to Surrey's wishes and only Ballance was now holding out against the county.

In May, the *Times* reported that Wilson's Education Secretary Reg Prentice approved the proposals over which Surrey and the churches had banded together: the county had petitioned him and he permitted the county to withdraw its funding from the grammar school—or its 'closing' as Surrey put it about ominously in the press for Keir and his parents to read—in view of the fact that Ballance refused the offer to amalgamate his school into one co-ed comprehensive with the Reigate County School for Girls. He approved Surrey's plans to cease eleven plus entry in Reigate and Redhill and to cease funding the school.

As Keir was finishing his second year, the pandemonium among parents and a wave of protests to keep the school funded and free crashed over the council. The parents had no idea what had taken place under Margaret Thatcher, and, in a conciliatory move, the council's education committee voted on what to do to make the outcry go away. Rather than abruptly withdraw state-funds from the boys and create an army of angry parents who couldn't afford fees to take their sons elsewhere, Surrey County Council voted for a staggered withdrawal from Reigate. It would pay for any pupil currently in the school so that he could either continue his O-levels for free, or his A-levels if he was already in the Sixth-form, the *Surrey Mirror* reported. Elegantly, it also voted to include the O-levels of pupils in the year after Keir as they had already sat their eleven plus but were strictly speaking not yet part of the school.

On behalf of the furious parents of pupils who were in similar position to Keir, however, the school governors demanded more funding as they wanted the county also to pay for the continuation of their sons doing O-levels to the Sixth-form. But Surrey declined. Reigate's parents felt deeply aggrieved about this negative response and hence their passionate appeal for more money to the new Education Secretary (Prentice, Mulley and Williams, in rapid succession). But all the department had to do was pull up the school's 1971 case file and revisit Thatcher's refusal to grant money to Surrey for their advice to the now Education Secretary Shirley Williams.

To Surrey the parents of O-level boys like Keir, Cooper and Sullivan must have looked like NIMBYs. Nationally, the Conservative press roared against Shirley Williams for taking 'choice' away from parents with regards to selective education for children. But in the case of Reigate, parents' choice in favour of a grammar-school education for their sons rather than at a comprehensive was being fully supported by the county for the 1970-1975 cohort. Every pupil could stay—regardless of whether parents could afford the fees or the fact that Reigate was going to charge fees as an independent school.

It was only continuation into RGS's Sixth-form where Surrey drew the line. But not because it abandoned the Conservative educational creed of giving parents like Jo and Rod and others the choice between going comprehensive or not—and certainly not in order to do Shirley William's bidding. The reason was because they had the new, dedicated Sixth-form-only school that was as exclusive as Reigate's Sixth-form. Keir, Sullivan, Cooper and Vickers could simply continue their education there without having to go comprehensive. Wilson had done so himself for his A-levels by going to a dedicated Sixth-form school.

This new school was called Reigate College and it was a lavish, well-funded co-ed Sixth-form college that opened its doors in 1976, the same year as the new RGS, in a park with a pleasant Edwardian building, 500 yards away from the grammar school. By its very nature it was selective and not an act of card-waving egalitarianism of the Tories in Surrey—

pupil selection merely happened at fifteen plus through the GCE. Surrey assumed that local parents like Jo and Rod, who couldn't afford private fees, would simply transfer their sons after his O-levels to the new Sixth-form college, which was, apart from free, a more modern take on the grammar school, and, in their considered opinion, of an equally high if not higher standard. Surrey didn't do things by half. In 2008, Ofsted graded the school as 'outstanding'.

Reigate College, Sixth-form only, founded 1976—where Norman Cook went

Keir's teachers at Reigate—who were still in the habit of calling each other by their surname—saw all this turmoil from the inside sidelines and watched what Ballance was instituting at the school with fascination as he juggled parents, the boys, and Surrey. One of them recalled that Reigate was 'a county grammar school and took boys from every social background, many of whom had little parental support'. 'Sometimes, of course, boys got themselves into trouble', and Ballance would have to 'ring the police before they charged him and use all a headmaster's influence'.

So they liked what they saw as the upshot of Ballance's fee-paying phoenix was that 'exam results and Oxbridge entry improved dramatically, the orchestra and drama productions improved, and the school began to build its reputation in rugby. Students began to achieve DoE gold awards', the teacher wrote about the fact that pupils were behaving less anarchically and rough around the edges.

Keir was there on the cusp of this change. When he was fourteen, Reigate's first year of independence, he first volunteered for the DoE Awards in a mental health hospital that would care for one of his grand-fathers, and for his last challenge was 'wandering around Dartmoor in a small team, with just a compass and a map in the pouring rain, frantically trying to find our way', he said in Parliament in 2021 on the prince's death.

But what this teacher most rated was Ballance's admirable vim in leading 'the school back to independence'. Under Ballance's leadership the school started acting like an independent from 1968 and from 1976 it spent money on private-school extras after its release from state oversight.

Though he preferred the RGS with fee-paying pupils, the teacher who wrote these words was warmly remembered by all pupils, state- or privately-funded. One pupil from a poor background said fondly that he was 'the "'toff"', who managed to convince me that even kids from the backstreets could aspire to a university education'. Nicknamed 'Aubs', the teacher's name was Aubrey Scrase, Reigate's popular Latin teacher from 1955-1995 and an ambassador for the school's Foundation until his death in 2015. At RGS's commemoration in 2016, the year Starmer is mentioned as RGS Foundation Ambassador, some 200 nostalgic former pupils were in attendance, but it was the newly elected MP who gave the final toast to all present by citing Aubs's favoured expression 'Silly sod'.

10. Oxbridge and Modest Backgrounds

'Somehow, the governors and headmaster scraped enough money together to go independent', wrote Sullivan in 2013—the 1975 need-to-know version for the parents and boys. By that year all the parents and pupils were in the know of the 'closure' and up in arms fighting for Ballance, and so were the teachers—some of whom were taken into greater confidence. But Keir, Cooper, Sullivan and Vickers were actually lucky in another way, too, that Ballance's daring what-if failed in 1971. Their headmaster's ignorance of the law hid a crucial keystone for success that would have made all the difference that year.

For all his grit and inventiveness, even in 1975 Ballance's eagle eye still failed to grasp the legal implications of Reigate being a maintained school of the 'voluntary-aided' variety, and that, quite separate from the misapplied letter addressed to Margaret Thatcher, this was of huge financial significance for the health of the school's balance sheet. It was to drive RGS from a likely failure after a short independent existence to success within the first year of charging fees—with sufficient extra cash to invest in its future even though RGS lacked an endowment like Hampton School or parents who created one in the year of it leaving the state system.

It was for the Charity Commission to point out to Ballance what the fine-print meant. Doing the sums in 1975, Ballance saw that a school with shareholders was not going to work profitably and that state support of some sort was needed to make ends meet. He told Aubs that charitable status of the new RGS brought 'certain advantages'—not having to pay tax would avoid yearly losses. Ballance yielded to the inevitable and when the Charity Commission came round to discuss his application they gave him the good news.

The charity inspector explained that, once the local authority withdrew its control under Butler's 1944 Act, the original charitable school would revive from suspended animation. This charitable school was a different animal from the new for-profit business that had been mooted to Thatcher in 1971. As the school was once again a charity, 'all buildings built or purchased for school use, should have been made over to the school governors'. Whatever had been paid for by Surrey County Council, the charity was the owner. In one fell swoop Ballance no longer needed to buy the land, existing buildings and attendant property.

All the financial anxiety, the ups and downs that had been spread amongst parents and the boys at the school was based on Ballance's misperception. Had Ballance realised this charitable loophole in 1971, things would have ended up very different for the history boys. With good legal advice in 1971, he would not have needed to get Crusader Life Insurance on board to buy and lease the buildings and to budget for annual rent. It would have hastened RGS's fee-paying existence by half a decade and history would have placed Keir, Sullivan, Cooper and Vickers on the wrong side of Reigate's fee-paying doors.

As it was, the commercial flavour of his 1971 venture had not made Ballance many friends at the county offices. Surrey may have been a Tory stronghold but—like Margaret Thatcher at a national level—its main interest was the education of the county's children like Keir rather than fall in with audacious for-profit plans of the headmaster of a school in their catchment area. While the county itself must have had a good professional understanding of what the statutory word 'voluntary' meant, it was trying hard to make the uppity Ballance trip up and bleed Keir's school to death.

Until the penny dropped for Ballance, the Conservative-led council were in tough negotiations with him about selling all the school property to his proposed new business at as a high price as it could get. They threw everything at him that they could find. The county even applied for planning permission to build garages on some of the land to put up the value and wished for 'the school gradually to die', as Starmer's favourite teacher Aubs wrote disapprovingly of Surrey's attempts to kill Ballance's plans.

Starmer's 2021 Labour Manifesto speaks of 'a recruitment and retention crisis' amongst teachers. It was this in particular that preyed on Surrey in the case of the independence plans of Keir's school. It saw Ballance as a new employer cannibalising the county's pool of experienced state-school teachers, a pool that the county had created over thirty years of state funding. The county was at pains to thwart

Ballance on this point and Surrey took painstaking care to interview each one of the 70 or so teachers and to offer them jobs elsewhere. It had many vacancies at Reigate College to fill and there were the other schools in the county.

Ballance had the last laugh, however. Acquiring all the school property for free had transformed RGS's finances. Released from state controls, Ballance offered Reigate's staff a modest 5 per cent raise knowing Surrey wasn't in a position to match it given Wilson's public-sector pay-cap in 1975 and Callaghan's in 1976, the one that would lead to the Winter of Discontent. With the going rate of inflation at 17 per cent in 1976, Ballance's offer was not generous but not insignificant either given the economic disaster sirens going off in the press.

For Keir, seeing all this from 3KU's prefab classroom, it meant that there was hardly any disruption in 1976, and nor was there for Sullivan, Cooper and Vickers. Only a few teachers left the school as a result of Surrey's campaign to peel them away. Those who did disagreed with parents like Jo and Rod who kept their boys at the school. They were mostly young teachers who went elsewhere 'on principle as they did not wish to work in a private school', wrote Aubs. With the deeds of the school buildings transferred to RGS, no rent to pay in the budget, the charitable tax advantages, uninterrupted quality of teaching as the school's experienced staff stayed put, enormous local goodwill created because of thrilled parents of the boys that he carried on the school, Ballance's poker game had turned into a full hand.

How much of a windfall the parents' ceaseless protests about closure to Surrey generated was reported in the *Surrey Mirror*. The council voted the school a lump sum of £289,000 in order to 'protect the futures of all pupils entering the Grammar School up to 1975', so that the last free students took their GCEs in 1979. This fixed gift from the county kicked Ballance's school off with a secure starting capital. Hampton School had, by contrast, relied entirely on the out of pockets fees for boys—a figure that could go up as well as down per year. Ballance didn't have to worry about it. His income could only go up from year one.

Though the legal machinery and the principle behind the school had changed beyond recognition, Keir's third year at the school in 3KU progressed as if nothing had changed. With no need for Crusader to purchase the school buildings at an end, all Ballance had needed was an overdraft, duly agreed by the local Barclays branch. Given the original involvement of a blue-chip company like Crusader in 1971, and all the good financial news about tax, rent and staff, it clearly wasn't a hard decision for the bank.

Invisibly, Ballance had executed an athletic summersault with the school. Over a period of eight years, using smoke and mirrors, charm and steely determination, making progress on a need-to-know basis, he had brought the staff, governors and parents on board to together make the leap he had planned all along. In the know by 1975, Aubs even grumbled somewhat about the 'lowish' amount Surrey used to budget per pupil as opposed to fees the independent school could expect, as well as, like parents in the position of Jo and Rod, the fact that it declined to pay for A-levels up to 1981.

With the buildings under his belt, there wasn't much scraping that Ballance needed to do in 1976. At liberty to plot his own financial course, he doubled the size of the fee-paying first year to add to the £289,000 and also added a fee-paying third form alongside 3KU—another reason not to mix up the new boys with the 'hard lads' in the following year and keep them contained in separate worlds—in addition to fee-paying girls in the Sixth form. Hampton School had not added girls, but again Ballance was pragmatic in adapting his objective of survival of the school. With the wall of Surrey funds behind him, Ballance was printing money. Later a junior school would be added, which siphoned of pupils from existing independent junior schools in the area and which thereafter would start to struggle. In 1977, Keir's fourth year at the school in 4KU, a year before his A-levels, RGS's finances looked very healthy indeed. Ballance poured Aubs a glass of sherry to celebrate.

In as much as he wouldn't let his staff disappear to Reigate College, Ballance wasn't going let his bright history boys disappear to Surrey's new Reigate College either. They were precious, carefully nurtured publicity cargo and worth many times over the loss of income from their A-level fees: Starmer, Cooper, Sullivan and the band of brothers burnished Ballance formidable reputation. He wasn't going to let Reigate College put that feather in their cap. As Sullivan said, Reigate 'sent more children from modest backgrounds to Oxbridge than any other state school in the country'. If Ballance could achieve such results with pupils from a 'hard' background in a state school, what might he not achieve with fee-paying pupils none of whom had, by definition, 'little parental support'?

Indeed one of Sullivan and Cook's fellow 3KU pupils, next to Keir's class, remembered that the headmaster almost bent over backwards to accommodate their financial needs. He recalled that RGS 'was very generous towards those going up to the sixth form, all manner of bursaries and scholarships / half scholarships and mixtures of them were used. Howard Ballance was very keen to ensure we had the opportunity to stay on'. Though this wasn't presented as blanket grants, but rather as means-tested ones, to grandfather the Surrey-funded boys from poor backgrounds was also a reward to all these boys' parents for continuing to support Reigate in its transition out of the state system and not take them for their A-levels to Reigate College instead.

Sullivan confirmed in 2020, 'Yes all of us were grandfathered in until we left. Neither Keir's parents nor mine paid a cent. If we'd been forced to pay we would have both been forced to leave.'

In 1982, the year after Keir left, a staff picture shows Ballance in his last year at the new RGS. He, too, was a new man. Seated in the middle of his staff, black-shoed among a sea of the seventy or so sensible brown pairs, blue-striped stockinged, with a broad confident grin, tailored suit and surprisingly black hair for a man of 63, he looked like a *jeune premier*. He had won his fourteen year battle to create an independent school, though he still would preferred to have started that in 1971.

Under Margaret Thatcher as prime minister grammar schools never made a return, though 'assisted places' were introduced at 296 independent schools such as RGS—a reincarnation of the 1945 'direct grant' system abolished in 1975 by Wilson. In the 1990-1991 school year when Thatcher left office, a total of 99 RGS places were free to students, or 11 per cent of the of 870 pupils who would have attended for free in Keir's time. Over eighteen consecutive years of power, the conservatives did not reintroduce selective secondary education either.

Wilson's question 'what do we have instead?' befuddled governments for a half century as they muddled through with marginal changes up to the present day. It is not that governments were hamstrung. In 2020, the Conservatives, with other parties in agreement, opened the spending spigot with £400bn in state aid to combat Corona, an infectious disease that mostly affects the elderly in Britain who make up 15 per cent of the population. It was the will to spend on secondary education that crumpled in the cash-strapped 1970s.

Howard Ballance, RGS 1982

Would Starmer, Sullivan and Cooper be the people they are today if history had placed them outside Reigate Grammar School from 1971 and in one of the comprehensives instead? By their choices, Starmer's working-class *Guardian*-reading parents who wanted the best for their children didn't think so.

Starmer's 2021 Labour Manifesto addressed the parents of working-class Keirs and eager-to-learn Jos and Rods of today—in 1970 a section of the parents of 1 in 4 pupils in England and Wales opting for selective education for their children—only where it said that Labour won't 'force schools to become academies'. Four years earlier, Corbyn's Shadow Education Secretary Angela Rayner, who thought little of school attendance as a sixteen year old, also thought selective education a 'vanity project' as an adult twenty years later on Radio Four's Today Programme.

11. Technicolor Dreamcoat

Despite Keir's overflowing school roster as a history boy, Saturday music lessons, and bi-weekly football, there was yet more time for other things in his busy schedule. Together with Cook—whose life already revolved like a tornado around music, collecting records, playing drums in a band called Disque-Attack age sixteen, DJ-ing and running a club night in Dorking— Starmer played as a band member with Cook in his spare time. As did another contemporary who recalled a dank basement called 'slugs' where Cook would meet.

Both Cook, the youngest of three siblings, and Keir were teased mercilessly about their names in their first year at Reigate. Cook said about 'Quentin', his name during adolescence, 'Two years after I was born, Quentin Crisp became the most famous homosexual in the world and people at school seemed to think that was really funny.' Keir also thought his parents had made a poor aspirational choice with his own decidedly unposh first name. Looking up the Gaelic meaning would lead to 'dusky; dark-haired, swarthy', and nor would being called after a Labour leader and miner have been an obvious winner. 'When I was at school, at about thirteen, I thought, why couldn't they have called me Dave or Pete?', Starmer recalled—'Rod', his father's name and his own second name, was not his favourite either. 'It's one of those names you hate when you're growing up but you grow to appreciate later', said Starmer of 'Keir'.

Blond-haired Cook was tall at six foot compared to the others, and, in a violent mix of 1960s and 70s styles, had a Beatles 'pudding-basin haircut' and 'enormous flares'. His coif was in an entirely different order from Keir's. Sullivan accused Starmer's haircut of having been a Bay-City rollers mullet, though judging by a 1980 Duke of Edinburgh Award photo in his bursary-funded Sixth-form—Starmer flute in hand—it later calmed down to a George Best meets Kevin Keegan canopy.

Unlike the others, Cook was genuinely middle class. He lived in Reigate proper and not in one of the humble villages that surrounded it, and so he was considered 'posh' by the others. His mother was a teacher and his father was a consultant who was to receive an MBE for introducing bottle banks in the UK.

Though a pupil with the typical background Ballance was after, Cook was 'anarchic', like his dress sense, in the words of Sullivan, and all round gunning for a position as rebel. He despised being middle class and desperately wanted to be working class like his grandparents and his band of brothers in 3KU. He hated every inch of Reigate and recalled, 'It's a suburban hell. Everything revolves around garden centres. It probably has the highest incidence of garden centres per capita in the country.' Cook's self-confessed big hope was to go on the dole after school. His grandad had been a window cleaner and had, Cook reckoned at the time, 'a much happier attitude' to life. None of this can have registered favourably with Ballance and Cook was stuck with the losers, hard lads, and villagers in the Kinnersley and Underhill prefab house.

Unlike Starmer, Cook had an avenue to rebellion—music. Punk had just arrived and he coloured his hair over the weekends with poster paints, washing it out on Sunday night, to look 'horrible and dangerous' despite the fact that his sister's witheringly suggested that it was 'more like Julie Andrews than Johnny Rotten'.

Starmer's band-friend also set up punk magazine *Peroxide*, a 'fanzine for modern youth' with photos, edgy lay-out, and no fewer than 28 stapled pages in black and red. Interviewing Spizz, Wreckless Eric, Captain Sensible, Goth-band Wasted Youth, but also the Surrey-based new wave band The Vapors—loved by Reigate's history boys—and other underground illuminati, it aimed to put Reigate on the map with 'Bristol, Brighton, Manchester etc'. Despite claiming sales of 700 copies, it folded after the second issue in 1980, but not before Cook had made contact with Adam Ant, who had considerable street cred as having headlined at Rotten's Sex Pistols' first concert and orbited Malcolm McLaren and Vivienne Westwood.

At home with the history boys, Cook disliked the rising damp of public-school attitudes that pervaded Reigate under Ballance. 'He once changed out of school uniform into jeans and t-shirt in the back of a car and drove past the school gates shouting, "I hate you fucking Grammar School boys!",' an artsy contemporary recalled. He disliked the middle-class's feeling of being better than others, Cook said. A rebel, he was not going to take the influx of fee-paying boys lying down. His teacher recalled that as a pupil Cook was 'instrumental in keeping 3KU together' as Sullivan wrote the petition to the headmaster that pushed against an open door.

In contrast to the working class history boys, middle-class Cook would promptly escape from the school after his O-levels, proving that his placement in 3KU was an accurate assessment as far as paying fees was concerned. He had no qualms about going to Reigate College. Changing his name from Quentin to Norman, presumably the name of his grandfather, Cook did his A-Levels at Surrey's new Sixth-form school, then in its fifth year of its existence. The College was considered 'cooler' than the rugby-obsessed grammar school and its rigid traditions. As, in fact, it was. There, Cook met musician Paul Heaton who went on to found the Housemartins, taking Cook on as bassist on their first tour and scoring massive world hits with R&B pop songs such as 'Caravan of Love' within a year.

In their first year of A-levels at RGS, now as bursary students, Keir and Cooper themselves on the other hand turned their hands to three performances of Andrew Lloyd Webber's Joseph and the Amazing Technicolor Dreamcoat. Bob Marsh, RGS's new music director, had just been appointed and this was his first production.

It had an ambitiously large on-stage cast, with girls in the female roles, a first, and it was supported by a more modest seven-man orchestra, including Keir on flute. Cooper had also been roped in off-stage and assisted the musical's stage manager, an English teacher at RGS. The lead was fourteen-year-old Nicholas Mansfield. He had arrived five years earlier as an RGS music scholar at the newly-minted private school and would go on to a professional career in opera.

In seven years, Jo and Rod's determination that Keir made the most of his aptitude for studying, but Reigate and Guildhall shaped Starmer's music with that eclectic depth and informed personal preference that musicians have. On the classical side it ranged from Beethoven's revolutionary symphonies to Shostakovich's ironic Stalinist pieces, caring deeply who was performing them. His favourite musician was conductor-pianist Daniel Barenboim and it was Starmer's sophisticated musical background that put him in a rarefied category on the world stage. In an interview in 2020 with the *Guardian*, Barenboim mentioned Starmer in the same breadth as Angela Merkel, whose love of music was 'the great exception' among politicians.

East Surrey Socialism

While Keir's history boys were soaking up knowledge, punk and Andrew Lloyd Webber, paroxysms of hatred convulsed the country. 'We Are the Champions' by Queen was released in October 1977, yet Britain was anything but. Inflation and strikes battered the UK as the Winter of Discontent drew closer. Wilson was able to persuade the unions to agree to national pay restraints of between Even within the unions, dissent brewed as the large minority of women and non-traditional members mistrusted their all-male traditional leadership. Starmer also got organised.

While Sullivan swung behind Thatcher and tortured 3KU's woke history boys, Starmer and Cooper made their own choices. As the Headmaster kept 3KU banded together for year four, they plotted to set up the East Surrey Labour Party Young Socialists to do more than have endless bus-trip debates duelling with their Thatcherite peer and instead go out to convince the world. Even as their school was being privatised, they aimed to think on a large political canvas that would benefit the rest of the country. But they were as yet the only two members. The branch was, admitted Starmer, 'very radical but not very big'.

As a Young Socialist, walking up the manicured front gardens of East Surrey, it was made evidently clear to Starmer that the path to his ideal world had practical hurdles in the shape of East Surrey's private estates. Starmer looked back bemusedly on his own tenacity: 'We sort of marched round East Surrey, up long drives telling people that we thought nationalisation was the answer. After we'd explained our views and asked 'well, how will you be voting?' there weren't so many that were persuaded with what we were putting, but we, you know, we passed resolutions. We took it all very, very seriously.' A lot of time was spent on proselytising nationalisation to a polite but highly sceptical audience, 'you know, it was hard work back then'.

In the deeply blue riding of East Surrey the young group was far from in an echo chamber. 'We were, slightly weirdly, young socialists in a very, very safe Tory seat,' said Cooper. 'We're talking about a time when the Labour party was Bennite. Whereas usually the young socialist group was further to the extreme, our group was very mainstream.'

Perhaps, then, because Starmer lived in blue Surrey but lived in a red house he developed an ability rare for a young person, the capacity to form his own opinions. At as young as sixteen Starmer was already throwing questions at the right, left and centre, shaping them into an original point of view. Given the dramatic headlines about rampant inflation and strikes like wildfire there was a sense of urgency, among the politically minded in East Surrey at any rate, that some powerful solution to the turbulence had to be found.

In 1979 the nascent East Surrey branch had a massive stroke of luck and suddenly doubled in size when they were joined by Jon Pike and his brother Tom, with the heady pace accelerating when they were later joined by another pair of siblings, a girl and her brother. At least that is what Pike recalled. In 2020, Starmer himself still hedged his Young Socialists' success with Surrey youth at a more conservative 'four in total'.

Pike joined after Leicester Square had been rechristened Fester Square in February following a strike of discontent London refuse collectors and Conservative-led Westminster Council's decision to dump garbage there and rats took over. Gravediggers and hauliers were also on strike and public services ground to a halt as NHS staff, including nurses like Jo, and other public workers worked on rule. In the bitter cold, the Winter of Discontent was in full swing and it was a muddled time for the far left. The Wilson and Callaghan governments had brought down inflation from 27 per cent in 1975 to a third of that in 1978 with national 'restraints' on wage increases agreed with the unions—5 per cent, 4.5 per cent, 10 per cent in consecutive years. Having promised a modest return of collective bargaining, Chancellor Dennis Healey U-turned and instead announced another 5 per cent nationwide 'restraint' in July 1978. Although union leaders agreed, their rolling over did not go down well at all on the work floor.

As with Starmer and Cooper, that was not the only reason for Pike's call to arms. 'There were large pockets of semi-rural poverty, ageing and neglected social housing, poor public services (including a terrible rural bus service)', recalled Pike, now a philosopher at Open University while his brother is professor of space-microengineering at Imperial College.

After catching shadow chancellor Geoffrey Howe unawares with a hostile NHS question at a Tory general election meeting in Caterham in the Spring of 1979, the long-haired fourteen-year-old Pike was directed to Starmer's youth branch of the Labour Party, one village over, by Labour activists in attendance at the back of the crowd. When he met the seventeen-year-old Starmer, Pike was immediately impressed. He thought, 'blimey, he's pretty cool. It was clear that he was a person of some substance and value.'

Apart from running 'jumble sales (very well attended)' and 'public meetings (not so well attended)', knocking on doors (Sisyphean), and poking fun at the Tories (gratifying), the main point of the East Surrey branch was to take vigorous part in the large-sweep national debates that drove the Young Socialists. There was also the small matter of how to win back control of Parliament after Margaret Thatcher had won with a slim majority in May 1979 by picking 60 seats off of Callaghan, who lost that year's General Election.

The junior branch of the Labour Party was at that time firmly in the hands of the Trotskys who had not yet absconded to the Communist Party. They were called 'the *Militant*' after the eponymous magazine around which they congregated, mainly in Liverpool, and they had developed a simple reason why they continued to put their faith in Britain's binary party politics. Revolution was very much still the goal, but rather than achieve it through conflict, the law was their secret wrench to liberate Britain's workers. The cunning plan was first to conquer the Labour Party, then to win the general election, finally to pass an umbrella law that would enable nationalisation and any other things that might be on the Trotskyite agenda from time to time.

It would be wrong to dismiss the power of either the Young Socialists or the militant in the Labour party at the time. Terry Duffy, a Young Socialist militant, was the one who at the Autumn Party Conference, proposed the motion that Callaghan stick to Chancellor Dennis Healey's promise made months earlier to let the unions negotiate their own wage increases. Set against a strike at Ford, where workers demanded a 17 per cent increase, twice that year's inflation, it was carried by 4 million to 2 million votes. MPs endorsed the motion in practice in November by removing Callaghan's power to back Healey up with the law. Grassroots strikes by rebels against union leaders began to snowball in opposition to Callaghan's Labour government into the Winter of Discontent and Spring of 1979.

The biggest battle for Keir's budding East Surrey politicians turned out to be, not with the unpersuaded Surrey voters, but with the militants at the Young Socialists HQ seeking to impose control over the new branch. As Starmer fronted the small group this 'was fairly straightforward because Keir was in the non-militant group from the off' recalled Pike. Starmer was not going to let his group be dictated from Liverpool as if it was another 23 Tanhouse Road. Unlike the militant movement, the East Surrey branch wasn't interested in following a rigid formula imposed by a distant Young Socialist committee. '[We] wanted to do our own political thing—and argue—a lot', Pike said.

The latter was Starmer's biggest contribution as the branch's young leader. He was in clear favour of exchanging views over merely expelling folk and so skewer the outcome of a debate to one that favoured a particular outcome, a favourite ploy in left left-wing politics. As a result, the group avoided drinking the cool-aid of one or other of the hard left's splinter groups and grew to be critical of what they were told. They endeavoured to make up their own mind on issues that affected Britain's industry and how to save it.

The big socialist talking points of the time were international brotherhood ('internationalism') and Britain's membership of the EU. According to Pike, the militants' formula was to organise whip-rounds in solidarity with foreign struggles—such as the one against Chile's Pinochet—while simultaneously using the international imagery to whip supporters into submission lest the same might happen in the UK. As to the EU, the militants enthusiastically endorsed Tony Benn's platform for leaving the EC. Benn loathed the idea that Britain might pool some of its sovereignty with other democratic states and with this sentiment the militants whole-heartedly agreed. Britain's joining the EC had strewn grit into the operation of UK law and it required an annoying extra move in their grand liberation scheme which now included: ditch EC to regain unfettered legal discretion, then pass the umbrella law that will crush the shackles of capitalism etc. The doubling of unemployment and wilting industrial output under Thatcher seemed to have been a closed case unworthy of deep discussion, presumably because it was considered the toxic by-product of a Conservative government's war on workers that would automatically disappear when Labour got back in.

The East Surrey branch thought the militant were, on the whole, 'boring' said Pike, particularly in their endless debates about nationalisation of this that and the other—though the four did believe in it enough to go out and knock on doors to explain why it was a good thing.

Starmer had a similar dim view of the 'tankies' who sought to infiltrate hard-left meetings of the Young Socialists. These hard-line members of the Communist Party earned their nickname as a result of enthusiastic support of the USSR's deployment of tanks in order to settle popular disagreement in Hungary and Czechoslovakia about the benefits of pan-Communism. They did not stand out much in the meeting of the Youth Socialists as there was little space between tankies and militants—except as to whether to liberate fellow men with the letter of the law or bullets.

Young Starmer and his branch were Bennite in their politics, and Starmer spent a weekend at a seminar hosted by Tony Benn during the second year of his A-levels. Benn was then at the height of his influence over the party, having been Britain's energy and industry minister for five years under both Callaghan and Wilson—still commanding the respect of a leading statesman. Benn had also been a member of the EEC Council of Ministers and small-town Starmer was starstruck, but not starstruck enough to agree with the ex-aristocrat's Euroscepticism. Even though he had never been abroad, he did not see Johnny Foreigner as a threat but in principle as a source of optimism—much like the gist of Jo and Rod's choice of music at home. 'European internationalism has always been very strong for me', Starmer said in 2020, in an echo of the wonkish lingo of the time when Eurocommunism was the polar opposite -ism.

This core outlook on the world was deeply shared by the tiny East Surrey branch of Young Socialists. Like Sullivan and Cook, Andrew Cooper would excel and through various peregrinations become a Tory peer keeping a fairly liberal outlook—he helped craft David Cameron's policy on same-sex marriage. But his liberal politics came at a cost to him in 2019, when his Conservative party membership was removed after he pledged to vote for the Lib Dems because of their anti-Brexit politics.

The East Surrey branch had to parry one further attack from a splinter group. This was from the other rump of the party's Trotskys, for whom the magazine *Labour Briefing* was its water cooler. Whereas the *Militant* looked for succour abroad, this group trained its eye on local and regional concerns, having started out with a London focus. Labour lefties such us Tony Benn, Ken Livingstone and Jeremy Corbyn all wrote for the briefing. But the magazine's head space was sufficiently out there for Corbyn as Labour Leader to go on the record in 2017 and deny that he had ever been on the editorial committee, and further to clarify—like Clinton's distinction between inhaling and smoking—'I didn't agree with it'. Judging by Labour's 2017 and 2019 manifestos and their long lists of nationalisations and the like in a blissful post-EU world, some of the militants' cunning plan had on the face of those documents come back from the dead under Corbyn's leadership.

Like the militants and the briefers, the young East Surrey socialists discovered from the word go that the real problem in politics is not the volume of ideas but first how to get to where you want to be.

'We were generally not old enough to drive, and there were two centres—Oxted and Caterham—and no easy way to get between them' as the towns were divided by the progress of junctions 5 and 6 of the M25 that were completed in 1979, East Surrey Young Socialists' first year in action.

Fortunately, Pike's mother and Jo knew each other from the rural-left, church, and both were studying for an Open University degree, solving that conundrum. The group hitched rides by convincing the parental network to help them out as they got on with the branch's executive work and busied themselves with exerting influence on East Surrey in general and national Young Socialist politics in particular.

13. 'You want to do law'

Andrew Sullivan's long bet as a history boy at Reigate paid off with a place in history at clever, studiously laid-back Magdalen College, Oxford, starting September 1981, where he briefly overlapped with Boris Johnson in 1983, who was at Balliol. Magdalen had also been Ballance's college, with his first year starting in 1940 while resuming reading history after the war in 1946. Andrew Cooper, having started school a year earlier than the other history boys, would sit his Sixth-form exams a year later and got a place at the London School of Economics in September 1982. A few years later he left Bennite politics behind and started working for the newly formed Social Democrat Party founded by the Gang of Four, one of whom was Labour's 'anti-parental choice' Shirley Williams. Vickers joined the RAF, and these three of the history boys knew exactly what they were after.

So did Cook, who got a place to at Brighton Polytechnic in 1981. Very up for becoming a popstar, it was really the music night-life he was interested in and he plunged headlong into the Brighton club scene, DJ-ing and playing in bands. Deep down, he never really hated his time at Reigate. When David Jones, a young English teacher for whom 3KU was his first class at the school and the dynamo behind school cricket, wrote to him in 2001 on behalf of two of his pupils, Cook responded immediately. He had just scored another no 1 hit with 'You've Come a Long Way, Baby' (1998) but promptly faxed back in handwriting to his former teacher inviting him over a forty-five minute chat and tea with his then wife Zoe Ball at their home in Hove.

Cook was well ahead of Vickers, Sullivan, Starmer and Cooper in reconnecting with the school. They seemed to have renewed their association with the school from June 2013 when Andrew Sullivan returned to Reigate on the 17th to give the first Henry Smith Lecture to its Sixth-form, attended by the former history boys, and another one to pupils in New York in November. BBC and *Private Eye* journalist Vickers provided the school with all the names of pupils in 3KU and their biogs. Starmer gave the Sixth-form lecture the year after, in 2014. He also spoke at the Chairman's Amicable Dinner in June that year, another phi-lanthropic event held under the banner of Henry Smith, who, too, was born in Wandsworth. It was held at the opulent Reform Club on Pall Mall and Starmer almost wasn't able to attend but for being given an emergency tie, without which he wouldn't be able to get in the club, and a taxi ride en route to Belfast to get to it. The first of these fund-raising dinners had taken place on 20 June 2013 at the Institute of Directors. Starmer seemed to be in the main picture covering the event, with a tie and glasses, though the then-Director of Public Prosecutions for another few months was not name-checked on this occasion. The next year, when he was the headlined speaker, RGS's public magazine printed that he had 'risen through the ranks of the Crown Prosecution Service', but did get his correct biog in on a third try.

Lord Windrush, Andrew Cooper, also became close once again to the school. In 2016, the former strategy advisor to David Cameron gave a lecture to 250 plus attendees on the political geographies of Britain. On 16 May 2019, he returned to speak at the Henry Smith Club dinner, whose members paid £1675 annually, expressing his gratitude two years after Starmer. He told his audience, 'No one in my family had been to grammar school before, and no one in my family had been to university. I was the penultimate year of the 11+ entry at Reigate Grammar School'. From his A-levels he said, 'It was only because the fees were covered at that stage that I was able to stay. My parents could not have afforded to pay'. The other after-dinner speaker was a foster mother talking about the assisted place of her son.

Addressing the Henry Smith Club on 25 June 2016 himself, Starmer fondly remembered what he got out of Reigate: 'Challenge and laughter'. Facing the couples in black tie seated at tables filling the ornate newly restored library of the Reform Club in London, newly elected MP Starmer was at ease and spoke 'eloquently and fluently' about 'the two words that described his time best', the school's public magazine recorded. Addressing Britain's voter five years later in the 2021 Manifesto, the new Leader of the Opposition seemed to have changed his opinion, signing off on the soundbite 'the Conservatives' grammar schools vanity project' and Jo and Rod's determination to keep him at RGS so that he would have a different life from their working class one.

Though always 'pretty driven and hardworking', Young Socialist Starmer seemed less certain as to what the next step should be. A Reigate contemporary recalled him as a pupil who believed 'in simple notions of goodness and decency'. But what did that boil down to in practice for an eighteen year old, particularly one who was at pains not to disappoint his parents and had a father who permitted no discussion. Compared to Sullivan, Cooper and Vickers Starmer himself looked directionless for all his earnest application.

In a radical move his inner young socialist must have rated, Starmer did not start at university that September. Instead he moved for six months to Bodmin Moor as a house parent in a Cornwall children's home for disabled boys and girls, looking after people in need in a role akin to his mother as a nurse. Upon his return to Oxted, he worked in Rod's factory operating a production machine. If Starmer hoped to find working-class redemption like Cook's flippant hope to go on the dole after Sixth-form, he was disappointed. 'DEAD BORING... Keir [Rod's ellipsis]', his father would write, ribbing his QC son in 2014 about the time he followed in his father's working-class footsteps the way Rod had done with his father Herbert and Herbert had done with his father Gus.

Starmer's choice was a highly unusual side-step in a time when only the British economy was taking gap years. When a Reigate pupil told Howard Ballance in 1974 that he wanted to work for a year at a South-African gold mine after sitting his A-levels, Ballance was underwhelmed and suggested he 'stay for a 3rd year Sixth and play some more rugby' at the state school instead.

In September 1982, the same year as Cooper's first year at the LSE, Starmer began law at the University of Leeds. He had not originally been keen on the subject, seeing himself more as a politician, and he wanted to study politics like Cooper. But his parents saw law as a sturdier career path and gradually encouraged him towards it in the same way they chose Reigate rather than one of the comprehensives in the area. The gainful impact of the East Surrey Young Socialists had been but modest.

In a Radio 4 interview Starmer talked about the discussion he had with his parents regarding his degree: 'Well, I wanted to go to university and do politics until my parents said no, you want to do law and I said, okay I want to do law.' Especially with his mother's health always uncertain, Starmer, who deeply loved her, wanted to fulfil his parents hopes for him. 'You'll get a decent job', they told him. They had made up his mind in the Sixth Form, according to *Prospect* magazine, but could hardly object to what he himself wanted to do during a year out.

This nebula of purpose—as opposed to being someone defined by circumstances or their parents—stayed with Starmer as an adult, even as Leader of the Opposition. It came across clearly in a Zoom interview with the British youth democracy organisation My Life My Say on 8 February 2021. The British-Zimbabwean Munya Chawawa kicked off the Q&A by asking Starmer in a friendly and gentle wrap of words, 'how do you define yourself?' Instead of a politician's crisp answer appropriate to their audience, Starmer's orbited his parents, his CV, human rights, the death penalty, dignity, a hatred of injustice and a dizzying list of other laudable things to boot. The twenty-eight-year-old comedian responded, 'OK, cool'.

This deflection from himself was not unlike that of his mother's, of whom Starmer said 'If you'd asked her how she was, she'd say "fine, how are you?"' Jo did it to be able to prevail over her painful and perilous physical condition. But in the case of Starmer it seemed that his deflections were invisible to himself once he got going. Whereas in the case of Jo this would be seen as exemplary fortitude given her condition, it seemed to exasperate Starmer that he was expected to give a personal answer that showed he was establishing a connection with his audience, rather than that they should do their homework in advance or who he was to them spoke for itself.

Starmer could have gone to Reigate College for his Sixth-form, like Cook, and given his 'left left left' views asked his parents that he stay within the state system. Instead, measured over four decades Jo and Rod's insistence on Reigate did not appear to be 'vanity': Reigate, Leeds, Oxford, QC, KCB. Nor did the Labour Party members appear to think so when it came to electing its Leaders over the same period of time; even if its educational policy against selection seemed to have been monopolised by those without a working-class education—either because it was paid for or left untended—telling people with one what was best.

Cameron's strategist Andrew Cooper observed that his Reigate schoolfriend could come across as 'self-important'. That seemed to be the case when comparing his address to people he was trying to look after and reach out to as opposed to the ease and succinctness with which he improvised on his own challenge-and-laughter years at the Henry Smith Club while speaking to philanthropists as successful as himself. Jo and Rod wanted their children to have better opportunities, but was that because their background made them prone to needing help to decide or because they had no money to spare to keep him at what they considered to be the best school in East Surrey: RGS rather than Reigate College? Starmer's mind seemed to idle at My Life My Say.

At freshers' week in Leeds in 1982, Starmer was signed up to join the Labour club by prominent student politician and archaeology student John Erskine. Much closer to the *Militant* Liverpool mother lode, there, too, was heavy factional fighting. But Starmer would refuse to be swept on in the tide. For him there were 'no enemies on the left'. Erskine recalled Starmer was of the 'non-aligned, conscience-driven left'— something approaching political Methodism. As at Reigate and the East Surrey Young Socialists, he enjoyed listening and arguing rather than raging against fellow travellers with a fractionally different hue.

But, as a young law student, Starmer was serious. I arrived at university. I had never met a lawyer. I didn't really know what lawyers did. I don't think I knew the difference between a solicitor and a barrister', he told Lauren Laverne on BBC Desert Island Disks. He shunned political infighting and student politics to buckle down and get on with his studies—as the first of his immediate family to go to university he was eager to succeed. He had done his fair share of passing of resolutions, knocking on doors and the like in East Surrey, where Pike and the others were still active. There had been many laughs and spirited arguments. 'Some of the life went out of the LPYS branch went out when he went off to Leeds to do his law degree', Pike said.

In Leeds, as the last of the history boys, Starmer too finally hit his stride. 'Once I discovered something like human rights, I so enjoyed it that it didn't feel like the burden it might otherwise have been', Starmer explained. Like Cook, his fellow musician, he had found what enthused him rather than looked like another set of hurdles to dispatch with hard work and diligence. When he studied international human rights law in the second-year of his undergraduate degree, he knew 'I wanted to be a human rights lawyer to change things for individuals who most needed my legal help and assistance'. It was a synthesis of the two conflicting strands he had explored during his year out.

In this corner of the law, all those slippery principles of human decency could be balled into a fist by a bright mind. It was a synthesis between the weaponised use of the law—whose levers the *Militant* hoped to grab as well, but in order to use them top down—and the sweeping ideas of radical social justice. Instead of passing endless resolutions, there was tangible progress if a court decided in one's favour after listening carefully without prejudice to arguments—as was his own habit. When asked in 2003 to give advice to anyone wanting a career in the law, he told the *Times*, 'choose an area of law that inspires you because the early days are long and hard'.

Once at Leeds, Starmer got first-hand experience of the ferocious political struggle that was going on in the country at the time. Yorkshire was the epicentre of the 1984-5 miners' strike where Margaret Thatcher's government slugged it out with Arthur Scargill's National Union of Mineworkers (NUM).

He naturally supported the miners, but it was clear by now that Thatcher was going to be in power for a long while and that the 1980s were not going to be the revolving door rule of Labour and Conservative governments of the previous decade. Despite the 3 million unemployed, Thatcher had tripled her Parliamentary majority in 1983 after successfully winning the Falklands War and bringing inflation down to under 5 per cent—obliterating Michael Foot and picking another humiliating 60 seats off of the Labour Party while leaving it for dead by a general consensus. The left started digging trench lines in the courts. New Parliamentary powers to suppress strikes created one of the legal battleground for the left in opposition. Labour lawyers were essential to hold the line and Starmer was successfully to represent miners when there was another strike in response to a further round of planned pit closures by the Conservatives in the 1990s.

In his Leeds undergraduate days, Starmer shared a six-bedroom house at 22 Chestnut Avenue in the Hyde Park area of inner-city Leeds which was just a short walk from the university and the Student Union.

Starmer's university antics became one of the ambivalent selling points of the house. 'There is a room available in Keir Starmer's old student house in Hyde Park,' bragged the Leeds students' *Tab*. However, there did seem to be some scepticism over whether this professional, put-together, father-aged man could ever have been a rambunctious Leeds student on a pub crawl: 'While refreshing to hear that Keir enjoyed his time here… Did he ever do an Otley Run? Did he ever go to Beaver Works?' the *Tab* queried.

Though absorbed by the study of human rights and excelling in exams, the challenge for which Reigate had prepared him, Starmer as a student did have a soft spot for pubs and football. Reflecting on his Leeds undergraduate years, Starmer recalled how, 'It was an incredible experience for me because I came from a very small town in Surrey to the city of Leeds'. 'We went to the Union most of the time. Back then, everyone used to drink snakebite', a mix of cider and lager, he told Leeds student paper *Gryphon*, and attend the Thursday night disco and its heady blend of indie music.

He picked Orange Juice's 1982 post-punk song 'Falling and Laughing' as typical of this time for BBC's Desert Island Discs. 'I've held Orange Juice and Edwyn Collins close to me for many, many years and I still play this song, but this absolutely captures those early years at university'.

'It was a fantastic period of my life and I've always been really, really fond of Leeds and Leeds Law School ever since,' he said. 'This was an incredible journey. Boy from Oxted goes to the city of Leeds to Leeds university. It was an incredible journey and a really important one to me and Leeds is a place now very, very close to my heart.'

14. Oxford Self-Management

Starmer graduated with a first-class law degree from Leeds University and went on to study in September 1985 for a BCL, a postgraduate degree at Oxford University. Fresh-faced, short-haired, clad in subfusc and a scholar's gown on the yearly freshers group-picture, he stood among the hundred or so new intake of students surrounding John Kelly the principal of his college St Edmund Hall—one over from Sullivan's Magdalen College.

St Edmund Hall, September 1985

One of Oxford's notoriously sporty and team-driven colleges, it would have suited him well if he allowed himself to take time off. Teddy Hall had a jovial nature as of one of the younger colleges, though its twenty-year-old eponymous saint already taught in its church in the 1190s where he charged for Aristotelean logic freshly imported by the crusaders—having cheated death by mortar, he would later preach for a sixth crusade only to become a reluctant Archbishop of Canterbury by the end of his life. The college's well and buttery in the bar were lined with sports jerseys and the church graveyard, where the young saint had once paddled round, was one of the few properties in the university where students were allowed to lounge on the grass.

It is unlikely, however, that Starmer indulged in many football games or sporty beer nights, even though the Middle Common Room for graduate students had its own team. In 1985, the university's Bachelor of Civil Law took two years and was the most prestigious common-law degree around the world and—having aged since its incipience from before the time of St Edmund—as selective among law students as Reigate was for eleven year olds.

Many lawyers who became top judges had taken the degree. Elizabeth Hollingworth, whose BCL overlapped for a year with Starmer at the college, was to join the Australian Supreme Court in 2004, a year after he himself became QC. The two young tutors at the college were themselves to become eminent professors and QCs. Derrick Wyatt (elected to the college in 1977 from Emmanuel College, Cambridge) was the first to put the EC division of the Strasburg court through the no-holds-barred paces of the common law and Adrian Briggs (1980, from the University of Leeds) tackled arcane lawyers' laws conflict of laws and private international law.

Structured like a barrister's prep for a day in court, at Teddy Hall the BCL piled on the pressure with reading materials, essays and one-to-one tutorials, leaving practically no time during term for anything other than law. Among others, the BCL tutors in the Oxford Law Faculty, who, arguing as barristers in London would on occasion be invited in court to consider dissenting views in books, some of them their own, approached the course as judges might. In the words of one of Teddy Hall's former law tutors, it was 'the best possible preparation for thinking on one's feet—or rather, pretending to, because nothing succeeds better in advocacy than preparation, preparation, and preparation'.

Like Cook, who filled his spare time with music as a Reigate teenager and a Brighton student, Starmer, his human-rights passion awoken, was in his element and filled his time outside term with debating, editing and writing about law and socialism. He joined Oxford University's Labour Club as well as a more fluid group of thirty or so left left-wing students and activists who called themselves Socialist Self-Management. The banner covered a lot of different ruffs: left-libertarians and ecologists such as Derek Wall of the Green Party, feminists, BAMEs, Trotskys, gay activists like Peter Thatchell and radical students such as Ben Schoendorff, 1984 chair of the Labour Club. The group was iconoclastic for its time and could be considered cutting edge even in 2021. If it were restyled as Intersectional Management its awkward terminology would easily fit in with the contemporary anesthetic jargon covering its 'space'.

In the late 1980s, sirens were finally going off in the left left-wing underground. After having exerted real influence on Britain through Callaghan, Benn and other sympathetic ears in government, and then even more so in the Party through Michael Foot, the body blows by Thatcher had shattered what remained of the party's ever-precarious unity. The 1986 printer's union dispute with Murdoch's newspapers was making it icily clear that Britain and history had moved on from Labour's remaining Trotskys. Murdoch produced his paper in Wapping, London, and needed fewer than 10 per cent printing staff on state-of-the-art machines. The strikes of the remaining 90 per cent meant very little to the company, which received ample police support to counter any attempts to sabotage Wapping.

Starmer's was also quite a sophisticated group of students, as it promptly produced *Socialist Alternatives* in July 1986. This was a new, well-funded, professional-looking 36-page magazine with a cover price of 90p, almost four times the cost of a newspaper. It was to have six or seven issues a year, a major commitment in itself (which would remain unachieved), apart from the equally ambitious plan by the neophytes of putting it together within a month of the deadline for submissions. Beautifully produced, it was typeset and printed in three colours by a professional academic press, and one of the members on the production team was also the financial supporter of Full Marx, a radical bookshop squatting in an empty commercial building on Cheltenham Road in Bristol (a Salvation Army branch in 2021).

The new magazine, published from 22 Charles Street Oxford by an editorial 'collective' of seven, including Starmer, was part of a gunshot of new left-left publications emerging almost as an act of sympathy to give Britain's unionised printers custom. The left left felt irrelevant in British politics, as indeed they were, and were desperately trying to regroup and claw a way back and dominate the stage once again. Starmer fit in with this goal. One of the thirty Oxford socialist self-managers recalled him in 2020, while being canvassed by Wall, as 'ambitious'.

The same printer produced and typeset the inaugural copy of *International: A Journal of Marxism in the Labour Party* (70p), whereas Frank

Furedi as Linda Ryan edited *Confrontation: Theoretical Journal of the Revolutionary Communist Party* (1986) in London, which flowed into *Living Marxism* after two issues, edited under his own name, and re-emerged phoenix-like as *Spiked* after a disastrous libel battle with ITN, all the while nurturing the *Militant*'s anti EU flame. Along the way, both the Revolutionary Communist Party and *Spiked* attracted Munira Mirza, today Boris Johnson's No 10 Policy Unit equivalent of Starmer's childhood friend Lord Windrush, Andrew Cooper.

Aiming high, layed-out on quality paper, these publications were nonetheless fringe enough to forget about depositing a file copy with Karl Marx's home from home, the British Library—except, that is, for *Living Marxism/Spiked*, which weighed in at £1.50 with a fine talent for enraging its readers in full colour.

Socialist Alternatives was Starmer writ large. Rather than prescribe dogma *Militant* or *Labour Briefing* style, it aimed to 'reflect the debates around a new socialist vision and paractice [sic] and keep you in touch with them'. Like Starmer, the magazine wanted to listen to what going on in the left-left. A similar idea of neutrality propelled the *Independent*, which also first appeared in 1986 with leading journalists such as Stephen Glover, and which aimed to introduce mainstream Britain to a paper that covered the news without a political preset—though it was viable only because it didn't use unionised printers and the precipitous drop in printing costs meant a new voice in newsprint.

Starmer's magazine was serious about the brotherhood of man and there were contributions on self-management from Germany Chile, France, Poland, Greece, Spain, Portugal, Argentina, Libya, South Africa, China, Russia, the US, Philippines, Fiji and Palestine. What 'self-management' really meant , however, was best set out by Tony Benn, Starmer's government idol who contributed a piece to the first issue.

'As for Labour, we have tended to think that all we have to do is to elect a Labour government or Labour council, and all will be done for us', he wrote. According to Benn, that merely reduced democracy 'to what the pollsters produce by telephoning a few people and describing them as "public opinion".' One word, 'electoralism', summed up the Labour's Party's (Neil Kinnock's) unhealthy obsession with the pesky voter. The real solution for socialists was to mimic wily Capital. 'Capital doesn't bother to put its major figures in the parliamentary arena at all, it works from outside the system by putting pressure on the system'.

The left-lefts alternative was therefore to create a host of self-management structures outside of Parliament to influence it. Though Benn himself was vague on how this worked out in practice, his was a solid analysis of what was to happen.

In 1987, France would sink Greenpeace's Rainbow Warrior, setting this 'self-management' organisation on course for a position of global eco-influence. AIDS/HIV tests had just become available and knowledge was increasing—as with Corona in 2021—and World Aids Day was launched in 1988 and its support organisations would become centres of 'self-management' influence outside of Parliament, and the medical research that followed in their wake would become the foundation of Corona testing and vaccines from 2020. The Green Party, christened in 1985, on the other hand, sought to work with the voter and consistently failed to gain first-past-the-post impact beyond exotic scandals. Ensconced in the SDP, a party that needed electoralism like a drowning man needed oxygen, Andrew Cooper would make a fair fortune after founding Populus, a research and strategy consultancy (later part of Yonder with a team of 175 staff), as he furthered himself as a 'pitiless empiricist', the term he preferred.

The real excitement of the magazine, however, was not Benn but someone called 'Michel Raptis', the pseudonym of Michel Pablo. He was advisor to Andreas Papandreou, Greece's first Socialist prime minister and, previously, of Marxist President Allende in Chile. Having won with a landslide in 1981, Papandreou continued to have a lock on genuine power and so, therefore, did Pablo. He hailed from a solidly Communist background forty years before Munira Mirza—also Trotskyite—and, importantly, he was a leading guru on socialist self-management. His ideas merited a dedicated magazine, because they were actually being used by a successful Socialist in government, as opposed to those of the left left in Britain or of Benn, who had in been in power.

Yet, *Socialist Alternatives* as a title alone riled Britain's left-left no end. Used to strong opinions and more prone to splintering than pine, it preferred the position of being the underdog to 'them', the people at the top. Former cabinet minister Tony Benn also put a deft finger on this sentiment and the left-left's own 'them' in the Labour Party. 'If we allow politics to be monopolised and controlled by the people at the top of the structures they will say: "Do nothing! Wait! Don't rock the boat!",' meaning the wet (as seen by the left-left) new Leader of the Labour Party Neil Kinnock. Benn also had a little dig at Raptis where he wrote in the same piece, 'we may even be seeing it with Papaandreou [sic]'.

Dismissed by the left-left as 'unprincipled' or worse, perhaps, as having a 'human face', the magazine wouldn't last beyond 1994 (with Starmer staying on till at least the Spring issue of 1989). Though this could also have been because, as one of the thirty members recalled, the Socialist Self Management group didn't wake up at 5.30am to sell copies at the factory gates. After putting their thoughts to paper, the group's hard work was done. It did, however, travel to celebrate Bastille Day and a revolutionary youth camp in the South of France—without Starmer. Cerebral in nature, the magazine still held out longer than more sectarian *International* covering Marxism in the Labour Party, which folded within two years as Labour's 'them', it seemed, was removing all the splinters.

Getting involved with *Socialist Alternatives* was a deeply-personal choice for Starmer, and, like its left-left editorials, which considered wet trade unions with as much disdain as Kinnock, Starmer dismissed their role under Thatcher crisply as no more than 'membership of the AA'. Even so, Starmer at his most stinging over these three years was: 'Appalling attacks by mounted police on demonstrators and the continued harassment of residents (including towing away of cars hindering the passage of the TNT convoys sweeping through residential areas at 60mph with no license plates)'. One could also count quotation marks in the same Wapping piece around 'property-protecting' as heat from Starmer's Oxford pen.

The group and the magazine were, however, defined who Starmer was. Like the Oxted and later London Starmer, it mattered that everyone who surrounded him pulled strongly in the same direction to champion the 'vulnerable', more so than whether their team views were strictly speaking sensible, utopian, extremist, realistic or unrealistic.

The latter was an invitation to the kind of passionate debates that he relished after he left the family home on Tanhouse Road and its lee from discussion. Focused on helping, his intellectual curiosity did not extend to—or it may have been invisible to him—those like himself at the university: the offspring of working-class parents like Vickers, Cooper and Sullivan, or any of the majority of others who didn't fall into the 'vulnerable' category. It was a personal variation on Tony Benn's single interest in the working classes to the exclusion of others as he moved further and further away from the ministerial responsibilities he once held for the country as a whole.

Beyond protection of the vulnerable, Starmer's views were eclectic. In Parliament, in his Party's tribute to Prince Philip Starmer said on 12 April 2021 that throughout the prince's life 'the monarchy has been the one institution for which the faith of the British people has never faltered'. It was a warm and lifelong appreciation but one that would surely have surprised Starmer's many peers committed in the 1980s to Marxist class struggle. In a 2005 clip uncovered by Guido Fawkes, Starmer joked in a pub, 'I also got made a Queen's Counsel, which is odd since I often used to propose the abolition of the monarchy'. He accepted a knighthood in 2014 where Benn had renounced the hereditary title given to his father in 1963.

It was the BCL's rigour that helped Starmer make up his mind. Jurisprudence as taught at Oxford asked both 'what is the law?' and 'what should the law be like?' Any radical position could be defended and sealed off as long as it followed the bright beacons set by established law. Although perhaps still considering himself more of a politician before he went to Leeds, by the end of his time at Oxford Starmer was firmly committed to a becoming a barrister. There was complete intellectual freedom inside the broad lanes of the law. Some who were part of the BCL even rushed to visit remnants of Soviet Communism before they were swallowed up whole by the purple dialectic of history.

As Starmer himself said, 'the idea of actually presenting an argument, being the person who got up in court, began to appeal'. 'When I arrived at St Edmund Hall, I had a first-class degree from Leeds behind me. But I was still not clear on the path I should take next. My time at St Edmund Hall—an intense year studying for the BCL—confirmed me in my choice of pursuing a career as a human rights advocate.' The BCL made Starmer understand that appellate courts didn't need to look at the law like Dickens's Mr Tulkinghorn but could be led by arguments.

For Starmer, this was his chosen, personal form of self-management outside of Parliament that former aristocrat Tony Benn spotted in *Socialist Alternatives*: 'the working class, far from shrinking, is incorporating into itself levels of managerial, professional and technical skills that were denied to the old working class... it incorporates people with a capacity to run, to organise, to manage, to develop which was simply not true of the old manual working class upon which the labour movement was built.'

Starmer's father had been a toolmaker and typical of the Marxian nineteenth-century working-class mould: a white, English male. The strikes in 1970s and 1980s had made clear, however, that this stereotype had become socialism's red herring and as attractive but nostalgic and misleading as an L.S. Lowry. Thus, in his first Oxford year, Starmer went back to Tony Benn to interview him for *Socialist Alternatives* at his house in Holland Park on the topic of realignment having been given a chair that once belonged to Keir Hardie by the ex-aristocrat.

What mattered if you were a Starmer-style socialist was whether you empathised with the subjects of power or whether you were on the opposite side and identified with those in power (even if Labour power or power at the hands of union leaders). As Rod's working-class son, his own tools were the sophisticated legal insights he was acquiring. It meant putting these at the disposal of those—individuals and the kaleidoscope of new self-management structures—lacking the resources to defend themselves in a vulnerable position.

This was not for some convoluted theoretical reason, but because he could and it was what he had discovered he wanted to do. His mother would not decline to nurse a patient of whom someone said they had disease A rather than B. Practical socialism was his mission—which in the 1980s he still couched in the nostalgic left-left terminology of the 'oppressed' and 'powerless' harking back to the time when 'them' and 'us' were groups who dressed, spoke and ate differently, but which he in 2020 replaced with a less anachronistic 'how we treat the individual'. In the same way conservatism needed to say no more than 'we're fine with things as they are', all he needed to say was, I will be there with you, like his mother. This Ignatian refusal to be pinned down on one of the -isms would again infuriate his left-left when he re-entered politics in 2014, whereas his Bennite championing of only a narrow section of the population worried his mainstream Labour colleagues.

While doing his BCL, Starmer went up to Wapping with some thirty others a number of times to act as legal observer for the National Council of Civil Liberties and first-hand spreads appeared in *Socialist Alternatives*. In a fierce debate at the Oxford University Labour Club, he disagreed strongly with both David Miliband and Stephen Twigg who represented its mainstream faction and gave but qualified support to the strike in a refined cocktail of ideology, class, and technology. But Starmer also didn't go along with Pike's proselytising for the nascent revolution-ary socialist Workers Liberty when his Oxted friend came up for a day. Instead the two former East Surrey young socialists bonded over pints at the King's Arms opposite the Bodleian Library. When P&O seafarers went on strike in 1988-89 Starmer once again headed out as a legal observer for the NCCL.

During his first BCL year, Starmer also joined the Haldane Society of Socialist Lawyers. This left-left society of barristers and solicitors was formed at the beginning of Ramsay McDonald's office as prime minister (1929-1935) to give the Labour Party in government desperately needed free legal advice—a Ministry of Justice was formed as late as 2007 in Britain as the machinery of the courts were considered extensions of the government. A quite separate Society of Labour Party Lawyers existed, which had seceded in 1949 to filter out Communists but it had become the stepping stone for Labour QCs eying a seat in Parliament. In 1986, Helena Kennedy was a Vice President of the Haldane Society, while Ben Emmerson was on the Executive Committee, both of them QCs today and go-to human-rights lawyers for the media.

The Haldane society came ready-made with sub groups that overlapped with Self-Management Structures discussed in *Socialist Alternatives*: women, race and immigration, employment and trade unions, northern Ireland, international, mental health, crime, and, a few years later, Africa and lesbian and gays. But with these subcommittees the Haldane Society addressed questions in the real world and not philo-sophical abstractions. As Starmer recalled, it was about how the left generally 'bound together the wider movement and its strands of equality—feminist politics, green politics, LGBT—which I thought was incredibly exciting, incredibly important'. Like a doctor, these lawyers' efforts made a tangible difference to the lives of people they were helping.

The Haldane Society, too, was in the process of setting up a magazine, *Socialist Lawyer*, whose editorial committee (not 'collective'). Starmer was asked to join early in his second year of his BCL at Oxford, the Spring of 1987. Three of its founding editors would become High-Court judges, most of the others QCs. The magazine, too, covered Wapping first hand and its first issue appeared in the Winter of 1986. The writers for the magazine over the years were mainly left-wing legal pinups, though after 1991 there were also occasional excursions written by, again, Tony Benn, Peter Thatchell, Chris Mullin MP, Clare Short MP, Arthur Scargill, Austin Mitchell MP, Sadiq Khan.

15. Pugilism

If Starmer was in any doubt about the Haldane Society's pugilistic nature, the group defined itself as 'socialists working together. We should unite ourselves like fists and hurl ourselves at the enemy'. At least that is what its President, John Platts-Mills QC, a New Zealander who had joined in 1937, reckoned in an interview with Starmer in the new magazine.

In its own words, the society described itself more placidly as a 'campaign within the existing legal system with the long term objective of transforming it into one reflecting the demands of a socialist society', though Platts-Mills's own set, Cloisters Chambers, was commonly referred to as the Kremlin. A pacifist, 'I was against the Cold War', Platts-Mills had been in favour of post-war alignment with Stalin, a friend of his, rather than the US. He was also among the first-ever barristers—a group of twenty from the Haldane Society—to join a picket line in 1976, armed with a bowler hat and *Times*.

The Haldane Society was the unlikely theatre for Starmer's only ever recorded act of rebel rousing in his life. While he was preparing to sit his BCL exams, he attended the society's 20 June 1987 AGM, one of the 'angriest ever executive committee meetings' in its history according to Bill Bowring, a barrister as well as, later, professor at Birkbeck College, who joined the society's Executive Committee at that AGM and would later become its President with Starmer as Secretary.

Starmer and Robin Oppenheim, a Manchester history student doing a Diploma in Law at Westminster University and later a QC, ambushed the society's members with the barn-storming proposal to drop the word 'Haldane' from its name. Correctly fearing a third Thatcher victory, the two radical students thought the society should appeal to a 'wider socialist vision'. They argued successfully at the 20 June AGM that the society's reference to Labour's first Lord Chancellor, the highest legal office in the land, 'obscures its central purpose'. Bowring, who seemed to consider Starmer a wet socialist in 2021, said that Starmer also proposed to drop the word 'socialist' and even blithely proposed to add 'progressive' or 'democratic' to the society's name. The magazine bears no record of such vicious knee-capping by Starmer and in his articles in the two magazines he continued to lock with the left-left's criticism of Neil Kinnock and union leaders Brenda Dean and Tony Dubbins.

The young Turks carried the acrimonious meeting and the resolution that passed proposed a new name, 'National Association of Socialist Lawyers'. It precipitated a ballot of the membership by post the society's leadership stipulated. And, possibly, a further two ballots. If Britain's socialist lawyers felt befuddled by this, 'free legal advice sessions to all members who find this procedure incomprehensible' would be made available by the solicitous leadership of the Haldane Society.

The entire top of the society past and present, a veritable legion of QCs and Vice Presidents including Platts-Mills and Helena Kennedy, lined up against the two students to thunder 'that this unfortunate step is reversed'. The name should remain as is. 'It would take away not only part of our history but much of our identity', the distinguished progressives wrote conservatively.

Sensitive to the insult to socialist DNA, but at pains to kick the proposal into the long grass nonetheless, the society's crime committee submitted a minority brief against the two students. While 'we are socialists and proud of it', they assured the reader, dropping the word Haldane would lead to a failure to capitalise on the defective nature of many Labour MPs who 'are much happier about relying on advice from organisations which are not overtly socialist. (The Society is, of course, usually referred to as the Haldane Society.) In our view a similar argument applies to the media.'

Of the 800 or so socialist lawyers who were sent a ballot, 70 keenly put their papers in a return envelope. These 70 ballots soundly defeated the 'question' by 51 (presumably mainly votes cast by the society's top collective) to 19. There were also six other questions with detailed procedural changes aimed to make the organisation more democratic, a meme bubbling up everywhere at that time. Even though lawyers by trade, a dwindling number of the 70 rose to consider the remaining six questions bringing up the rear, and the results pointed to both the hard boundaries of participative democracy and the art of notification. In the same issue, Marina Wheeler castigated 'Tory hypocrisy' and was to rekindle a year or so later her close childhood friendship with, leading to marriage with,

Boris Johnson, then separated from his glamorous first wife Allegra Mostyn-Owen.

Even so, the revolt Starmer had co-led did reap a reward for him. The society's members knew who he was and at next year's AGM he was co-opted as secretary on the Executive Committee. Several years later, in another rare sighting of Starmer sucking on a lemon, he would use the word 'farce' to describe the society's AGMs, saying that 'Largely irrelevant and wordy resolutions are passed and then forgotten'.

Piercing the level surface of his prose, he inserted the farce word in his 1990 *Socialist Lawyer* piece about how best to organise the Haldane Society with a view to the future. Covering three pages, it was close to the longest essay he ever wrote in either *Socialist Alternatives* or *Socialist Lawyer*. This tail would wag one more time, 31 years later when in January 2021 an upset AGM decided that Starmer 'does not qualify for membership of the Haldane Society of Lawyers because he is demonstrably not a socialist' after a resolution proposed by Chambers 'rising star' and young socialist lawyer Nick Bano.

Indeed, as Starmer embarked on a professional career in the law, he also began to stuff away his adolescent voracity, love of the absurd and appre-ciation of a good Python joke behind the veneer required of Britain's legal priesthood. John Curtice, a politics professor at the University of Strathclyde, complained about Labour in 2016—Starmer's freshman year as MP—that there was no one able to grab the attention of the wider public.

Even so five years later the junior common room of Starmer's Oxford college was adorned by the freshers class of 2021 with a cut-out of the college's honorary fellow and Leader of the Opposition. The undergrad-uates weren't aware of his Young Socialist past, his riding the 410 bus to Reigate with his mates, or campaigning long drive to long drive in Oxted and left-left activism in Oxford. To most he was the measured serious man taking on Boris Johnson's Corona response and cuts to the NHS. Not as radical as Corbyn, Starmer was even accused of being a 'centrist'. Yet, despite this, there was a certain attachment to the new Labour leader. In January 2021, the college's snow-man building competition winner was a seven-foot-tall entry nicknamed 'Skeir Starmer'.

How was this different from Starmer's first year at the college in 1985?

The big debate then among its undergraduates concerned cuts in student benefits, the novelty of the newly installed computer and phone system and watching video reruns of Brideshead Revisited, the 1981 TV series set in an elegiac past of Oxford with Jeremy Irons. There was also the fatal drug overdose in the rooms of Otto von Bismarck, a member of the self-elected public-school Bullingdon and Piers Gaveston clubs, following a sordid binge of cocaine, heroin, amphetamines and alcohol, of Olivia Channon, heiress of one of Margaret Thatcher's cabinet ministers. Our 'meetings remain as unpolitical as ever', the president of the St Edmund Hall junior common room exclaimed, however, to his satisfaction that year. The only real political issue was whether Murdoch papers should be banned, which resulted 'in us taking an extra copy of the *Sun*', he recorded, a measure duly reported on in the tabloid itself.

Elsewhere in Oxford, Boris Johnson became president of the university's debating club on 15 March 1986, three years after Andrew Sullivan. He would sit for his finals at the same time as Starmer in Trinity term of 1987. Olivia Channon herself was not a member of the Bullingdon Club. She had gone to the right type of school like Bismarck and could easily afford the club's lavish benders resulting in flying crockery, but she was a woman and only men were allowed in. Her college was St Hilda's where Emma Foote, one of Starmer's *Socialist Alternatives* co-editors, was also based.

In the Spring of 1989 when Starmer interviewed Haldane Society's John Platts-Mills for the *Socialist Lawyer*, Johnson was writing for the *Telegraph* as correspondent in Brussels and the famous banana story would be written a few years later. Like Starmer's absorption with Oxford's left-left underground, these early years were also to become a story for Johnson, in the *Mail on Sunday* and the *Times* in 2019, following national reports by neighbours of an altercation and a police knock on the door of the house where Johnson was living with his partner Carrie Symonds. After a row with Johnson in 1989, his then-wife Mostyn-Owen moved in with her friend Louisa Gosling. Gosling met up with Johnson in a bar to mediate and he instructed her not to repeat what 'Mostyn-Owen had told her about their relationship' and she claimed to both papers to have remained fearful of Johnson ever since. Symonds got engaged to Johnson in the same year and their first child was born on 29 April 2021.

16. Archway and the Israelites

In an interview for the *Times* in March 2003, three years after becoming Liberty human-rights lawyer of the year, Starmer was asked why he became a lawyer. Not yet a politician guarding the vulnerable his answer was relaxed, 'Because I realised that I would never make it as a football player.' Good for a few laughs, Starmer went on to emphasize that his position as a footballer reflected his political life and shaped his career. He said he saw himself 'in the middle of the park, on the left, shouting a lot of instructions.'

'Feels better in my head afterwards than it was on the pitch but there are things you can actually learn from football,' Starmer repeated as politician. His appreciation for the 'basic rules which really matter' on the pitch hint at what would materialise throughout his career as a deep commitment to human rights. 'As soon as you're on the pitch nobody gives a damn what you do for a living and the only rule is don't be an ass. That's quite a good rule for politics. Don't be an ass.'

Despite having a law degree from Oxford it still took Starmer years to reach the prominence that would garner him the *Times* interview. In 1987, the training required for becoming a barrister, was still an unpaid pupillage and by and large a self-selecting system for those of means to enter the profession. Students like Starmer, who had no funds, tended to become solicitors as large and small firms would cover the cost of legal training as they hoovered up talent to man their desks. Indeed, Starmer said, 'I thought I'd become a solicitor but then the idea of actually presenting an argument, being the person who got up in court, began to appeal'.

Fortuitously, the year before he started his BCL, the Queen Mother had dined at the Middle Temple and a scholarship fund had been created by its benchers—announced by the temple's treasurer Lord Justice Acker. The Queen Mother's Scholarship was the top award that 'shouts excellence' according to the inn's education department in 2021, though the one founded by her daughter in 2017, the Queen's scholarship, had since been given pole position among a by then collection of bursaries of all shapes and sizes. Even so, in the first few years it was by no means the case that the Queen Mother's scholarship was awarded on need. One of the inaugural scholarships in 1986 went to a student who had attended of one of the 'great nine' public schools and Oxford colleges.

Starmer gained one of the bursaries awarded in 1987, having received his BCL on 1 August, two months after the fractious revolt he led at the AGM of the Haldane Society held at the London School of Economics.

Though finance to become a barrister was no longer an issue, the 25-year-old still had to apply to a chamber that would take him as a pupil and where he could act on what he wanted with young like-minded lawyers. As it so happened, several Haldane members were part of the chambers of Liberal peer Emlyn (Lord) Hooson QC and John Mortimer QC, author of the Rumpole series of crime novels at 1 Dr Johnson Building, including the society's secretary and two editors of the first issue of *Socialist Lawyer*.

And so Starmer found himself one winter facing Gavin Millar, Edward Fitzgerald, Helena Kennedy, Geoffrey Robertson, Stephen Irwin, Peter Thornton—all since QCs, except for Irwin who joined the Court of Appeal and Thornton who became Chief Coroner. Starmer was dressed informally in a cardigan rather than his Oxford subfusc minus gown. He was 'nervous and awkward' and 'looked about 14', remembered Robertson as they congregated in a cramped, Dickensian book-lined room of 1 Dr Johnson Building.

'He was obviously brilliant', remembered Millar, who six years senior and was to share a room with Starmer. Also, Starmer was, recalled Fitzgerald, who was ten years his senior, 'very seriously left-wing and very idealistic'. He would also work closely with Starmer, who was often his junior barrister.

'I remember very clearly that he gave a powerful and thorough critique of the prison system and how it didn't work', said Millar. Fitzgerald QC thought that Starmer even quoted the Marxist maxim that 'property is theft' and that Starmer had queried whether there was a point in sending non-violent burglars to prison—adding as rider that it was a 'famous story' about Starmer's first interview at the chambers.

Either way, Fitzgerald said, 'one or two people thought, "We can't have this terrible lefty in chambers".' Being visible on the editorial board of *Socialist Lawyer* before gaining a pupillage at 1 Dr Johnson Building can't have helped Starmer much with these tenants of the set. In 2021, the Haldane Society still said on its website, 'We have had many distinguished members but judicial appointments and elevations to Queen's Counsel have been conferred despite, not because of, membership in the Haldane Society.' Without either a Labour or Tory affiliation, the society successfully aimed to be a 'legal thorn in the side of every government'. As a matter of fact, three years before taking silk in 2002, Starmer would retire from the society's executive committee after twelve years of active and very visible involvement and he resigned as member in 2007 upon becoming Director of Public Prosecutions.

But Starmer's sharp mind pushed the scales in his favour at the liberal leaning 1 Johnson Buildings. 'His pupil master Stephen Irwin intervened and said, "He's absolutely brilliant and he may have got carried away",' recalled Fitzgerald QC. His other pupil master—today called supervisor—was Helena Kennedy. This was unusual in its own right. By 2021, the division of male to female barristers had fallen to 2 to 1, with the occasional Mx thrown in, but it was 1 in 5 thirty years earlier when Starmer became a barrister.

Starmer was called to the bar on 11 November 1987, joining the Middle Temple and 1 Dr Johnson Building, and started shadowing his pupil master for six months before gaining right of audience.

Senior barristers who weren't of the 'lock-'em up' variety were still rare in 1988. There was former Labour MPs John Platts-Mills QC, the Haldane president, and before him Denis Pritt QC, both close to Stalin, and of the same generation, Labour Lord Chancellor Gerald Gardiner QC, then in his late eighties, as well as liberal QCs in their sixties such as Louis Blom-Cooper, John Mortimer and Hooson, who had famously defended moors murderers Ian Brady and Myra Hindley, with Hooson calling out some of the evidence in the trial as 'flimsy'. But their culture was still very much as portrayed in Mortimer's Rumpole series—lots of port, claret, and references to the wife as 'she who must be obeyed' twinkle in the eye—and lampooned on TV by John Cleese plus bowler hat and unfurled umbrella in Monty Python sketches.

Millar QC, called to the bar six years before Starmer, recalled that all the young barristers in their set were of 'that generation who had been radicalised by Margaret Thatcher. We wanted to change the world, and we wanted to do it by using the law to entrench stronger human rights and civil liberties'.

A few months after joining the chambers, Starmer interviewed Millar and another barrister for *Socialist Lawyer* about the monochrome nature of judges, a problem that plagued the judiciary as much as the top of the trade unions in their eyes: 'The make-up of the judiciary is notoriously white male and educated at Oxford or Cambridge. It is class-based and cannot be said to reflect the aspirations and anxieties of ordinary people in any way. But what should we do about it?', he asked as Millar offered various solutions, including training.

Starmer queried, 'Isn't it a bit too optimistic to expect much progressive change to result from simply changing the face of those who administer justice unless the actual content of that justice is also tackled?' That was the key task at hand. It was as to the latter where Millar and Starmer and the other young barristers aimed to carve out a real difference in their careers.

'Keir is the hard workers' hard worker', Millar said and Starmer brought to his chambers the extraordinary work ethic of his parents. Other lawyers who worked were impressed how he was extremely organised, meticulous, detailed and strategic in planning everything out that a case would need in advance. He also inherited from his mother the unwavering inner compass as to what he set out to do without mission creep. Close to the end of her life, when her son could afford care outside the NHS, the former nurse gave Starmer a stark warning that he remembered well, 'In that high-dependency unit, near death, where they weren't sure they had the facilities for her, she held my arm and said: 'You won't let your dad go private, will you?''.' Starmer, too, had that bee-line integrity, while his former pupil master Kennedy observed of him, 'there's just a little area of distance which is self-protective'.

Young, and idealistic, Starmer kicked off his career living in a sketchy four-bedroom flat with his school friend Paul Vickers. The flat, which Starmer described as a 'hovel,' was in Archway, London N5, above a dubious sauna and massage parlour. The windows were broken and there was a big hole in the kitchen floor, which grew in size over the years.

Another flatmate who was there before was Andrew Cooper and he said it was 'really incredibly cheap' but 'really grungy', and their landlord was eventually sent to prison for living off the earnings of prostitutes.

'Keir and Paul lived there for several years, and then I believe it was condemned as unfit for human habitation by Haringey Council,' Cooper recalled, 'But it was incredibly convenient, right opposite the tube.' Any decision in the flat had to be made collectively insisted Starmer.

'Sat surrounded by boxes of thousands and thousands of *Socialist Alternatives*', as Vickers recalled, this decade was also the beginning of a string of girlfriends until Starmer married in 2007. They were fiercely bright and included the formidable feminist lawyer Phillippa Kaufman, a Haldane Society member and writer for *Socialist Lawyer*, who is now also a QC. 'Unfortunately, more copies of that magazine ended up under my bed than actually distributed to the world at large', Starmer himself conceded about the beautifully produced Self-Management magazine.

This groovy new London life was set to new music and a new style of dancing, Northern Soul. On BBC Desert Island Discs Starmer chose 'Out on the Floor' by Dobbie Gray as most representative of this time. Though more than redolent of his mother's favourite musical era, Northern Soul was in fact about all-nighters to trippy music played by fiercely competitive DJs who were able to put together sets that their rivals didn't have. Gray's hit had been released in 1966 in the US but had never made it to the UK until Northern DJs started picking over his and other soul music from dusty music catalogues in order to spin perfect dance tunes. Years later the all-night style would effortlessly flow into Acid House raves—which Starmer would find himself defending a few years later.

'I love Northern soul' Starmer told Laverne about the song, this reminds me 'of my sort of early days in London, with a group of friends in a really grotty, flat above a sauna or a massage parlour that kept interesting hours. And I was sort of trying to make it as a lawyer, having a lot of fun and forging lifelong friendships. So it evokes a particular period of my life and, and a love of Northern Soul.' Starmer's dancing, then, came with the required athletic backdrops, high kicks and handclaps later perfected by street dance. He would not try and repeat his younger self's exuberance in 2021, he conceded.

94

17. A Band of Revolutionaries

From Archway Starmer was trying to change the world politically, contributing articles, interviews and book reviews, using *Socialist Alternatives* as a platform to rail against 'the authoritarian onslaught of Thatcherism'. The magazine's editorial collective also called for a 'radical extension of common ownership over wealth and power', that 'prisoners should have much greater control over the conditions of their own imprisonment' and, given the massive unemployment at the time, a 'nationwide campaign of struggles' to reduce the European working week to thirty-five hours. Under his own name, Starmer was adamant that the Labour Party needed to embrace the burgeoning social movements of the time, including those pushing for women's equality, green policies and gay rights.

But, as university peers such as Cooper and Miliband were being sucked into party politics, becoming part of the cogs, wheels and levers, Starmer himself was being seduced by the frontline of hand-to-hand legal combat in court.

His 1987 pupillage at 1 Dr Johnson Buildings was either lucky, astute or both. Underneath the veneer of all that centuries-old beeswax polished wood, the ballooning school gowns, horsehair wigs, green-leather chairs, granite class distinction between clerks and tenants, purring accents, dining-rooms, roast beef, spotted dick and custard, and other institutions of public-school life perpetuated into adulthood, a revolt was fomenting among almost two dozen activist barristers, constituting about half of the barrister in his chambers.

Led by Australian-born Geoffrey Robertson, who had just taken silk in 1988, 21 civil-liberties barristers, including Stephen Irwin, Peter Thornton QC, Helena Kennedy, Ed Fitzgerald, and three associate lawyers, including Blom-Cooper QC, broke off in July 1990 among a blaze of publicity in the legal world. Revolutionary for barristers they set up tenancy in Doughty Street, outside the footprint of the inns of court—an unheard of and staggering innovation since the seventeenth century—and left their criminal and commercial colleagues behind.

Though now famous for being famously the chambers of Amal Clooney, the wife of a Hollywood film star, 54 Doughty Street was hardly on the national radar then, and civil liberties even less so. Jonathan Cooper, who joined Starmer's chambers a few years later for his pupillage recalled how unusual this was then, 'There were very few of us interested in human rights at that time and during and after my pupillage'.

Instead of Starmer having to adjust to a life without his cardigan, it was his new chambers who instead made a determined effort to break out of their traditional mould. Gone were the cramped, over-crowded rooms in the inns, 'It is light and airy here, with modern art instead of all that wood and heavy gold. We have a waiting room, lots of flowers, and serve clients coffee and tea. We are making conscious efforts to break away from the Bar traditions that impede progress and be forward-looking, Christine Kings, Doughty Street's practice manager, a novelty position in itself, told the *Times*. Kings herself made history as the first woman ever to manage a set.

Set in Bloomsbury, 54 Doughty Street is just north of Gray's Inn and within the constituency of Holborn and St Pancras, which Starmer went on to represent. Charles Dickens lived in Doughty Street as a twenty five year old, writing *The Pickwick Papers* at no 48. While Bloomsbury is famous for its artists and writers, Sydney Smith and Vera Brittain among them, and actress Gillian Anderson also lived in the street, it also had its association with radicals—even Lenin lived nearby for nine years. Also, for almost as long as Starmer was at his chambers, the neighbour two doors down at no 56 was The *Spectator* magazine. Boris Johnson, its editor from 1999 to 2005, used to be seen regularly wobbling up the street on his bike.

Stephen Irwin QC was the new chamber's co-head who had invited Christine Kings to take the job, even though she had no experience at the inns and worked at the Campaign for Nuclear Disarmament CND. The new set wanted someone intelligent in charge who had no prior knowledge of the historical way of the barristerial process. Thus, all 21 tenants were given a fixed salary, another revolution, and she herself was paid £44,000, a modest amount at the time (in 2017, a senior clerk made around £500,000 or more).

But Kings's real problem was finding a clerk to work underneath her to process the legal admin with the courts down the road. Whoever she asked assumed she would be working underneath them, and they refused to take her calls, while one spat at her. She finally found a woman who was a second junior clerk elsewhere but willing to make the move. And, with Helena Kennedy and not much time to spare before the launch, Kings went to IKEA to get furniture for the new but as yet empty building.

Starmer's new set used Christian names as in pre-Norman times instead of 'Sir' and dressed colourfully rather than in shades of grey. Others, large commercial sets, followed not much later down the same path—setting up shop outside the inns, but more so because the inns had started charging market rates since 1987 and the move was a way to rationalise their lucrative commercial business and pay structure on the clerks' side. At Doughty Street things were done more on a wing and a prayer. 'They had made a huge personal commitment to it—they had put in money and had taken a big risk, including with me and the staff—and they were going to make it work. We all were', Kings recalled of the set which was in 2021 probably as crowded as 1 Dr Johnson Buildings was in July 1990.

In a sign of the times, Starmer's pupil master Helena Kennedy became QC in May 1991, a few months after the move, together with Dominican-born barrister Patricia Scotland—who would appoint Starmer as DPP in 2008. Margaret Thatcher's Lord Chancellor, the very Scottish-kirk Lord Mackay, made the two female barristers up, and Kennedy said the chamber's joke was that 'I got it because I was Scottish and she got it because he thought she was Scottish'.

Echoing Starmer and Millar's discussion of the judiciary in *Socialist Lawyer*, Kennedy told the *Times*, who ran a lifestyle feature on her in 1991, that as judges 'are making decisions about others' discrimination, we should make sure we have a clean record from the point of view of women and ethnic minorities'. At that time, there were two female High Court judges out of 83 and 20 female circuit judges out of 428. But, as a sign of a growing number of humiliating government defeats in the courts, the *Times* noted that anywhere but in the law such views would be dismissed as coming from 'talking loony leftie wimmin's committees'.

Robertson QC, graced with a bouffant like Starmer, invited junior barrister Starmer to co-found Doughty Street as one of the twenty one. Like Starmer, he had done the two-year BCL and needed an assistant with an academic bent for appellate cases on pure points of law.

The duo scored one of their first successes while they were still based at 1 Dr Johnson Building. It involved a landmark case defeating Denmark and it struck down its government's utter confidence in the long-standing impartiality of Danish due process. The legal issue was whether the person who investigated the crime could also be the judge. This happened still to be the case in Denmark and the state's hubris was so great that it had offered a free trip to more than a hundred Danish students to witness this key plank of its legal system win acclaim and admiration before an international court.

'I had brought only my new secret weapon, a brilliant young junior, Keir Starmer', Robertson recalled in one of several memoirs of his life. Though Starmer had forgotten his passport on his first trip abroad, in those less centralised times Robertson was able to persuade French customs officers to *laisse passer* and the Strasburg court handed down a ringing victory to the two man team from Doughty Street on 24 May 1989, with TV cameras from European countries in attendance during the hearings.

The defendant himself was a bullion trader based in Switzerland, who had brought in Robertson in on the Strasburg stage of the appeal relating to a tax case in order to assist his Danish counsel. While the case underpinned an important principle on what exactly a fair trial meant, it was not really the type of client Starmer had in mind for his human-rights work at 54 Doughty Street.

'You would not find Keir customarily in wing collar and stripy trousers', Millar QC said. 'We both came into the profession in the 1980s when there was a generation of young lawyers concerned about miscarriages of justice and making the law more accessible, not speaking arcane language that no one could understand.' Specifically, 'Keir's purpose when he became a lawyer was not to make a fortune, or to build a glorious reputation', recalled Millar. 'Most of the work in those days was legal aid work. Some of it was *pro bono*'.

Where Starmer thought he could make the biggest contribution was from the inside rather than on the streets as one body among the many waving flags in protest against the high inflation, austerity and unemployment. 'Keir has always subscribed to the view that you have to get into the system and not stand outside it', said Millar, 'he would want to be on the inside, not out on the barricades.' They were lawyers driven by 'Thatcherism, the miners' strike, industrial conflicts, cuts to public sector and welfare budgets. It was a terrible, terrible time. Our reason for being there was to fight it.'

The cudgel for Britain's young civil liberties lawyers was the European Convention of Human Rights. If it could be used to strike down crusty Danish legal shibboleths, the same was true of those that existed in Britain.

The United Kingdom, where in particular Winston Churchill had been a driving force behind the convention, was one of the ten founding members of the treaty and its attendant Council of Europe—if not, as a result of Churchill and the Second World War, the leading nation among Belgium, Denmark, France, Ireland, Italy, Luxembourg, the Netherlands, Norway and Sweden.

Churchill's idea was historical and simple. The Second World War hadn't been fought merely as a random clash of empires. In the West, it had been a fierce existential fight of democracy and its system of peaceful transition of power between nationally opposing factions, against a totalitarian way of life.

'In the centre of our movement stands the idea of a Charter of Human Rights, guarded by freedom and sustained by law', he said, and the convention, drafted mainly by British lawyers, came into effect during his post-war years as prime minister. Close to 100 million citizens had lost their lives in this fight, half a million in the UK, and its entire population had suffered fourteen years of war rationing. From 1966, four years after Starmer's birth, the convention also conferred to every British citizen the individual right to petition the European Court of Justice in Strasburg if they felt a basic democratic right had been violated after exhausting legal appeals in their country.

Both Margaret Thatcher and John Major expressly affirmed their support for this individual right of British citizens to petition Strasburg, in 1989 and 1993 respectively, though both Prime Ministers were entitled to terminate this pledge and its self-imposed curb on national sovereignty for the purposes of democracy.

In fact, Starmer's human-rights inspiration drew in part from the same well as Churchill's. At Leeds, his deep interest in human rights, as opposed to the rule of law as such, came from the fact that at the end of the second world war and its atrocities of the second world war countries had voluntarily come together to say 'never again'.

'I became fascinated and really taken with the idea behind human rights really', he recalled of this time. 'It's not so much the individual rights, but it's the human dignity that sits behind human rights. How we treat individuals, how we treat them fairly equally', he told BBC's Laverne in 2020.

As with the Denmark case—the European Court's Treaty Division in Strasburg became in the 1990s the ultimate forum for British lawyers to test civil liberties at home within the framework set up and ratified in cross-party unison. Human-rights testing was, in fact, happening across Europe as a consequence of the franchise of the individual right to petition Strasburg throughout the member states of the convention.

It showed in the rise of petitions to the court under the treaty. In the 1960s, the court produced 10 judgements, 26 in the 1970s, 169 in the 1980s (one of them the Danish case), and some 65 a year from 1990s, rising to 950 a year from the noughties, arising from petitions brought in the 47 member states. From 1966 to 2010 there were 14,460 Strasburg petitions from the UK, 14,029 of which were rejected, and of the 431 the Court allowed 271 judgements found against UK law. For example, another famous Robertson case of 1996—in which Starmer wasn't involved, but John Mortimer QC from their old chambers was—was Goodwin vs the UK, which established the right of a journalist to protect their sources against the government's legal pressure, a hitherto unheard of right under Britain's common law.

What set Starmer apart from many of his fellow civil-liberties barristers at the time was one thing. He was not that captivated by the art of lawyering itself. He disagreed with lawyers who either thought—like the Danes—that Britain's legal system was subtle enough for a body of human rights law to be created within the existing frame work, or that legal codes existed to be thoroughly mistrusted by legal professionals. By nature not inclined to accept a solution by halves, he said, 'What I can't stand is when people walk around a problem and can't solve it so I have resolved not to do that.'

Familiar with Marxist theory, Starmer saw through Marx's sociology of Britain that the common law was essentially a collection of inventive riffs on the theme of my 'home is my castle'. Fine if you had one, but prone to lawyerly myopia if it wasn't about pounds and pennies. Despite its name, even in history the common law had been anything but common. It had left a whole host of private issues that fell outside its (extremely costly) framework to the devices of the patchwork of local courts covering Britain. Only partially, and after an inexpensive fashion, were these subsumed under the common law through Justices of the Peace and the like.

Truth be told, even the European Convention of Human Rights itself could be a bit dodgy for the socialist in Starmer. He reckoned in the *Socialist Lawyer* of Autumn 1995 that any attempt to bring about change through abstract declarations—e.g. those of the French and US revolutions, *La Déclaration universelle des droits de l'homme* and the Bill of Rights—was 'obsolete verbal rubbish' according to Karl Marx, who 'was, of course, right', Starmer concurred.

Though hardly universal in Starmer's eyes, the European Convention of Human Rights was nonetheless better than 'our hopelessly inadequate legal system' and it offered an opportunity to include rights that didn't just cover limitations on political power but also positive ones touching on economic power. So it allowed socialist lawyers at least to make a head-start with the ideal of equal distribution of jobs, food and housing and with corroding those 'common-law rules governing the property entitlements of private parties which for almost a thousand years judges have been to regard as pre-political norms'.

In short, the problem, as Starmer pointed out in the Millar interview on the British judiciary, were the 'parameters of laws which pay much more attention to individual property right than they do to the collective rights of ordinary people'.

It didn't help either that, although they had been abolished, common-lawyers still continued to think of legal issues like specific writs with a course of action that you sped off with a runner to court: no writ, no law, tough luck. Even, for example, as distinguished and brilliant a civil-liberties barrister as Geoffrey Robertson QC 'did not see gay rights … but then again nobody saw them and those who did kept them under the blanket' according to Robertson's mentor, former Australian Justice Michael Kirby.

Robertson's junior Starmer—a generation younger and coming at the common law from a radical left-left angle—considered them, however, an indivisible part of the panoply of human-rights surrounding women, the environment, housing, public order, peaceful protest and street campaigning, the right to silence, anti-terrorist legislation, police powers, trade unions, the right to strike, evidence, death penalty, free speech, race, evidence-gathering, torture, miscarriage of justice. Protest groups, like women groups, who were actively supporting the coal miners during the strikes, were from the start part of the Socialist Self-Management discussions, as were gay rights, represented by activist Peter Thatchell, one of several Australians in the movement, who wrote for both *Socialist Alternatives* and *Socialist Lawyer*.

Jonathan Cooper, the first openly gay barrister doing a pupillage at Doughty Street in 1992, recalled Starmer, a junior tenant at that time. Cooper had a history degree from the University of Kent and worked for years as AIDS co-ordinator at the Haemophilia Society trying to obtain compensation for sufferers of this genetic disease—infected at an industrial scale due to the blood-transfusions they required as treatment—at a time when there was enormous fear surrounding AIDS and very little sympathy for its patients. As part of his work, he came across people who fell between the cracks, such as a pregnant woman with HIV who was pressured to have a termination and be sterilised. When Cooper's society drafted a declaration of rights for people with HIV and AIDS he became interested in the law and retrained as a barrister.

'These were the worst years of the AIDS crisis', Cooper recalled. He knew many people who had died from AIDS, gay and straight sufferers from haemophilia, after a grim and excruciating death from funguses, germs and mutating cancerous cells that the immune system of an uninfected body would be able to protect against. It was a deadly version of the lethal risk that came with Starmer's mother's steroid medication that her doctors prescribed to switch off her over-active immune system and auto-inflammations caused by Still's disease and which made her 'very, very prone to infections', Starmer recalled. He had spent his youth, adolescence, and many times as a young man, in the NHS's high dependency units with Jo near-death, and Starmer had first-hand experience of the suffering that failure of the body's immune system brought.

'Keir knew I had good friends with AIDS and showed compassion and concern. He wanted to know how the law could help, and was quick to recognise that without a human rights-based approach to HIV/AIDS, there would be no solutions. AIDS troubled him profoundly, not in any hostile way, but in how to guarantee the dignity of all those affected, especially those who were dying. He also offered something that was unique to the debate. He was particularly concerned for the vulnerable already caught up within a marginalised community', Cooper recalled.

Starmer's response at the time was instinctively inclusive of small minorities. At a mid-1990s event they attended, 'A young trans/non-binary person stood up and shared their difficulties. In the face of some hostility, Keir leapt to their defence pointing out that human rights mean no one is excluded. He was clear: to trivialise gender identity undermines the human rights project', Cooper told Justice in an interview.

Starmer saw no distinction on a personal level either. He knew pupillage was tough on barristers and treated Cooper as the others. 'Keir made sure my boyfriend was as included as everyone else's partner', Cooper remembered. 'Keir wanted to know what my boyfriend and I had got up to over the weekend. Though it may not sound it, this was remarkable', Cooper recalled. 'Plenty of us would be gently teased because of our sexuality. Others might not mock but would still focus obsessively on our sexuality. Others found it easiest to ignore us.'

By a fluke, Cooper met Boris Johnson socially a few years before Starmer while he was still working at the Haemophilia Society. 'One night we ended up in a small private club in central London. Boris Johnson was there. My boyfriend wasn't. The banter was fun.' Johnson was totally at ease and referred fondly to Cooper's boyfriend 'Oh that shirt-lifter', a word which Cooper didn't know and that was explained with rising hilarity. A decade on, when they happened to meet again, Johnson retold this anecdote ending with a tongue-in-cheek punch line, 'I didn't say that'.

18. Strive Mightily

At 54 Doughty Street, the one-time Sixth-former who had never met solicitor or barrister before and had but a dim idea of what they did was surrounded by the chambers' idealistic barristers and its three associate tenants: Louis Blom Cooper QC, a South African and a Mauritian silk. They specifically aimed to prevent that the rule of law Britain became a mere slogan covering up pockets of arbitrary power, and for Starmer it was an unusual and once-in-a-life-time occurrence to be at the birth of this nascent legal-power movement.

In Starmer's eyes, in particular, the divining rods for those pockets of undemocratic rot were human rights. As much as democracies, totalitarian and oppressive regimes have written constitutions and promulgate laws, but only in order to deceive the real power relations between the state and citizens. In those countries the rule of law was a perversion, 'an outright deception' he wrote. The Doughty Street lawyers were determined to put before a British court every suspected violation in Britain if they could in order to scrape them off like barnacles from the hull of a ship.

Apart from Geoffrey Robertson QC, the store of excellence among the other senior barristers at the infant chambers was towering. But it was Ed Fitzgerald, a genial man with an enthusiastic beaming smile, who became Starmer's mentor and a close friend. Fitzgerald was a passionate and fearless human rights lawyer who had a knack for taking on unpopular cases. Apart from defending the Moors murderer Myra Hindley, like Hooson, the lead QC at the set they had left, there were child killers Mary Bell, Jon Venables—one of Jamie Bulger's killers— various IRA prisoners and Abu Hamza, the controversial Muslim cleric with a hook-hand who was extradited and convicted as a terrorist in the US, as well as Abu Qatada, the suspected terrorist acquitted of charges in Jordan. He became a QC in 1995, four years after Kennedy.

Like his mentor, Starmer was not afraid to take on unpopular defendants during his career and was to represent a convicted paedophile in 2002 who sought to have his face pixilated or otherwise altered so that he could not be identified in a BBC documentary. Starmer told the court, 'We say there is a real risk of physical attack if his name and image are shown together, along with adverse comment from police officers about the leniency of his sentence.' The judge did not agree, though he did impose a ban on any information which would lead to identification of the part of the country where the man lived.

Their life-long collaboration would be celebrated by Starmer as guest editor of a special issue of *European Human Rights Law Review* in honour of Fitzgerald's sixtieth birthday. David Pannick QC, often Fitzgerald's opponent for the government, called Fitzgerald on the occasion in his *Times* column, 'a Rolls Royce in the cab rank of barristers' saying how he himself would be the sacrificial lamb over whom submissions poured out while Fitzgerald emitted 'noisy and impressive quantities of passionate commitment. As he warmed to his task, his arms would increasingly take on the form of a windmill, his voice rose in volume and his facial expressions conveyed his disagreement, disapproval, astonishment, disgust and contempt'. Starmer was to develop his own style, though.

It was on the dramatic occasion of Salman Rushdie's *Satanic Verses* that Starmer saw these three leading men perform in court in 1990— only a few months before Doughty Street opened its doors. Robertson QC, Fitzgerald and Pannick, flanked by Robertson's 'secret weapon' Starmer as junior barrister, squared up with Penguin to defend the publisher's release of *Satanic Verses*. After Iranian leader Ayatollah Khomeini had issued a death warrant against the novel's author Salman Rushdie, he was secretly living in hiding under police protection in Lonsdale Square, a mile from his home in Islington and would remain fearful of his life for decades to come. At stake was whether the publisher could be prosecuted further to the common law offences of seditious libel and blasphemy, or under the Public Order Act—prosecutions that were being petitioned by Muslim activists.

Rushdie and Penguin's bevy of lawyers were given police protection on their way to court in recognition of the gravity of the situation. In the heat of the reports about global mayhem and deaths surrounding the novel, there had been a number of failed attempts to set fire to bookshops that sold the novel. When some protesters alerted the press that a group were going to burn a copy, echoing infamous book burnings in the past, and called for national censorship, the lid seemed to have blown off. Correspondents were sent to Muslim areas, especially to Bradford, to report on the sentiments among its population about the book's commotion and what the local view was of the fatwa that Khomeini had proclaimed over Rushdie's life. In the event, the lawyers were successful and limited any prosecution for blasphemy to Christianity only and the year after Robertson argued its antiquated prosecutions out of existence.

Starmer watched the young Doughty Street chambers score other heady victories set against the backdrop that same year of the surprise resignation of Margaret Thatcher at the hands of her own party and Blom-Cooper QC's Royal Commission exposed the shady links between Pablo Pablo Escobar's Medellin drugs cartel, the Israeli arms industry and US protectorate Antigua.

Ambitious as he was, it spurred Starmer on to lay the foundation for one of his own first major successes at the young chambers while protecting the underdog. Perhaps remembering that his great-grandfather had been invalided after service in the First World War, in 1991, he represented the families of six British soldiers killed in Iraq during the Gulf War in friendly fire. The distraught relatives of the privates from the 9th Royal Fusiliers Regiment had received a report from the US on what had happened, but all the relevant sections had been blacked out. Nine British soldiers had died in total while eleven others were injured when an American A10 aircraft fired on two British armoured personnel carriers.

In a legal coup, Starmer petitioned the Oxford Coroner successfully for a jury trial given the fact that British military details of what happened conflicted with US reports. 'It is clear that the death occurred because the system of communication between the ground and aircraft broke down. This was not the only incident of so-called friendly fire. An alarming number of deaths were caused by fire of some sort from the same side as the people who died', he said. No fewer than forty per cent of British casualties fell under this category and that meant NATO procedures urgently needed to be reviewed and changed, he argued.

'Just brilliant', the families responded to the news of a jury inquest in the *Times*. At the trial Robertson QC scored Starmer's pass to him by persuading the jury to return a verdict of 'aerial manslaughter' in a blaze of publicity. Asked on the occasion of Doughty Street's thirtieth birthday what the chambers' triumphs had been, it was this case that he included among the handful of early key victories of his set.

But Starmer was a different type of lawyer from his more theatrical mentors. Whereas Robertson and Fitzgerald were captivating jury whisperers, much like Michael Mansfield QC, who was older but also wrote on occasion for Starmer's *Socialist Lawyer*, and many other famous courtroom performers, Starmer himself was more of a judge whisperer. 'I've never seen him make a rabble-rousing speech, I don't think that would be in his nature', said fellow barrister Professor Bill Bowring and Haldane Society president at the time.

'There's something slightly missing where the rousing stuff might need to be,' said another fan of Starmer's who wanted to remain anonymous. 'Keir's real speciality is getting it right. He can unpick an argument brilliantly, but he's not such a natural at the passion behind the argument.'

At Doughty Street, Starmer's superlative skill was his limpid understanding of the law. Even though he might have lacked the verbal flair or even lack an innate interest in pressing a jury's psychological buttons like the star advocates, 'he was', said Gavin Millar QC, 'very good at spotting the winning point in a case'. He might lose in lower courts where a jury would decide issues of facts, but on appeal, with the facts out of the way one way or another, he could focus on points of law that would woo the judges.

It wasn't just Doughty Street barristers who saw that early legal promise. It was clear to the wider outside world of campaigners as well. Jane Winter of the British Irish Rights Watch, who met Starmer in his first years at the new chambers and who wrote for *Socialist Lawyer* on the legal issues in Northern Ireland, recalled, 'He could win cases that everyone else thought nobody could win'. Through the jumble of facts and the common-law's habitual torrent of legal citations and cases, Starmer saw with 20:20 vision where the broad avenues of the law lay that judges felt duty bound to observe in their judgements and ferried through the clients he represented.

19. Judge Whisperer

From the start, Starmer set out a blue-print for his own work from when he joined the team at Doughty Street and it divided into two distinct parts. The first was to hunt for cases that could successfully be litigated, if need be all the way to Strasburg—not easy given the European Court of Justice's very picky approach in hearing only 1 in 35 petitions. Not many of these cases would involve well-heeled Swiss bullion traders and a lot of them would have to be argued *pro bono* and would even require contributing his own money apart from time (fifteen years later, Starmer would receive the Bar Council's prestigious Elland Goldsmith time award for his contribution to pro bono work in 2005).

The second line of strategic attack was to start making the case in the wider legal world for the introduction of a Human Rights Act. Starmer considered the common law incapable of handling human rights organically. 'The legal system, which is orientated almost exclusively to individual rights, has erected huge obstacles, whether legal, procedural, financial or cultural' to wider human rights, he co-wrote in the second issue of *Soundings*, a magazine launched by a Marxist press in 1995.

Given the expense alone, a more open and fair system of justice, required an act of Parliament authorising the courts to adopt out new 'parameters' that they could apply. The parameters would be enshrined a Human Rights Act based on the treaty Churchill had espoused and after the royal assent the real work would start. Assimilation into the common law was a gradual process as it required Britain's judges to establish, case by case, bright lines of a new and different nature from their nineteenth-century mercantile traditions. This meant continuous feeding of the system with the right cases after the Act became law.

Starmer was not the only one who saw this need, but through his deep political conviction he was a relentless collective force for change from the inside. 'His modus operandi is unity. He cares about the collective', said Gavin Millar QC.

It was this single-minded, sometimes absent-minded, concentration that made that him the stuff of legends for his Archway flatmates.

Starmer was 'very driven and focused', Paul Vickers recalled in 2009, before his death. Starmer was constantly at his desk, and out came the books and files over which he pored to his own marching tune. 'He was very keen on Desmond Dekker['s reggae]: His favourite record was 'Israelites'. We'd have to listen to it dozens of times a week'.

It led to another famous Starmer anecdote. One day, Vickers returned home to find their television and video recorder in the hands of two men passing him on the way down. 'I ran upstairs thinking I was going to find an empty, ransacked house—and there was Keir sitting at his desk working,' he said. 'He was so obsessed with his books, so buried in his texts, that he didn't notice two burglars walking round the house, helping themselves to our stuff.'

As Starmer himself said, 'I think it was an Amstrad or some sort of bashing away, deep in thought. And then one of the other people in the flat came back up and said, Keir, what are you doing? Did you not notice?' He was sitting in the room next door as the two men started carrying off their belongings until Vickers intercepted them. Would they have continued to ply their trade if Starmer's non-custodial sentences had been their punishment after being caught red-handed by the police rather than Vickers?

From behind this desk, Starmer unleashed an explosion of words and energy to achieve the two goals he had set out to achieve. He became secretary of the Haldane Society in 1988 and, working closely with its new chair from 1990 Bill Bowring, organised the society's legal activities over the next five years of its subcommittees, much like a field marshal advances his troops. He put the Society on a robust financial basis, obtained premises for it, and set up an outreach trust with a paid member of staff. He remained on the editorial board for the same period until 1992, and during this busy time still every now and had the time to write about his own cases or about the nuts and bolts of the society. Afterwards, he stayed on as the Society's treasurer until 1996 and was a member of the Northern Ireland and International subcommittees. Bowring, chair until 1994, was full of praise for Starmer as a 'very good organiser'.

More and more, Starmer researched in detail the case for a Human Rights Act in order to put on paper why one was needed, writing, editing and contributing to a torrent of legal books over the next decade. He taught and was to become as human rights research fellow, member or chair at the Human Rights Centre of the University of Essex, the London School of Economics Centre for the Study of Human Rights, and the Human Rights Unit at King's College, London. Given time off for his writing, he completed as author, editor or co-author *Justice in Error* (1993, with Clive Walker) *The Three Pillars of Justice* (1996, with Francesca Klug and Stuart Weir), *European Human Rights Law* (1999), *Miscarriages of Justice* (1999, with Clive Walker), *Criminal Justice, Police Powers and Human Rights* (2001), *Blackstone's Human Rights Digest* (2001) in addition to a raft of legal articles, chapters and talks for lawyers organised by Justice.

Starmer in such a full-on activism trance of doing good could come across as a little stiff and wooden, noticeable even to other workaholic barristers who inhabited London's legal micro planet. Charlie (Lord) Falconer QC, who started out alongside Tony Blair as a commercial barrister and became his Solicitor General and later Lord Chancellor, often interacted with the young Starmer on Labour Party matters.

The Starmer he met was 'utterly committed to the causes of the left'. As the object of Starmer's lobbying, however, Falconer did not meet the 'team player' Doughty Street colleagues knew so well and who enlivened their meetings at the Duke pub around the corner on John Mews, or Salaam Namaste in Millman Street, another favourite place for the chambers' silks. The person he encountered was a 'loner who thinks things through for himself'. Starmer's unrelenting-drive often rendered him working late-hours alone and Charlie Falconer described the young Starmer as a 'very intense, committed, slightly isolated figure.'

'He's not a particularly clubbable figure; he is a man alone,' Falconer added. But, 'He is the real deal—every time you would speak to Keir, he would be engaged in a particular cause. He was completely motivated in all he did in the law by politics.' The man he encountered, 'could have made all the money he wanted. He never did. Politics always dictated the work he did,' said Falconer.

The sense of being more comfortable with his own company than was optically acceptable for a political leader was one of the things the young Starmer had in common with the young Boris Johnson. Jeya Wilson, president of the Oxford debating society before Johnson, recalled how his first attempt to win the presidency ended in complete failure.

He was too sure of himself, having come from Eton where he had been a member of 'Pop', another self-elected club with a thing for waistcoats like the Bullingdon but at Eton rather than at Oxford. Johnson quickly learned from his mistake, however. 'During his first attempt at the Oxford Union, Boris was often seen prowling the streets of Oxford by himself. Chastened, on his second time attempt he accepted that solitary walks were verboten and his election minders saw to it that he never walked alone but had at least one political heavyweight with him', Wilson said about their heady days of student politics.

The work Starmer and others put into lobbying the Labour Party on human rights bore fruit five years later in 1995 when the Labour Party Conference adopted the plan to incorporate the European convention into domestic law through a dedicated act of Parliament. The year before The Criminal Justice and Public Order Act 1994 had been passed by John Major's Home Secretary Michael Howard, which, in Starmer's legal prose, 'swept away rights such as the right to silence and the right to peaceful protest. Save for so-called "anti-terrorist" legislation, it marks the low-point of this government's respect for civil liberties'.

But Labour's commitment to a Human Rights Act provided Tony Blair with a clear pivot to put to the voter in view of the many new restrictive powers the Conservative party were introducing under the rule of law, and whether the electorate agreed or not. Starmer wrote in *Socialist Lawyer* about his prime example of Conservative excess under Howard's Act, where 'police officers can banish any individual from a given area of land on the basis that they think that person is going to commit an offence of "aggravated trespass". If that person comes back within three months he or she commits an offence. Worse still, there is no appeal from the police officer's order (save for the hopeless remedy of judicial review, which essentially means that the applicant has to show that the police officer took leave of his or her senses).'

20. Hippies in Hedgerows

With his Doughty Street colleagues Starmer could deal direct hammer blows aiding the protection of the vulnerable. Here lay the fundamental difference between Starmer and politicians Andrew Cooper and David Miliband. Being a barrister meant forcing through reform at the coal face of human rights. In court he could help forge decisions that advanced or moved back the rule of law one precedent at the time.

This process had immense advantages for someone practical with left left leanings. Instead of joining endless debates about choice utopias creating ever-smaller fractals of like-minded committed committee visionaries—Tony Benn, twelve years out of power, wrote in *Socialist Lawyer* of Spring 1993 about his 'Commonwealth of Britain Bill' for a republic to be founded with a 'Peoples House'—Starmer's advocacy in a court of law funnelled his views into a binary outcome. As had been the case 23 Tanhouse Road, once the court had spoken that was the way it was and you moved on. He could work with that. Although he might have preferred more complex terminology, this fair and sincere hearing in court was the plain and simple embodiment of decency that he looked for in human rights, socialism and civil liberties.

It did mean that Starmer himself had to become visible to those in need of legal help and create a name for himself. His first steps down this road started as early as 1989, as he was still doing his second 'six' months as a pupil under Irwin and Kennedy at 1 Dr Johnson Building. Shaping his name as a legal activist was key and in his first year he was legal officer of the National Council of Civil Liberties, as well as ad hoc spokesperson for the Children's Legal Centre, Legal Action Group, The Haldane Society, The Liberal Movement (an early Homeric nod of Starmer's pragmatism as a left leftie), National Association for Care and Resettlement of Offenders, and the National Association of Probation Officers with his name appeared several times in national newspapers from the *Guardian* to the *Times* while commenting on matters as diverse as proposed changes to the right of silence and use of video in parades and questioning, as well as the police use of blockades and no-go zones.

With Nick Cohen interviewing him for the *Guardian*, Starmer's name appeared prominently on page 5 of the paper where he objected on 29 June 1989 on behalf of the NCCL to the presence of 800 police aiming to prevent hippies from congregating around Stonehenge. The monument was situated 500 feet off the A303 and the police had been as successful in dispersing the crowds on the 21 June summer solstice as the hippies were hopelessly disorganised, and Starmer's quote stood as proxy for the druid fiends or hippy 'vagabonds', depending on which side of argument you stood.

Spokesperson for the NCCL, 1989

It was the police's behaviour that irked Starmer and the NCCL. Under the freshly-minted Section 13 of the Public Order Act 1986, the police had created a four-mile henge exclusion zone for 'groups' of two or more people that covered the fields and fringes of the tiny villages in close proximity to the stone-age monument. Of the 250 or so people who pitched up at the blockade, half were charged and half were cautioned and released. Whisked off to special courts in Salisbury, those who pleaded guilty were given substantial fines of £30 to £50 while the others were released on bail conditional upon respecting the exclusion zone.

And even beyond the zone, a group of 50 stragglers was hastily escorted back from the perimeter and police 'snatch squads' picked off druids from the nearby village centre of Amesbury with much running by both sides and disgruntled swearing and shouting by the revelling prey. Hippies hid in hedgerows, and at night the police swooped round with a helicopter and a powerful search light rounding up all but six, who were caught in the end by Stonehenge's private guards.

Starmer's and the NCCL's interest here was less with protecting druids on a stone-age mission than with the legal use of blockades, a device pioneered against Wapping workers on strike. They were the self-appointed answer to ancient Rome's *quis custodiet ipsos custodes*, or as Starmer put it in *Socialist Alternatives*, 'the question of the role the police should play, if any, in civil society. Who are they protecting and from what?' The NCCL was an Ur-version of the meta-political structures Benn and Starmer's Self-Management movement envisaged. Before 1986 police no-go zones had been far and few between, but in 1989, after the 1986 Act, there was one almost every week, which the NCCL considered as so many likely instances of unlawful restraint.

As Starmer wrote in the Winter 1990 *Socialist Lawyer*, it was established from the first-ever case litigated under the 1986 Act that 'contrary to popular opinion, the police have no general power to set up roadblocks. Whilst people and vehicles can be stopped and searched if certain conditions are satisfied, there is only one circumstance in which people can be physically prevented from continuing their chosen journey. A roadblock can be set up when a police officer has reasonable grounds for believing that a breach of the peace is imminent'.

Thus, on behalf of the NCCL, Starmer told the *Guardian* the police had no right to create a no-go zone and he added tartly that a 'gross infringement of freedom of movement' had taken place. Quite a few villagers heartily agreed with Starmer, as they had been indiscriminately caught in the blockade after going out for a drink or take-away and the police officiously blocked them from going back to their homes in case a druid might wander in sheep's clothes. To their huge irritation, they had to wait until the blockade was lifted. Presumably, their number was the half of the 250 reaching the barricades who were cautioned and released rather than charged. The manager of the local hotel, Mary Hard, was deeply underwhelmed with the local constabulary and said, 'This is over the top. I can't see why they just can't let them go to Stonehenge.'

Hidden behind 1989 Summer-Solstice-gate lay in fact a long-running commercial negotiation in which the police was moving pro-actively for the owners, much like at the Wapping strikes. Over a decade and a half, the Conservative government did seem to have it in for druids as much as miners and printers. The year before, owner of the site English Heritage had failed to persuade 60 celebrants, who planned to officiate at the 4.47am sunrise by blowing on rams' horn trumpets, to create an event under escort with 1,100 tickets. The use of police power and public money for private purposes after a failed business negotiation by English Heritage irritated the NCCL no end.

The year before druids had conjured up 4000 followers who were repelled by 1,000 riot police while they were being pelted with stones, bottles and anything else the rowing visitors could find to gain access to the ancient site, leading to 70 arrests and 10 injured. This charge in turn had followed on from the infamous 1 June 1985 Battle of the Beanfield, when 1,300 police prevented 600 New Age revellers from setting up camp for the Stonehenge Free Festival after English Heritage had closed public access to the site.

In 1985, in the process of enforcing a high-court injunction—not a matter of criminal law as such—in favour of English Heritage, Wiltshire police arrested 537 people—a battle-scalp number almost worthy of the *Guinness Book of Records* as the highest since the Second World War. The druids claimed that the police clubbed pregnant women and women with babies, while the police alleged that the revellers rammed their perimeter with cars and were armed with petrol bombs. In part as a response to this battle, Thatcher's Public Order Act 1986 aimed to create blanket no-go zones with police cordons over private or public land, breach of which was punishable as an offence.

In 1989 there was no society of druids to defend in court and Starmer could only suggest in the *Guardian* that the hippies should each individually get a lawyer to challenge Wiltshire's bobbies. That would change with the much more clued-up organisers of Acid House raves, including Guido Fawkes.

21. Acid House and Druids in White Cotton

Another chance for the NCCL to litigate cases under the Act and for Starmer to profile himself as a legal campaigner against what he saw as government oppression came with the sudden craze for Acid House parties in 1989.

These rural raves for many thousands of revellers were—in Starmer's dismissive eyes—gatherings of 'Thatcher's children, middle-class youths clad in designer labels and Reebok trainers' and wealthy enough to have cars. As there was no serving of alcohol, these raves were valuable to the NCCL's cause. It was not hard to make the case that the police was exercising its new powers unlawfully when it tried to prevent the raves with no-go zones merely in order to spoil the Thatcher youths' fun, as Starmer wrote in *Socialist Lawyer*. They were very well behaved and, being Thatcher's youths, there was no chequered history of clashing violently with the police, unlike the druids.

Like hippies at Stonehenge, the raves got Home Secretary Douglas Hurd very hot around the collar. Yet the Court of Appeal had just interpreted Hurd's 1986 Act in such a way that, if the police wanted to create a no-go zone it could do so, but only if there was a likely breach of the peace—meaning imminent assault, affray or riot. Legally, that clearly excluded teenage twists to music, or just noise. Ergo, the Acid House blockades were illegal.

Following the Court of Appeal's decision, the NCCL successfully helped promoter 'Lost in Space' to claim for damages after Thames Valley police had set up a roadblock on the M4 and elsewhere to turn dancers away from Lambourne, Berkshire, and 60 officers supported by a helicopter confiscated £40,000 worth of goods among the lasers, lights, video screens, sound systems, take-away food, mobile lavatories the organisers had set up protected by a security firm. To stop the event Thames Valley police had even taken the owner of the land to the police station, having threatened to lock up another land owner at an event elsewhere.

Speaking to the *Guardian* in August, Starmer upped the ante and called it 'an incredible abuse of police powers' and said 'what happened was outrageous and unlawful', as indeed it was after the Court of Appeal's decision.

Having to forego its public-order powers, the police now desperately tried to deter raves by prosecuting promoters under licensing laws that regulated public parties. Starmer, ostensibly engaged on his own rather than acting through the NCCL, again stood in their way. He had by May 1989 gained the right of audience as a barrister and defended a promoter called 'Sunrise Productions'/'Back to the Future' in court with regards to its mega-successful party of 7,000 in a disused aircraft hangar on the outskirts of Maidenhead.

Here, too, Starmer was successful and argued ingeniously that the £15 fully-insured access was restricted to members of the clubs organised by the promoters' (who had been told to create a members list that had grown in size from 200 to 12,000) and therefore this was not a public event that was subject to a license. The court agreed.

This case blew the lid off raves as the police were now largely unable to stop them in time. Not everyone minded as much as Home Secretary Douglas Hurd. 'There's much more trouble at Young Farmers' dos', one land owner had marvelled about the thousands of youths, 'It was the most fantastically well-behaved crowd I've ever seen'. The estimated 50,000 curiously docile, spacy people that attended raves in 1989 had caused fewer than five instances of violence, though the organisers did hastily regroup in January 1990 to ensure that 'the only thing our party-goers get high on is Lucozade and music.'

After their fifteen minutes of Acid House fame, a Conservative Private Bill, however, closed off the club loophole later that year. 'Sunrise's' 24-year-old Tony Colston-Hayter was to end up in prison in 2018 after pleading guilty to hacking banks and fraud for over £1.3 million. The organisation's other promoter was 22-year old Paul Staines, a student at Humberside University, member of its Conservative association as well as author of a 1989 report on human rights in Nicaragua published by the International Society of Human Rights, headquartered in Strasburg. Staines later became a professional gambler and would cross swords again with Starmer as popular blogger Guido Fawkes with a self-confessed hatred of politicians and a bracing promise—'I pummel them until they beg for mercy'.

Having successfully shut down countryside raves, the Conservative government did not give up on Stonehenge either. After Margaret Thatcher's quick tumble from power in November that year, a procession of Home Secretaries under John Major culminated in the appointment of Michael Howard. Even according to right-wing Conservative colleague Anne Widdecombe he 'had something of the night' over him. He certainly became a formidable foe of the dawn-seeking druids to whose defence Starmer rose once again.

Howard's difficulty still was that Starmer and Liberty, as the NCCL had been restyled, had killed off police roadblocks in the courts. In theory, English Heritage could serve individual injunctions for trespass, but the state of technology in the 1990s (and still today) made this a paper lion. Howard's answer was to create a new criminal offence called 'trespassory assembly', which he did in the Criminal Justice and Public Order Act 1994. In effect, this was version 2.0 of Hurd's Public Order Act 1986.

It was now King Arthur Pendragon, the Honoured Pendragon of the Glastonbury Order of Druids, Official Sword Bearer of the Secular Order of Druids, Chief of the Loyal Arthurian Wayband, who sought Starmer's support. Since the bruised losses at the Battle of the Beanfield in 1985, he and fellow druids no longer went up to the monument and respected English Heritage ownership of the site. But they did come together every year to stand along a road-side fence of the A344 near Stonehenge. Waiting for sunrise, he would touch the outlying 'sacred' Hele Stone with Excalibur in a pared-down ceremony from the more full-on one they really wanted to celebrate.

Armed with Howard's Act's new provisions, Wiltshire County was the first to deploy them and issued an order to prohibit assembly of twenty—giving locals a break—or more trespassers around five miles from Stonehenge for a four day period during the 21 June 1995 summer solstice. When King Arthur, surrounded by a band of 20 of his druids, declined to disperse before sunrise, he was arrested under the Act, refused bail, and flung into jail until dawn had passed. The police took great care this time not to be seen to be acting heavy-handedly.

Starmer, in the words of Liberty 'left the Act in tatters'. He defended

King Arthur's not-guilty plea before Salisbury Magistrates, while Arthur himself, clad in white, wearing an Iron-Age head band, swore on Excalibur to tell the truth and conceded he was age 52 instead of his more usual given age of 937. The magistrates were persuaded that the druids were exercising their fundamental human right to religion and that a string of druids did not amount to an 'assembly' under Michael Howard's new Section 14.

It was still more of a blue eye for Michael Howard than quite the knock-out blow that Liberty said it was. K.O. came with Dr Margaret Jones and Richard Lloyd, neither of them druids in an official capacity as Dr Jones was a Marxist praxist, poll-tax veteran, veal-trade protester and also a forty-six-year-old senior lecturer in American literature at the University of the West of England, Bristol, while Mr Lloyd was her twenty-five-year-old student. Supporters would in 2011 describe her as 'Swampy's Sister', after the tunnel-digging eco-warrior, and as a forty-nine-year old.

The two protesters stood with 19 others armed with banners on a footpath near Hele Stone but just outside the henge's perimeter on 1 June 1995 to commemorate the tenth anniversary of the beanfield battle when they were arrested by the Wiltshire constabulary. Using ad absurdum an 1892 case of a one-man protest against the Duke of Rutland's grouse-shooting that would have made his game-keeper ancestors grumble, Starmer argued that 'a clear trend towards recognising peaceful, non-obstructive assembly as a reasonable use of the highway'. On appeal at Salisbury Crown Court, Starmer won again under common law and without having to appeal to the incorporation of human rights. 'Common sense 1, Michael Howard 0', Starmer gleefully said in *Socialist Lawyer*.

He wrote a little too soon, however. Michael Butt, who had called Starmer a 'time waster' in court, prevailed before the Queen's Bench in 1997 whose judges decided that a right of passage on a public highway did not come with a right to assemble as Starmer had argued.

Ultimately, Starmer triumphed with his colleague Fitzgerald QC before the House of Lords when three against two of the law lords found in 1999, in time for the Summer solstice, that times had indeed moved on from the Duke of Rutland and that peaceful protest did not amount to 'trespassory assembly' under the 1994 Act after all. They disarmed Howard's law quite broadly by stating 'that the public highway was a public place on which all manner of reasonable activities might go on'. To the extent that the police itself was minded to block a public road it meant in effect that it, too, had to come up with more than 'because I say so'. The judges agreed with the common sense of judge-whisperer Starmer.

Though couched in the common law's confetti of cases and words, the House of Lords' ruling had in fact secured the protester's freedom of expression, a right included in the 1998 Human Rights Act that had just been given the royal assent. There would be several further Starmer iterations of the right to protest on public roads further new offences created by Labour. With his Doughty Street colleagues he would constantly successfully bat these away for peaceful protesters.

Swampy's Sister and Mr Lloyd were free once again to protest and Dr Robert's Marxist *praxis* graduated in 2011 to pleading guilty to resisting an officer during another road protest in a case beyond the shield of human rights. She was trying to prevent the completion of the last section of Bristol's Avon Ring Road and had barricaded herself in an aerie in the rafters of a disused warehouse surrounded by a 20 feet tall metal fence in a muddy field. She had never before aimed to break settled law, but this time she had, she accepted, 'I'm going to plead guilty because I am. In fact, I wish everyone else was guilty too.'

22. 'Rightness'

In the year that Starmer was its legal officer, the National Council of Civil Liberties had technically already changed its name to the more aspirational moniker Liberty by 24 January, 1989, the last year of its General Secretary Sarah Spender. Although the name change was the upshot of a review by management consultants, which thought the council was firing on too many cylinders, it reflected an ideological shift from fighting citizenship impediments to the broader aim of enabling citizenship.

This would have suited Starmer at this time, who co-wrote in *Soundings* in 1996 that collective action by the working class has 'been largely suppressed, often in the name of the defence of democratic rights. It is precisely because these forms of action are so potent that they are so strongly resisted, and for that reason it is vital that they are defended'. Together with Beverly Lang (a high court judge since 2011), he attended Liberty's two-day AGM in April 1991 on behalf of the Haldane Society, as Liberty was launching a Justice Reform campaign. The society's proposed changes to the judiciary were accepted by Liberty, and, 'as in previous years, the most controversial issues at the AGM were pornography and a Bill of Rights', the *Socialist Lawyer* reported drily.

The NCCL was not averse to picking trickier fights than the freedom of druids and raves as proxies for the right to strike. Early on its active members had included writers E.M. Forster, Rose Macaulay, Virginia and Leonard Woolf, C.P. Snow, magistrate Margery Fry and historian R.H. Tawney, all lining up for freedom of expression at a time when communists were seen by many as the enemy within.

A 1975 NCCL meeting about prevention of terror legislation in Manchester led to hospitalisation of eleven members after attacks by the National Front and the Ulster Volunteer Force. Even so, and notwithstanding the violent attack, the NCCL stuck to principle and twice gave free-speech advice to the National Front under the NCCL's 1985-1986 General Secretary Larry Gostin, a American mental-health lawyer.

Surprisingly given the number of writers, education, the elephant in the room, was never much on the NCCL/Liberty's radar during its century-long existence, nor was it on that of the left left, or Starmer for that matter

Starmer was by now a go-to person for comment in the national press and happy to speak out where the issue wasn't going to win him many dinner invitations. On 19 December 1990, just after Margaret Thatcher had resigned, the High Court handed down its verdict in R. v Brown, further to a police investigation that led to the prosecution of sixteen men with convictions ranging from fines, suspended sentences, and twelve months to four and a half years for the ring leaders for causing consensual actual bodily harm.

It was the time when Starmer was still more ambivalent towards sentencing, and the police operation was spear-headed by Scotland Yard's Obscene Publications Squad. Eighty-year old cultural crusader Mary Whitehouse was frequently in the news—so much so that an eponymous youth programme launched the careers of several young comedians, David Baddiel, Steve Punt, Hugh Dennis and Jo Brand among them, in the wake of the spoof success of Spitting Image. There was also the government's 'Don't Die of Ignorance' AIDS campaign that had run in election year 1987, followed by Margaret Thatcher's Section 28 further to her Election Party Conference promise to prohibit promoting 'the acceptability of homosexuality as a pretended family relationship' in schools. In one of its campaigns, the press reported gleefully, the Obscene Publications Squad had raided Soho seedy video-rental shops and bagged a comedy horror film.

It was however the recovery of a home-made video tape among a total of four during what was termed 'a regular house raid' in Manchester that led to the Scotland Yard operation across sixteen of Britain's local police forces. With the certainty of someone young still convinced of their 'rightness', the twenty-eight-year-old Starmer gave the *Times* on behalf of the Haldane Society a very strong condemnation of the verdict and said in bold terms that 'morality was a question for Parliament not judges'.

The Obscene-Publications Squad established that sixteen defendants had privately circulated and produced a multitude of home-videos shot in various private locations and, while no money passed hands, that the video ring involved a total of forty-four men including an international lawyer, a missile designer and a lay preacher, and several who were married or lived with girlfriends. The images the men shared showed scarring and spanking, hence national headlines such as 'Torture Vice Gang' (*Daily Telegraph*), 'Vicious and Perverted Sex Gang' (*Times*), 'Horrific Porn Ring' (*Daily Mail*) 'Pain Brigade' (*Sun*) and 'Sado-Masochists' (*Guardian*).

Contrary to Doughty Street's junior barrister's thoughts on the matter, the judge in charge of the proceedings had been clear. Handing down his verdict against the sixteen on charges of actual bodily harm, Judge Rant said, 'no one who had heard what had happened would say "men should be free to practise this kind of thing on one another".' The video tapes were evidence relied on to convict the group and invited to view the most graphic videos, the press reported, the judge's face had gone white and asked for an adjournment.

A number of the ring leaders took their convictions to Strasburg for an appeal under Section 8, the right to privacy, with Pannick QC arguing against them for the government. They thought they had a strong human-rights case as there had been no financial gain and all participants agreed consent had not been coerced. A few months before the 1997 General Election, the Strasburg court rejected their appeal with David Pannick QC representing the government.

Liberty's new secretary general, Andrew Puddephatt, a Cambridge English graduate, was interviewed alongside Starmer in the *Times*. He pointed at a sophisticated legal anomaly in the verdict. Some of the sentences exceeded ones handed down for men convicted of violently raping women and also exceeded instances of actual-bodily-harm, referred to as 'queer bashing' by Puddephatt. It suggested, he concluded, that, since these rape and queer-bashing victims objected to what had been inflicted on them, their objection to being violated was a mitigating factor for sentencing the perpetrators under the common law. 'We urgently need a law of privacy enshrined in the law which would a basis for assessing what is or what is not permissible in private', the Cambridge graduate, who was also one of Starmer's co-campaigners for a Human Rights Act, added more fuzzily.

Surprisingly, six years later the Court of Appeal seemed to take its own step in the direction of recognising privacy in 1996, John Major's penultimate year in government, in a case where a Mr Wilson used a hot knife to scar the capital letters 'W' on one and 'A' on Mrs Wilson's other buttock. Judge Rant had ruled earlier that anyone faced jailtime, whether 'heterosexuals or bisexuals'. However, what happened 'in the privacy of the matrimonial home' was not 'a proper matter for criminal investigation, let alone criminal prosecution' Lord Justice Russell said in the Court of Appeal's decision, adding that these acts were instances of marital 'desiring'—a ruling that would apply post same-sex-marriage introduced in 2014 further to the policy Cooper, Lord Windrush, designed.

By sheer coincidence, months before Baroness Scotland announced in July 2008 that Starmer would become the new Director of Public Prosecutions, Home Secretary Jacqui Smith shepherded a new offence through Parliament that made good on Starmer's 1990 comment in the *Times*. It was a new crime she brought on the statute book as Section 63 of the Criminal Justice and Immigration Act 2008 and it wrapped like a glove around the verdict of the sixteen men. Although the prompt for Section 63 was a horrific murder case that dominated the news five years earlier, the new offence also covered the facts of the 1990 case Starmer had criticised.

No longer a critic on the outside but working on the inside of Westminster, it was Starmer's job as DPP to execute the Crown Prosecution's policy on the new offence when his five year term started in November 2008. Human-rights poacher turned gamekeeper, what would Starmer do eighteen years later on the Westminster side?

Possession of a single real or realistic-looking 'grossly offensive' image was punishable with a maximum of three years, and the burden of proof regarding exceptions to possession were on the defendant (to which Liberty had objected in a submission). Nor did prosecution have to prove that such an image would 'deprave and corrupt' someone as in the famous *Lady Chatterley* case against Penguin under the Obscene Publications Act. Parliament also put on the statute book an eye-watering description of the images they were criminalising.

It was a formidable real test of Starmer's earlier beliefs as it meant that, if a similar prosecution were to come up under the new DPP, in principle all of the forty-four ring members would be charged under new Act instead of the sixteen prosecuted under Margaret Thatcher's government. As DPP Starmer would have to give consent to such prosecutions. By an unrelated coincidence, Home Secretary Smith, Starmer's Westminster colleague for a few months, would be tripped up in her job when her husband charged two pay-per-view X-rated videos to the tax payer. Though these were licensed images that had clearly nothing to do whatsoever with the new offence, the media recalled the Home Office press releases sent at the time of the royal assent. 'Frozen rather than angry', Smith told the BBC Five Live in 2011, as well as, 'my 17-year-old son said: "Dad, haven't you heard of the internet?"'

Twenty years later, Starmer left behind his 1990 *Times* opinion and was 'a Trot but professional', as a Conservative minister said in 2020. A month and a half after he started out, the Criminal Law Policy Unit circular sent to up to 10,000 lawyers, days before the offence went live in January 2009, set out the law as the Ministry of Justice saw it and its relevance to the Obscene Publications Act, which had hitherto criminalised imagery.

In addition, Starmer gave a greater number of prosecutors than expected the required consent to proceed. The Labour Ministry of Justice estimated that there would be 10 or so convictions in 2009. But by 2010, when Starmer was DPP working under Conservative Attorney General Dominic Grieve, he consented to what amounted to between 950-1500 prosecutions a year, marginally more than under the DPP Grieve appointed after him. The majority of these convictions were guilty pleas brought in as ancillary charges to prosecution for higher-penalty crimes—as, for example, in the 2016 case of England football player Adam Johnson for grooming a fifteen-year-old girl.

Stand-alone prosecutions for the novel offence went less smoothly under Starmer, however. An early prosecution in 2010 concerned possession of two clips by a Welsh defendant who insisted they were dirty jokes. The criminal case against him had to be withdrawn after the Crown Prosecutor played the clip called 'Sex with a Tiger' in court, and realised that its audio had a humorous Frosties' cornflakes ending, 'that beats doing adverts for a living', followed by a similar outcome for the second image. Another case brought in Starmer's last year as DPP against a fellow barrister and former aide to London Mayor Boris Johnson was also reported as misfiring.

As early as 1993, Starmer was dialling down his work at the Haldane Society to devote more time to his own pro bono cases and work on the human rights act with the team at Doughty Street.

He worked particularly closely with Jonathan Cooper and together they would hunt for both cases and eddies in the law where judges would be comfortable with being prodded to create a new writ to add to the utilitarian pigeon holes of common law and its at times self-righteous users. Without a defined set of core values the common law's rigid transactional approach, prone as it was to ossification, would be indistinguishable from any other naked machinery of justice, and the rule of law could not remain true, they imagined with Winston Churchill. Though Cooper was a barrister, too, he was more interested in the policy side of the law and combined his practice with working as legal director of Liberty and later of Justice, a more law-technical charity that had lots of contact with the Blair and Brown Labour governments. He, too, wrote pieces for *Socialist Lawyer* and for *Soundings*.

One particular case brought to Cooper was the one of Irene Ivison, who had approached him. Her daughter Fiona had, despite going to a good school, fallen in since the age of fourteen with an older abusive boyfriend in Doncaster. After being bullied at school she had morphed into a withdrawn teenage girl who craved protection which she mistook for affection. Irene had repeatedly asked help from the police and the social services. They were unable to help her and, after being murdered by her 'boyfriend' in 1993 when she was seventeen, Fiona, it turned out, had been groomed by him as a prostitute and she had been working the streets. Ivison set up a charity to pressure politicians called Coalition for the Removal of Pimping (CROP) but had got nowhere until she contacted Cooper.

Starmer and Cooper both sensed that here was one of those lacuna in the common law given Fiona's young age and vulnerable circumstances. Irene, a minor who had been repeatedly sexually abused during her short life, had clearly deserved help and so had her mother Irene who had desperately but in vain tried to enlist the help of the authorities to peel her daughter away from her groomer. The police and social services had told Irene, however, that Fiona had to come forward herself and there was nothing they could do. According to Cooper and Starmer, it was simply not an answer to shrug and turn away. As Starmer said later as DPP, 'what is wrong is wrong'.

They pored over their legal books to find a way to help Irene, but could find no precedent under English law. Without this first step in the legal process, there was nothing to appeal from. But Starmer, working *pro bono* on the case, then devised an ingenious way of petitioning the Court in Strasburg in a way that centred on a member state's obligation to protect the vulnerable.

Irene also wrote a successful book about Fiona in 1997 and 'showed the police and social services that when it comes to child prostitution, families are part of the solution, not the problem', a CROP member of staff said. Unfortunately, Irene died before her petition was heard by the Court of Human Rights, but changes in the law were made in 2003 and the Home Office funded CROP to act as a national coordinator. In 2004, the organisation was looking after 63 cases and trialled runs with authorities in Irene's native Sheffield to help parents under the Child Abduction Act.

Starmer remained aware of this blind spot in the law with regards to minors and when he became DPP took action proactively after being alerted by one of the CPS's regional prosecutors, Nazir Afzal. Afzal had watched police footage of an old case in Rochdale where a young victim described a brutal gang-rape by two men. Because of her age and other circumstances, the case had not got any further, essentially because CPS prosecutors decided that in court her testimony would likely not be considered sufficiently 'credible' by the jury. In a vicious circle, the girl's brave decision to go the police led to the men being interviewed and their denials, but also to their discovery that there was no further follow-through from authorities who considered themselves powerless to act, which the two men interpreted as a license to continue and create a ring of nine groomers who, by 2011, were abusing forty seven underage girls.

Though there were some 100,000 Crown Court prosecutions and 700,000 in magistrate courts in 2011, Starmer's office passed on Afzal's case to Starmer and he personally consented to Afzal prosecuting the ring which led to their successful conviction. Instead of ducking and running from what else might have fallen between the cracks, Starmer also concluded that there must have been other vulnerable girls whose complaints had been screened for the wrong reasons. According to Afzal, Starmer said, 'look that can't be the only one we got wrong, what about the other cases that didn't get to the stage where we prosecuted?'

The analysis of old cases that came back confirmed that complaints of abuses of minors were being missed because of the guidance standard that had hitherto been applied as to whether a case should be prosecuted or not. Starmer rewrote it so that vulnerable young girls who came forward to the police would be taken seriously when the file filtered through to the CPS stage. As with Irene, who was implicitly blamed by authorities for the way her daughter's Fiona's life was careening out of control rather than seen as a potential ally in addressing a problem within their purview, a point of skilled consideration had crystallised into a systemic triage against the underage who were asking for help but were not ideal witnesses because they, for example, worked the streets or had a drink problem.

Afzal went on to prosecute predator Stuart Hall for indecent assault against 13 girls between 1967 and 1985. The broadcaster had previously been able to operate with impunity because of the not being 'credible' rule. The same applied to Rolf Harris and Gary Glitter, who were also successfully prosecuted. Mindful of the problem in the case of Irene, Starmer also created a right for victims to challenge a CPS decision not to prosecute their case as an additional step in creating a set of legal tools around the problem of girls like Fiona. As Operation Midland, based on the testimony of Carl Beech against for example former Thatcher minister Leon Brittan which resulted in Beech's own conviction for perverting the course of justice, showed, there were pitfalls.

23. The Road to Northern Ireland

Starmer, as a youthful left-wing barrister, was deeply drawn to Northern Ireland, with its legal system under decades' long fierce pressure due to the Troubles. Starting out as revulsion at the failure of justice under the rule of law in Northern Ireland, his interest would ultimately rekindle his first love for real-life politics and prompt his first political appointment in 2003 since the East Surrey Socialist Youths. This part-time appointment as human rights advisor to the Northern Ireland Policing Board covered the Good Friday agreement and the time he spent there made a deep impression on Starmer as a novice QC.

According to his mentor Fitzgerald it was Starmer's long engagement with Northern Ireland that became his road to Damascus and caused the 'watershed'. As advisor to the Policing Board he saw that the hard-fought Good Friday Agreement had dramatically changed for the better the rule of law for everyone in Northern Ireland and, generally, in the rest of the UK, in a way that outpaced even a cascade of favourable human-rights judgements. Life for everyone was transformed by the Agreement, not just for those who tangled with or got entangled by the law. The coming together of sworn enemies, buffered by the US, Irish and British governments, with Labour's Mo Mowlam slugging it out in endless, thankless meetings, showed that the East-Surrey Young Socialists' and Haldane Society 'farce' of passing resolutions could, in the right hands at the right moment, have a transformative effect on kindling national decency and cooperation.

The job, which was only part-time, was an epiphany, and 'probably when he got the taste for politics in a world wider than the bar', said Fitzgerald.

Northern Ireland also had its own soundtrack for Starmer—The Edwin Hawkins singers 'Oh, Happy Day' (1968). 'There's an expression in Ireland used a lot, which is "happy days". As an expression, it's a fantastic expression. And it just reminds me of all the challenges we went through the ups and downs', Starmer said.

It was the region's spate of unsafe convictions from 1989 to 1991, during Starmer's first years as a practising barrister, that kickstarted his passionate interest in the region. In rapid succession, the convictions of the Guildford Four, the Maguire Seven, the Birmingham Six, and Tottenham Three (a racial case) were found 'unsafe and unsatisfactory' in rapid succession, and this following long spells in prison for the convicted.

At the time, the lawyers of the Haldane Society considered the regional rule of law in Northern Ireland an egregious miscarriage-of-justice-waiting-to-happen factory and a nefarious influence on the rule of law in England and Wales to boot. Under the emergency legislation passed, Starmer himself co-wrote critically in *Soundings* that under Northern Irish circumstances the first victim was always inevitably the law: 'first internment without trial, then the removal of the right to jury trial, and finally the removal of the right to silence. So fundamental are these human rights breaches that Britain has frequently been found to be in breach of the European Convention on Human Rights'. Even the Major government agreed to the extent that it created a Criminal Cases Review Commission to investigate miscarriages a year before the General Election.

In April 1990, though no longer its legal officer, Starmer himself attended a new miscarriage trial as Liberty's legal observer. This was the case of the Winchester Three—Martina Shanahan, Finbar Cullen and John McCann—who had been found guilty in 1988 of a plot to murder Northern Ireland Secretary Tom King. Their silence in response to police questioning had been relied upon to corroborate their convictions with 25 year sentences. It was this that lay at the heart of the appeal.

The case's wider implications ran like high-voltage current through left-wing legal circles: Thatcher's Lord Chancellor Lord MacKay was preparing to change the law in England and Wales as well to allow silence to speak for the prosecution in criminal cases. Moreover, the judiciary were compromised. Exploding the appearance of impartiality, before taking his seat with the other judges on the bench to hear the legal arguments pro and contra, Lord Lane, Britain's most senior member of the judiciary as well as the man thought to be one of his generation's most brilliant legal minds, had managed to spread discomfort to all the isles by inexplicably letting slip in advance that he agreed with the government's legal position.

The Court of Appeal, without Lord Lane who had recused himself, found for the defendants and quashed their convictions. Starmer, commenting for Liberty to the *Guardian*, said mildly that 'The government should abandon its proposals and reinstate the right of silence in Northern Ireland'. In *Socialist Lawyer* he expressed himself more raucously, as in the druid and Acid House cases, that it was a 'glaring example' of what was going wrong in Britain.

It was through Jane Winter of the British Irish Rights Watch, that Starmer and other Northern Ireland subcommittee members of the Haldane Society received regular updates on what was happening legally in Northern Ireland under its Emergency Provisions Act (EPA), Northern Ireland's own version of the Police and Criminal Act (PCA), and the Prevention of Terrorism Act (PTA), which applied equally in England and Wales. Her reports fed the deep disquiet felt by the Haldane Society at large about Northern Ireland.

Her reports so shocked the *Socialist Lawyer*'s editorial committee that a feature by her was given the front cover. In it she revealed her intel that, because solicitors representing Protestant PTA detainees were mainly Catholics, Northern Ireland's police officers would suggest in so many creative ways to detainees that their solicitor was in fact an IRA loyalist. If the local police were indeed guilty of this, it would ostensibly be seriously endangering the lives of these solicitors given the February 1989 death of North-Belfast solicitor Pat Finucane. He had been killed with two shots on a Sunday morning following such a rumour: the door of his home was rammed open with a sledgehammer and his face received another twelve shots at close range.

One Catholic firm of solicitors, Winter said, had tallied the instructions they received from Protestant detainees as follows: 'Of 268 clients seen between March 1989 and October 1991 no less than 238 mentioned such matters in their instructions. In 143 cases, more than half, the solicitor was abused. In 34% of cases police officers claimed the solicitors had IRA or other terrorist connections. 29% of clients said that the police had made reference to Finucane's murder. One in ten said that police officers had made a specific death threat against their solicitor.' Under PACE and EPA legislation, interviews of terrorist detainees without a legal representative were permitted in the region, and the Northern Irish solicitors were not present to counter or report on the veracity of these complaints themselves and tallied from what their clients told them.

Starmer himself was so disturbed about the news that was seeping through that he set off for Belfast himself on 26 September 1992, together with thirteen other Haldane lawyers who were part of the committee, including Phillippa Kaufmann. The delegates visited the Beechmount area in West Belfast, to speak to families, the Maze prison, and Casement Park. Potential violations of the rule of law might have taken place there and Kaufmann, who was for a while Starmer's girlfriend in the 1990s, also noted that 'independent medical advice of maltreatment' was brought to the delegation's attention.

During the visit, the delegates met in person with seventeen-year-old Damien Austin who had recently been detained at the Castlereagh holding facility. He testified to shocked Haldane delegates that, 'He had been arrested twice in recent months. He had been verbally abused, punched in the stomach, slapped and spat upon by detectives; choked until he nearly fainted and then kicked and punched again. A detective placed his boots between his legs and applied pressure to his testicles. He was burned on the face with a cigarette, had his trousers pulled down and a lighter held towards his pubic hair. His ears were pulled so that stitches from a previous injury came out. He was interviewed some nine times a day before being released and received threats on more than one occasion.'

In 2020, Starmer's Belfast trip was still able to cause controversy as a result of what had been passed at the society's April 1992 AGM. This meeting—at which Starmer also resigned as the society's Secretary to become Treasurer—was the one that had sanctioned the delegates to act as official observers of the Society in Belfast. But at the same time, the AGM accepted a far more partisan political resolution, 'calling for the withdrawal of British troops and a United Ireland', as Kaufmann said. This was meant to be a 'hard-line' position, Jane Winter confirmed. Fuelling the flames, the then society's chair, Bill Bowring added that the delegates 'did not hide the fact that we had such a policy'. He also wrote up the official report of the trip afterwards and published it with the society. An anonymous source close to Starmer, however, countered that neither the political resolutions of the AGM nor those in Bowring's report 'represent Keir's views now or then'.

The Belfast visit prompted Starmer to edit his first book in 1993, *Miscarriages of Justice: A Review of Justice in Error*, with Clive Walker of Leeds University. Still in print, in 2021 with Oxford University Press, it gathered chapters from academics, campaigners and practitioners, including Michael Mansfield QC, involved in the cases.

At Doughty Street, however, not everyone stood wholly behind Starmer's belief in the miscarriages of English law. The human-rights chambers' associate tenant Louis Blom-Cooper QC wrote his own more equivocal book further to his friendship with Lord Bridge, who had presided over the trial of the Birmingham Six and who had exchanged his private views with him. Entitled *The Birmingham Six* the book's cancelled press conference made the front-page of the *Guardian* and it rapidly disappeared from sale further to libel letters, followed by a successful libel court-case against the author in Ireland after a few copies went on sale there. Blom-Cooper was ultimately able to save his finances from the libel verdict's most ruinous consequences against him by taking it on a technical appeal to the court in Strasburg.

Starmer's own book set out his own battle cry for legal decency as a Doughty Street civil liberties barrister: 'A miscarriage occurs as follows: whenever individuals are treated by the state in breach of their rights; whenever individuals are treated adversely by the state to a disproportionate extent in comparison with the need to protect the rights of others: or wherever the rights of others are not properly protected or vindicated by state action against wrongdoers'. A review in the *British Journal of Criminology* retorted tartly on behalf of the traditional common law, 'what rights?'.

In the wake of the 1998 Good Friday Agreement, Starmer squared up on behalf of a Protestant soldier, Lee William Clegg, whose controversial case he joined in as junior counsel. It was a *cause célèbre* among Unionists and heavily criticised by Sinn Féin's Gerry Adams. Starmer's decision to switch sides from the Northern Irish Catholics so surprised left-wing London solicitors that he had to call on his judge-whispering skills to stop them from withholding cases from him.

Clegg was a private in a patrol unit of sixteen, the standard army protection given to a police constable in Northern Ireland. Within the unit, he was part of a 'brick' of four called V10A, which consisted of himself another private, a lieutenant and a corporal. Their brick had just left behind a 'VCP' checkpoint of army vehicles in the process of creating a chicane at a small bridge on Belfast's Glen Road when, late in the evening of 30 September 1990, a Vauxhall Cavalier approached with its headlights on, slowing down and then accelerating as the soldiers shouted at it to stop.

Clegg's unit subsequently fired three shots at the car coming at V10A but also, it was alleged, once more after it passed and retreated. Tragically, for those inside the car, as opposed to the patrol itself on this occasion, it led to the death of two of the three young Catholics in the car. They turned out to be joy-riders and not terrorists. Under the army's shoot-to-kill regulation, issued in plain language to every private on a Yellow Card as to what was lawful in case of danger, when in danger soldiers were in effect permitted to do the first but not to shoot at a retreating car.

Three years later, in a hugely unpopular verdict among his Protestant army peers, Clegg was jailed for life for murder in 1993 as forensics showed that a bullet from his gun was lodged underneath the liver of the eighteen-year-old girl who died on the back seat. Bullets also hit the other passenger and the driver, a seventeen-year-old boy, who died in hospital of his injuries. Clouding the case was testimony given by the unit's patrol officer that the other private of V10A was struck on his leg afterwards to make it appear as if the car had hit him. Riots combusted in Belfast's Catholic areas when Northern Ireland Secretary Patrick Mayhew released Clegg from prison on license in 1995 after Tory MPs had taken up Clegg's case. Back at his post in the army, Clegg's numerous appeals up to the House of Lords to quash his conviction on points of law remained unsuccessful, however.

When Starmer joined Clegg's defence team in 1998, new facts had dramatically prompted a retrial. Clegg's solicitor said that there was new 'forensic and ballistic evidence which proves that not only did Lee Clegg not fire after that car passed him, but identifies the soldier by name who did fire the shot that hit the back of the ear'. His defence QC revealed in addition that, after an alert about and imminent attack, the constable in charge had 'decided to go on an "anti-joyriding" patrol instead'. The judge only very partially agreed with the new facts and testimonies put to the court, but did agree that it was possible Clegg thought the Vauxhall Cavalier formed a 'real and present danger' and thus acquitted him from the murder charge beyond reasonable doubt. The guilty verdict on the manslaughter of the driver for four years was overturned in 2011 under a double jeopardy argument and Clegg's name was cleared of this too, though Starmer—months away from becoming DPP—was not involved in this leg of Clegg's rehabilitation.

Clegg himself said in 2011 about what happened that night that he had been in active service for five months and that he was 'bloody frightened'. This was his first live round in anger as a soldier and saw 'literally in a flash' that a colleague was struck: 'I thought, "Bloody hell, it has hit him"'. When it had done that it came across to my side of the road. It was coming directly across to my position'.

Starmer himself said about his interest in the Clegg case, 'Well, I think everybody was sympathetic to him, the predicament that he had found himself in. It was very much there but for the grace of God went any squaddie.' It was for him more than just a legal case. In order to release the stress of the trial while he was in Belfast working on the appeal for three months, Starmer went out weekly to the garrison to play football with Clegg's regiment.

Solicitor Mark Stephens, Starmer's colleague and friend added, 'He's making clear that actually there's a systemic problem with shoot to kill policy and that you shouldn't be blaming individual soldiers like Clegg for carrying out a policy which frankly the generals and the politicians have imposed on them.'

The lead barrister actually didn't think the case was about what was on the Yellow Card, but did agree that Lee had suffered a 'sort of moral injustice' which had uncommonly affected him, too. For Starmer it was a small first step that broke away from the framework of battling for hard-knuckle legal precedents that he had set up for himself in 1989 Archway. Although he may not yet have regarded his own seemingly settled early life at 23 Tanhouse Road as flotsam—like Jo and Rod's youth—in the currents that prevailed at Westminster, his interest in a wider canvas than Socialist Self-Management as a lawyer was taking shape.

24. 'Who the f*** does he think he is?'

Through working on many other human rights campaigns, Jonathan Cooper got to see glimpses of the person on the other side of the dedicated barrister and even got to consider him like an older brother who he could turn to for advice.

Starmer was highly attuned to loss as someone who grew up in a household where one of his parents might not live any moment but who survived for half a century against the odds. The empathy it demanded could so consume him that he at time failed to read obvious runes. Another instance of Doughty Street lore Cooper recounted was how, as a very junior barrister, Starmer was due to meet a leading QC in an important case but asked to reschedule. 'Of course, is everything OK?' the silk asked smoothly, only to be told that one of the Starmers' donkeys had died and his mother wanted him to attend the funeral.

Cooper had his own first-hand donkeys' story, too, and how the animals stood for the concern Jo wouldn't accept for her own illness from her family or others. Around 1995, he and Starmer had flown from back from a legal conference in Geneva to Gatwick and Starmer had wanted to drop in on his parents on the way to London. It won't be long Starmer said to Cooper, but why don't you come in?

Over tea and a biscuit, Jo gave her son an update. 'It quickly became clear we'd not be heading off immediately. There was something wrong with one of the donkeys. This was a family affair and required Keir's undivided attention. We'd have to go up to the donkey field', Cooper said.

'On came the boots and she led the way through the back door along a path from the back garden to the donkeys' field. Walking was clearly not easy for Keir's mum, but this procession as we all joined her on her way to see the donkeys was something very familiar and normal to all there.' Totally absorbed mother and son resolved the crisis together after which the journey resumed. For as long as Starmer was at Doughty Street donkey news was one of the fixtures, skirting along Jo's health.

Family was the sole reason where Starmer made exceptions to his

Rod-style sense of duty. During his Labour leadership campaign, his mother-in-law fell and ended up in intensive care. While she was in hospital he took time off from the campaign in a rare move for a politician seeking to be elected. She died after two weeks and, just before a speech he spoke to his wife, who was dealing badly with the loss of her mother as did their children, for whom his mother-in-law was the regular babysitter.

It was another moment he struggled with his new role as politician and dealing with the voter, a year after his own father had died. 'I think I'm finding it harder to watch my wife go through this', but he had to go back to the stage to take questions.

'I had been trying to be the best husband I could be to my wife, the best dad I could be to my grieving children. Then I'm asked, "What's the most exciting thing you've ever done?" And I'm judged on that. I know who I am.' The QC who always had the perfect answer for justice in others' intricate problems, was almost dismayed by people's uncomplicated and less than perfect interest in him.

Victoria, who married Starmer in 2007, had her own Keir story of how they she met Starmer QC a few years before. She was working as a solicitor on one of his cases and he was a demanding silk. In his zone on the way to court, he rang her up and, having never spoken to her before, queried whether the brief she had sent him was less than '100% accurate'.

Her measured approach to him was not unlike Starmer's lawyerly approach to Jeremy Corbyn. As to this, Lord Falconer relayed the professional trope that you 'can't ever say that my client's the most appalling f***wit, because that's not allowed'. Unflustered, Victoria firmly held her ground against the caller on the other side of the line, reassuring him that she really knew her job and crossed all 't's and dotted all 'i's, and, after putting the phone down, said, 'Who the f*** does he think he is?'

Her not being cowed by his reputation didn't prevent, or may have increased the chances of him asking her out on date, which he did by casually taking her out at the Lord Stanley pub on Camden Park Road, with inexpensive pizzas, smashed avocados, grilled aubergines, halloumi, and other items dismissed by a pub-traditionalist as 'one of the most arty-farty menus I've ever seen'. His low-cost approach left his eldest, too, underwhelmed. 'My son says I should have taken her for a nice meal', Starmer conceded.

Not only his wife and son expected more of Starmer, his daughter was similarly minded. 'Yes, it's true, especially my very strong-willed four-year-old daughter who makes it her business to contradict everything her parents say', he said when he became MP in 2015.

He made a conscious effort not to be the absent workaholic father Rod was and tried hard. 'I always think I'd like a bit of peace and quiet, but, um, I'm not sure that's going to last very long.' On desert island discs, he chose a song by Stormzy 'because my children love Stormzy'.

He considered good parenting far more difficult than the toughest legal battle. He wanted his relationship to be communicative and far more like that of his mother with him, and he regretted that Jo was never able to speak to his children. 'We've got two young children, but my mum has never spoken to my children because she was too old', he said. When she died in May 2015, Toby was seven and his daughter was four.

One of Starmer's greatest difficulties was that he remained Rod's son and found it hard not to let work dominate his time.

'It is difficult', he said as DPP, 'The only way to do it is to be really disciplined. I tried to ensure there were a set number of days a week I was home for bath time and that I had some preserved time at the weekends. If you speak to my wife she'll say that didn't work very well. But that was the intention and sometimes the practice.' Victoria changed her job to mentor deprived children in the NHS and is governor at their children's school.

He tried to do his part in the school run and bed-time reading. It worked better when his five-year stint as DPP ended in 2013, but lapsed again when he was elected to Parliament in 2015. 'It's a struggle to see a lot of them during the week', he said.

He made up for it during holidays and as a result started his first day as MP on crutches having torn his ACL while playing football with on a beach in Cornwall. 'It's bloody painful', he told reporters, and, as a mock apology for being a father rather than Oxted's answer to Roy Keane, he added, 'It's about as unglamorous a story as you can imagine.' His first appearances in the House of Commons—as he was finding his way around the new rhythms and flows of its debates—were considered not much better.

It was an iron law, that he refereed the football game at his son's school in Kentish Town on Monday morning at 8 am. 'My job is keeping the peace and ensuring that the scores are fairly even', Starmer said. Not wanting to be the side-line parent egging on their child, this as far as he took his own passion for the game, though under Corona he took to playing computer game FIFA with them as real games were out of the question.

The Starmer-Alexander marriage had its own tune: the second movement of Beethoven's fifth piano concerto—very unlike the 'incredible noise' of the ninth symphony and a virtuoso piece that is 'beautiful' Starmer said. Nicknamed the Emperor Concerto, for Starmer 'it's the music that my wife walked in to at our wedding'.

'She's an incredible, warm, wonderful woman who is my complete rock'. Although she left the law, he continued to relied on her profession-al point of view and while preparing for the last interview with Attorney General Baroness Scotland for the post of DPP, he wanted to run his ideas for the Crown Prosecution Services by her in the morning. Their first child Toby had been just born in 2008.

'It meant that I was doing the interviews for the job three weeks after Toby was born, so I was obviously not sleeping. I had to do a five-minute presentation at the final interview on the future of prosecution services in the next five years. On the morning of the interview, I said, "I've got to try it out for time on Vicky." I got about halfway through it and Toby threw up, and that was it', Starmer said.

Toby's input notwithstanding, he got the job, 'Then the first time I took my son into my office as DPP, he picked up a copy of the code for crown prosecutors and started eating it, much to the amusement of all the staff', Starmer recalled.

When Starmer's children started taking centre stage in the new DPP's life instead of football and donkeys, Gavin Millar QC said about the change, 'He is getting rather boring about nappy-changing'.

It was always his one vice outside of work. 'Mad about Arsenal', a colleague said. His own moment of ecstasy was 1996 and David Baddiel and Frank Skinner's Three Lions song. It is, Starmer said, 'the iconic football song in order to really appreciate this song, you had to be in

Wembley in the crowd. I was in the upper tier for the semi-final of Euro 96, when we're playing Germany and two for the whole stadium to be jumping up and down, rocking to them.'

Heather Williams QC, who was also an early member of the *Socialist Lawyer*'s editorial committee, recalled Starmer's rigid schedule when she was deputy head of Doughty Street under him. 'He would be at chambers 6am Sunday morning, then played football at 10:30am, then he'd come back afterwards.'

After changing career to become DPP and MP, Starmer continued to play five-a-sides and eight-a-sides with friends and friends of friends religiously on Sunday and Monday at Talacre, between Gospel Oak and Kentish Town, and Muswell Hill. Starmer is the one fronting the responsibility and sending out the emails and texts and collects the subs.

'It's fun and no one really gives a stuff', Oxted's Roy Keane has claimed, somewhat disingenuously. Patrick Stephens, one of the teammates and international director at the Crown Prosecution Service when Starmer was DPP, described him as 'a midfield general', adding, 'with a silky left foot'. Making the same point but more colourfully an aide described him as 'Chopper Starmer'. Starmer himself realised this 'just brings chuckles now from those that I play with' though he was certainly the driving force behind the matches.

Not having his football fix during Corona was a hardship that was remedied by scouring the TV for games. I'm an Arsenal fan, yeah. But I would watch any football game, whoever was playing'.

Not surprisingly, Starmer has two season tickets to Arsenal, on the Upper Tier West Stand. In fact, taking his two children to a game was one of things he was most thrilled of doing with them as a father. But ordinarily, continuing the habit of a lifetime, he and his friends congregated in a pub before an Arsenal game. 'He goes with the same group of his mates to a pub off the Holloway Road before every match', said Stephens. One friend of Starmer's said that he was essentially, 'a man of hidden shallows'.

Whereas Chelsea used to be the place to be for legal footie darlings, it was now Arsenal—particularly for civil liberties QCs. 'We are clearly the team of choice among high-flying human rights silks', an Arsenal fan said, noting their greater dress sense than the average football-scarf-wearing crowd. One game, they noted, counted a four-a-side of Arsenal QCs—Ben Emmerson, Peter Thornton, Ken McDonald and Keir Starmer—rooting against Borussia Dortmund. Starmer was also adviser to the Football Association and, surprisingly, the Jockey Club. 'His weaknesses were pretty boring', said Gavin Millar QC. As his luxury item on Desert Island Discs, Starmer chose a football and a detailed Atlas as the one book.

While football was for relaxation and losing himself, for stress Starmer played squash with fellow barristers such as Robert Latham, an associate tenant at Doughty Street Chambers who specialised in social housing and was a Camden Councillor. Latham said, 'I play squash each Friday with Keir. He takes out his aggression that has built up over the week because of the government's war on terror, while I rail against the maladministration of local housing authorities.' Starmer was also good for a half-marathon for relief in disaster-struck Bangladesh in March 2008, just before his interviews for DPP started.

Starmer's mentor Ed Fitzgerald, too, could get livid in the courtroom. Pannick QC recalled an instance in a frosty courtroom in Trinidad where Fitzgerald exploded about a passage by Britain's first Supreme Court president, 'that's just not true'. He had to be calmed down by a fellow QC on his side.

Starmer controlled his emotions in court, but outside he could let his feelings get the better of him. Fitzgerald said of Starmer that on one occasion while lawyering in the Caribbean against capital punishment, 'we had to restrain him from a fight with some American who was advocating the death penalty rather loudly in the bar. Keir said, 'I'm going to go and get him.'

25. McFilm Star

Starmer's commitment to success was paying off and he impressed other colleagues in the profession with his increasing name-recognition in the field. Starmer was name-checked in lists of 'ones to watch,' and in August 1995, he got his first mention in *The Lawyer* magazine. As a junior barrister of some eight years standing, he was cited in a list of some of the profession's leading advocates, in which it was said that he was 'instructed in a wide range of civil liberties cases and a very good specialist in this expanding area for lawyers and barristers'.

In November 1996 he was noted as one of a crop of the most promising juniors alongside others who went on to great things, including Rabinder Singh and Michael Fordham, both of whom became judges—Singh becoming the first non-white Court of Appeal judge in 2017. In November 1997 the magazine quoted peers as saying he is 'a radical with a good reputation'. By 1998, he was described as 'head and shoulders above everyone else'. On 30 June 2009, while DPP, he was elected as a Bencher, a life member of the 'parliament' of 500 or so at Middle Temple, its own local authority since the Middle Ages, with Prince William as Royal Bencher.

As the successes started rolling in there was a pressure not to squander the opportunities it gave him. The push to take more and more high-profile cases increased. And so did the pressure to win them.

One of his most famous victories was in the 'McLibel' case, which was even to give him his own entry as film star on IMDB in a 1998 feature film. Lasting over a decade, it was the longest British libel trial. In it, he acted for environmental activists Helen Steel and David Morris, often referred to as the 'McLibel Two'.

In 1986, they handed out a leaflet called 'What's wrong with McDonald's: everything they don't want you to know' to McDonald's customers in The Strand in London. It accused the company of paying low wages, of cruelty to animals used in its products and dozens of other malpractices. This type of case was right up Starmer's street: it included the environmental issues he had espoused as central to the new left in *Socialist Alternatives*, his passion for fair treatment of workers, and his affinity for free speech.

McDonald's sued Steel and Morris for libel. It was an uneven fight. While the company had a worldwide turnover of over £10 billion, Steel was earning £65 a week from part-time bar work and Morris was on income support. Other defendants in the case, including three other members of Steel and Morris's group London Greenpeace, backed down an apologised—which is all McDonald's were asking for—but the McLibel Two refused to do so. They were denied Legal Aid and so Keir Starmer offered *pro bono* assistance. It was 'very much a David and Goliath,' he said. 'There's an extremely good legal team acting for McDonalds at great expense and Dave and Helen have had to act for themselves with me as a sort of free back up whenever possible.'

In Starmer's mind, the unfairness of the legal procedure was becoming an issue of human rights. In his 1999 textbook on the subject Starmer would include a section on the right to access a lawyer: 'Although article 6(3)(c) guarantees everyone charged with a criminal offence the right to legal assistance, it is silent on the question of when this crystallises.' Starmer was adamant that legal assistance should begin early in the process, even when it came to explaining the charges and procedure to the litigants. The attempt of McDonald's, to intimidate Steel and Morris with their highly-qualified team of lawyers ,did not sit well with human rights advocate in Starmer.

Starmer maintained that it was impossible for the defendants to keep on top of the material without proper support. In an adversarial system he would like to see a duty being placed on the judge to explain the legal procedures to the 'litigants in person'—that is, those who defend themselves. This was a growing problem because so many more people were taking their own cases to court as legal aid was shrinking and solicitors were too expensive.

McDonald's spent several million pounds on the case, while Steel and Morris could only raise £40,000 from supporters to help cover expenses, such as making transcripts and photocopying, and were unable to call all the witnesses they needed. While Starmer and solicitor Mark Stephens gave their advice pro bono, McDonald's not only employed Richard Rampton QC, a formidable libel specialist and solicitor on gravity-defying hourly rates and the services of a full legal chambers. McDonalds' had access to anything it wanted, and thought nothing of flying in witnesses and experts from all over the world.

In June 1995, as the case came up to its tenth anniversary, McDonald's offered to settle the case. They offered to donate a large sum to any charity named by Steel and Morris, provided they stop criticising McDonald's in public, though they could continue to express their views in private. Steel and Morris responded by saying they would stop criticising McDonald's, if McDonald's stopped advertising in public and only promoted its restaurants in private.

On 19 June 1997, Justice Rodger Bell delivered a thousand-page judgement which largely found in favour of McDonald's. He said that some of the leaflet's claims—that the company was to blame for starvation in developing countries, for example, and that its food caused cancer—were untrue. However, he found McDonald's 'culpably responsible' for animal cruelty and that the company exploited children through its advertising.

The judge also found that McDonald's paid low wages, but that the company had been libelled because other aspects of the material were defamatory. The couple were ordered to pay £60,000 in damages. Both refused to pay. However, the case was estimated to have cost the fast food giant £10 million. It had lasted 313 days and has been described as the biggest corporate PR disaster in history. The case brought Starmer into the attention of the media and afterwards Keir Starmer appeared in *McLibel*, the film about the case made by Ken Loach and Franny Armstrong.

But that was not the end of it. Starmer was back to arguing police abuse when Steel and Morris sued the Metropolitan Police for disclosing confidential information to investigators hired by McDonald's and received £10,000 and an apology for the disclosure. They also appealed the verdict. The three Appeal Court judges ruled it was fair comment to say that McDonald's employees worldwide 'do badly in terms of pay and conditions' and true 'if one eats enough McDonald's food, one's diet may well become high in fat, etc., with the very real risk of heart disease'. They cut the damages to £40,000.

The House of Lords—the forerunner of the Supreme Court—

refused to hear the case. Mark Stephens and Keir Starmer took the case on. By then, Keir had written a number of books on human rights and filed a case with the European Court of Human Rights in Strasbourg, contesting the UK government's policy of withholding legal aid in libel cases, particularly when McDonald's deep pockets biased the case so much in its favour. The lack of access to legal aid, Starmer argued, breached the pair's right both to freedom of expression and to a fair trial.

In Strasbourg, Starmer told the court that 'without legal assistance, the [defence] case was underprepared, unready for trial and was advanced by two inexperienced, untrained and exhausted individuals who were pushed to their physical and mental limits. In short, it was patently unfair'.

On 15 February 2005, the European Court ruled that the original case had breached the defendant's right to a fair trial and their right to freedom of expression, and ordered that the UK government pay Steel and Morris £24,000 in compensation. Starmer said that the judgement by the judges in Strasbourg was a 'turning point' in the law of libel that would force the government to take steps to redress the balance between rich and poor in defamation cases.

'Until now, only the rich and famous have been able to defend themselves against libel writs,' he said. 'Now ordinary people can participate much more effectively in public debate without the fear that they will be bankrupted for doing so. This case is a milestone for free speech.'

Starmer was unafraid of taking controversial cases, but now they came paired with intense media coverage, and grand links to human rights issues.

Doughty Street Chambers specifically became well-known for their commitment to negotiating the ins-and-outs of human rights. The *Independent* acknowledged that Starmer and Doughty Street chambers were at the forefront of bringing cases under the 1998 Human Rights Act which incorporated the rights set out in the European Convention on Human Rights into domestic British law.

'Knowledge of the European Court is low at the Bar in general,' Starmer told the newspaper. 'But Doughty Street has done so many cases at Strasbourg that we have become experts in the field. We will begin to get cases from a broader range of solicitors than we do now.'

They were also advising public bodies on their liabilities under the Act and to provide training for judges, magistrates and police.

'The idea of Doughty Street training magistrates and police is bizarre,' Starmer added. 'But we are writing the manuals.' The bizarreness of the situation, certainly rang true, once a vocal advocate for curbing police power Starmer now worked with the police attempting to create the guidelines that would govern them. Yet, perhaps it was not as big a stretch as one might assume, Starmer's understanding of human rights was based on the Strasbourg system where the protection of human rights was seen as a dialogue between multiple facets of the state: the executive, the legislative, and the courts. It would be not too drastic an assertion to add into that dialogue the police.

As legal director of the Human Rights Act Research Group, Keir Starmer QC, from 2003-2008, was appointed as advisor to the Northern Ireland Policing Board to develop a framework for handling the Police Service of Northern Ireland. Accepting the post, he said the integration of human rights principles into all aspects of policing ensures the rights of all are fully protected at all times. He believed the framework would allow the board to effectively monitor the extent to which the integration of human rights is being achieved.

As early as 1999, in an essay on the right of silence published in his book *Miscarriages of Justice,* Starmer had criticised methods of policing in conjunction with how evidence was brought forth in court trials in Northern Ireland. Starmer discussed how in the *Gamble* case, Carswell J drew an inference based not on the accused silence during police questioning but his refusal to testify in court. Starmer found that this was in violation of article six of the European Convention on Human Rights which guarantees a right to silence without the risk of self-incrimination. It is clear that Starmer felt that there was both a role for revising police procedure and court procedure in ensuring the protection of human rights.

'It will enable engagement between the board and PSNI so that good performance can be recognised, harnessed and shared and when it is identified, bad practice changed,' he said. 'This is not about critical assessment. This is about intelligent engagement to ensure effective application of human rights standards in everyday policing.'

He held that post until 2008 as they oversaw the implementation of parts of the Good Friday Agreement. He had already been acting as a consultant to the Association of Chief Police Officers. These official positions could be seen were as stepping stones on his way to becoming head of DPP.

However, although Starmer was still looking to reform the police, it was also his first brush with controversy. His role in Northern Ireland invited controversy when the police chiefs were heavily criticised by both unionists and nationalists after riots broke out during an Orange Order march. Sinn Fein claimed that PSNI tactics had triggered the worst rioting in the city for two years.

Keir Starmer and fellow human-rights advisor Jane Gordon said: 'We are satisfied that the PSNI properly took all the relevant factors into account in deciding that they could not prevent the group of followers/supporters from moving up the contentious part of the route.'

SDLP member Alex Attwood accused the pair of producing a flawed report as they were English lawyers, even though Ms Gordon was from Ulster. Attwood said he contacted Starmer to stress any upset caused was not intended.

'If I said something in haste that has angered anyone, I will acknowledge that,' Attwood said. 'There was something I said that was inaccurate, that one of the lawyers was from England when she was from the North.'

Starmer and Gordon went on to praise the PSNI for their efforts to comply with human rights demands, publishing a report that said: 'In our view, the PSNI has done more than any police service in the UK to achieve human rights compliance, and in many respects we have been very impressed with the work the PSNI has undertaken in the human rights field.

'The fact that a range of recommendations have been made does not mean we have found widespread lack of compliance with the Human Rights Act.'

Sinn Fein took exception to their findings. At the launch of the report in the Stormont Hotel, ten protesters unfurling a banner asking: 'Who sanctioned British death squads. Time for the truth.' But Starmer and

Gordon were not uncritical of the PSNI. They urged the Chief Constable to study footage allegedly depicting two cases of officers beating or kicking people during a riot that July. Later they forced the Chief Constable to rethink plans of arming his officers with Tasers.

'We are concerned that none of the official bodies charged with considering the use of Taser have publicly addressed the legal and human-rights frameworks within which Taser can or should be used,' they said. It was eventually decided not to issue Tasers to officers in Northern Ireland.

However, Starmer and Gordon also found that key recommendations made in their two previous reports had not been acted upon. In particular, they complained that the PSNI was not properly updating its policy on issues such as dealing with deaths in custody, bail and arrests, ensuring a professional relationship between police and defence lawyers, and keeping up to date on equality legislation. Even so, Sinn Fein complained that their report justified the use of plastic bullets, albeit in restricted circumstances.

In the later report, Starmer and Gordon asked for an independent police team to investigate the collusion between loyalist terrorists and RUC Special Branch officers that may have been responsible for as many as thirty-one murders.

Reviewing the work he did in Northern Ireland, Starmer said: 'We're really worried about the Good Friday Agreement, that was an incredible period because we worked over five years I was there trying to transform the RUC, the Royal Ulster Constabulary into the Police Services of Northern Ireland—a massive change, and in particular to get Catholics into the police service. No Catholics had joined the IUC for obvious reasons and that meant getting Sinn Fein on the policing board and courts. It was a real eye-opener on how you could work with different institutions on the Good Friday Agreement to make some real change and that made me want to work nationally if you like....'

A glutton for unpopular causes, Starmer's commitment to human rights led him to represent an alleged terrorist in 2000. He made an application for habeas corpus for Khalid Al-Fawwaz who had been arrested under the Prevention of Terrorism Act. He was under indictment in the US accused of helping to prepare the 1998 United

States embassy bombings in Dar es Salaam and Nairobi. While he was alleged to have conspired with others in an Islamic terrorist organisation to murder American citizens, officials, diplomats and other internationally protected persons, as well as American soldiers deployed in the United Nations peacekeeping missions, Al-Fawwaz had never been to the United States of America. The alleged offences had taken place outside the US, so Starmer argued that extradition could not be ordered. The magistrate had also erred in law by admitting the evidence of an anonymous witnesses and it was wrong to find a prima facie case against him. Nevertheless Al-Fawwaz had been sent to prison awaiting the decision of the Home Secretary. Al-Fawwaz was eventually extradited, but not until 2012, and sentenced to life imprisonment in 2015.

After 9/11, there was increasing pressure for the Britain's laws to be toughened to allow fringe or second-tier suspects to be picked up and held, but it was argued that this would fall foul of the Human Rights Act 1998. Keir Starmer said: 'Under the Terrorism Act, we now have extremely wide powers of arrest and detention where people are suspected of conspiracy to cause damage to property or people—and these are more wide-ranging than elsewhere in Europe.'

Similar to his work on the Rushdie affair, Starmer's defence of Khalif Al-Fawwaz indicated an increasing internationalism to Starmer's human rights work. Of course, this didn't come as a surprise as Starmer had been an internationalist ever since his days at Leeds. 'European internationalism has always been very strong or me,' Starmer said. He was a Remainer before Britain even joined the EU—or EC as it was then.

Instructed by the Refugee Legal Centre, Starmer stuck up for asylum seekers in a judicial review of the handling of cases of six refugees fleeing oppressive regimes around the world that included Iraq, Angola, Rwanda, Ethiopia and Iran. He told the court that many had to sleep rough on the streets, and were so 'cold, hungry, scared and sick' that in some cases they were mentally distressed. None had had their claim for asylum determined. One had been spent the night in a telephone box and a tunnel. The court granted injunctions providing them with emergency shelter and food during the hearing.

'It is inhumane to subject someone to that sort of destitution. There is no way they can prosecute their claims,' said Starmer.

He also disclosed that a draft Home Office leaflet recommended that asylum seekers reduced to living in telephone boxes or car parks should register with their nearest post office to receive official letters about their case. Once again citing the European Convention on Human Rights, he said they were allowed no funds, no accommodation and no food, forbidden to seek work, denied access to benefits, were without family or friends, and had no control over when their asylum claim would be determined.

'One is not looking at the ordinary healthy barrister and how they might survive on the streets, but a group which by definition is vulnerable,' Starmer said.

Asked about the wider implications of the case, he said: 'First, there is the development of the notion of dignity and humanity in our law. It doesn't matter whether the foundation of that notion is the European Convention on Human Rights or the common law, it is simply unacceptable in a civilised society to prevent a vulnerable group of individuals from working, to exclude them from the welfare benefits system and then to deprive them of a roof over their heads and of food. The other, wider, implication concerns the relationship between the government and the judiciary. Like many others, I was shocked at the personalised and ill-informed response of the government and some of the press.'

Starmer also became embroiled in a large case regarding the death penalty in the Eastern Caribbean, which he would go on to say was one of the greatest successes of his career. Working with like-minded lawyers from a leaky loft in Soho, Starmer had long been a campaigner against the death penalty. They took a series of cases to the Privy Council, which is the final court of appeal for the Caribbean and some other former British colonies. In 1993, he represented three prisoners who were on death row in Jamaica, but the Judicial Committee of the Privy Council held that it had no jurisdiction to hear their appeals against sentence. It found that, after many years' delay, their executions may be unconstitutional, the appellants had not yet exhausted their potential domestic remedies. While the death penalty remains legal in Jamaica, no one has been hanged since 1988.

Starmer was also becoming increasingly vocal in the media becoming counsel for the *Guardian*, alongside Geoffrey Robertson, and began writing for the paper. But despite this increased media presence he was still unafraid of criticising the giants of British politics. On the occasion of the Queen's Golden Jubilee in 2002, he contributed a piece calling for the reform of the 1701 Act of Settlement, which prevented Catholics, or anyone married to a Catholic, succeeding to the throne and discriminated against women, favouring male heirs over female ones.

'Surely, therefore, the time is ripe for reform,' he wrote. 'For republicans reform offers the opportunity for informed debate about the continued existence and role of the sovereign. For monarchists, there is the happy fact that there is at present an heir apparent with two sons; succession for the foreseeable future is unlikely to be affected by any alteration of the law allowing it to be passed to the eldest child of the sovereign irrespective of religion or sex. In the meantime, no doubt Prince William will take comfort in the fact that his idol, the princess of pop, Britney Spears is a Baptist. One day she may be Queen.'

But despite this unabashed criticism, as Starmer's law career grew things would change. Whether a result of the newfound lime-light, the need to maintain an exterior of perfection or merely an increase in age, a clean cut professional character, that Starmer needed when he would later become the measured Director of Public Prosecutions, was beginning to develop.

26. Starmer QC, Rushing

Interviewed by the *Times* in 2003, Starmer had a clear plan and was looking towards his future. When asked where he saw himself in ten years Starmer responded: 'Not rushing from case to case, I hope. Perhaps mixing law with policy a bit more and doing more strategic work.' Though he had dotted between absurd and noteworthy cases with passion through-out the 1990s, he was now starting to formulate a clear view on Human Rights, grounded in a desire for structural change.

In the interview Starmer perceived his greatest successes to be those that would have a lasting change in regards to policy. When he was asked what his most memorable experiences were as a lawyer he said, 'In 1992 I was part of the legal team that successfully challenged the Conservative government's scheme to close numerous coal mines. And earlier this year I was part of the legal team that successfully challenged the mandatory death penalty in the Eastern Caribbean as unconstitutional.' This sentiment was shared by Robertson QC and Fitzgerald QC, who consider these cases in the former colonies Doughty Street's most resounding victory for human rights.

The East Caribbean case was a landmark judgement. In April 2001, after years of campaigning by Starmer and other human-rights lawyers, the Eastern Caribbean Court of Appeal ruled that the mandatory death penalty in murder cases was unconstitutional. This judgment was upheld by the privy council in March 2002. As a result, the mandatory death sentence was outlawed in Antigua & Barbuda, Belize, Dominica, Grenada, St Kitts & Nevis, St Lucia and St Vincent & the Grenadines. The privy council also accepted that the mandatory death sentence was unconstitutional in Jamaica.

The significance of the East Caribbean case in Starmer's personal recollections of his career allude to the growing inclination towards internationalism in his work. Starmer had never backed his work on human rights into a British corner. Perhaps as a result of his affection for the European Convention on Human Rights and Strasbourg Case Law, in the textbooks and case studies Starmer wrote in the late 1990s he often made reference to French and German cases. Now, he was moving beyond a conception of human rights informed by European models, switching continents and cultures as he advocated for the end of capital punishment.

In June 2005, working *pro bono*, Starmer helped overturn the mandatory death penalty in Uganda saving the lives of 417 people, including twenty-three women. With a party of other lawyers, he visited death row in Uganda which was a heavily fortified prison on top of a hill west of Kampala.

Reporting in the *Times* Starmer and colleague Saul Lehrfreund and Parvais Jabbar said: 'After the usual administrative procedures, we were led along a long corridor to a small door. What happened in the next few hours will stay with us for the rest of our lives.

'We were greeted by a small group of prisoners, all in white shirts and white shorts, all wearing flip-flops. They introduced themselves and led us towards a small yard. As we stepped through an archway, we stopped in our tracks. Before us were all the male prisoners on death row— hundreds of men standing, sitting or squatting in a space no more than ten yards by twenty-five yards. When they saw us they burst into song and clapped as we sat down on the benches set up so we could speak to all the inmates at once.'

Starmer and his colleagues were escorted by a former minister, who introduced them to various people including the 'headmaster' of the school the inmates had organised and the 'prime minister'. Each took a bow and said a few words.

'Then groups of individuals were asked to stand. Those who were eighteen or younger; those who had been in the condemned section for twenty years or more—this group included the 'elder', an old man who had lived there for twenty-five years; those who had not had representation at trial were not asked to stand because there were too many of them.'

What they found most extraordinary was that the prison superintendent and guards supported the case the lawyers were bringing on behalf of the prisoners under his command. He had just four other officers with him, none of whom had handcuffs or truncheons.

'When at work, they lived with the prisoners, supported their initiatives and had all signed affidavits opposing the death penalty and describing the anguish that they would feel if called upon to execute those whom they had got to know so well. The idea that prison conditions cannot be alleviated without considerable resources had been shot through.'

For three hours the delegation sat in the hot sun talking.

'Most inmates thought that they had been brought into the condemned section for one reason and one reason only: to be hanged. Unsurprisingly, the mood had been grim for many years. But the case had given them hope. They sang, they talked, they laughed. Having worked on similar cases elsewhere in the world, we thought we were fairly hardened, but no one could have left that prison unmoved.'

The case was brought in the Constitutional Court in Kampala. It was argued, first, that the death penalty was inhuman and thus contravened the Constitution of Uganda. Secondly, even if the death penalty itself was not unconstitutional, the automatic or mandatory nature of the sentence of death was arbitrary and disproportionate—death was the only punishment that could be imposed for murder and other serious offences, whatever the circumstances.

Thirdly, death by hanging was cruel as many of those executed fail to die immediately and are actually throttled to death. The final argument was that those who had been on death row for long periods should have their sentences commuted to life imprisonment.

'Some of these arguments have been run with varying degrees of success in other Commonwealth countries, particularly in the Caribbean,' said Starmer and his colleagues. 'The stakes are high. In the Eastern Caribbean hardly any death sentences have been imposed since the mandatory death penalty was declared unconstitutional in March 2002. On the other hand, in Trinidad and Tobago, execution warrants have been read to several prisoners since the controversial decision of the Privy Council last year in the case of Mathews v State reopened the path to the gallows.' The British introduced the death penalty in a large number of their former colonies, many of whom are yet to remove the death penalty from their statute books.

However, in Uganda, humanity prevailed. In a landmark judgment the majority of the Constitutional Court declared that the death sentences passed on the 'condemned' were unconstitutional. Although the court did not strike the death penalty down altogether, it found that the mandatory nature of its imposition was unconstitutional because it did not provide the individuals with an opportunity to mitigate their sentences. The court gave the Ugandan government two years to put the judgment into effect. After that, all death sentences would be set aside. The Constitutional Court also ruled that prisoners who had been on death row for more than three years were entitled to have their sentences commuted to life imprisonment. That amounted to three-quarters of the population of death row.

For Starmer and other human-rights lawyers, the judgement was another victory in their long campaign against capital punishment. A few months later, the judicial committee of the Privy Council struck down the mandatory death penalty in the Bahamas. Starmer said: 'This case marks a new dawn for human rights in the region and has given hope to all those sentenced to death in the world.'

Then the High Court of Malawi declared the death sentences on all prisoners on death row unconstitutional in another landmark judgment that spelt the end of the automatic death penalty. Again Starmer was involved. Starmer also worked on the appeal against sentence of three death-row inmates from Barbados and one from Trinidad. The appeals were dismissed but Starmer said he would take the cases to the Inter-American Court. He also took up torture cases in Saudi Arabia.

Starmer's commitment to the international protection of human rights often acted as the basis for his outspoken criticism of government. Although he clearly had political ambitions, he had no qualms about making enemies. In the run-up to the 2003 Iraq War, Starmer took on Prime Minister Tony Blair. In a comment piece in the *Guardian*, Starmer warned that UN Resolution 1441 did not authorise the use of force without a further resolution doing so. He said with British troops about to be committed to battle: 'They, their families and the public have a right to know what the 'proper legal basis' for their action is.'

But Starmer did not foresee Tony Blair going to jail as some have wished, saying: 'The idea that the prime minister would end up before the international criminal court for participating in a US-led attack is far-fetched. But military commanders on the ground will not thank the government if any action they take is later judged to have been in breach of international law.'

Starmer, QC

He spelt out the legal arguments: 'According to the UN charter, there are only two possible situations in which one country can take military action against another. The first is in individual or collective self-defence—a right under customary international law which is expressly preserved by Article 51 of the UN charter. The second is where, under Article 42 of the charter, the security council decides that force is necessary 'to maintain or restore international peace and security' where its decisions have not been complied with. In other words, where a UN resolution clearly authorises military action.'

Starmer felt that neither of these were fulfilled.

'The question whether the Article 51 self-defence route justifies a pre-emptive attack has been keenly debated. Article 51 itself is silent on the matter. But even if it does justify a pre-emptive strike, which is surely the sounder position in a nuclear world, any threat to the UK or its allies would have to be imminent and any force used in response to that threat would have to be proportionate before Article 51 can be relied on. The mere fact that Iraq has a capacity to attack at some unspecified time in the future is not enough,' he said.

The problem for the government was one of credibility.

'No one believes that Iraq is about to attack the UK or its allies, and any self-defence claim by the government would sit very uncomfortably with the US position that military action is justified to destroy such weapons of mass destruction as Iraq may have, and to bring about a change of leadership.'

Having disposed of the provisions of Article 51, he went on: 'The second route, which depends on Article 42 of the UN charter, appears more promising for the government. There are two strands to this argument. The first is that resolution 1441 itself authorises the use of force against Iraq. It warns Iraq that 'it will face serious consequences' if it continues to violate obligations spelled out in that resolution. But, critically, the words 'all necessary means' have not been used.

'They are important words because they are the formula used by the UN to indicate that the use of force is authorised. They were the words used to justify military action against Iraq in 1991 and, subsequently, when the security council authorised intervention in Rwanda, Bosnia, Somalia and Haiti.'

It would have to be shown that all the security council members, including France and Russia, intended to authorise the use of force when they voted for resolution 1441. This was hardly compelling when France and Russia were threatening to veto any further UN resolution making this explicit. The British and American governments may grumble about the position of France and Russia: 'But that does not justify the US or the UK acting outside the UN. It merely highlights the need for reform of the undemocratic security council structure which they put in place at the end of the Second World War. Article 2 of the UN charter requires all states to refrain from the threat or use of force that is inconsistent with the purposes of the UN, which emphasises that peace is to be preserved if at all possible.'

The only other recourse was to argue that Iraq's failure to comply with the ceasefire requirements of UN resolution 687, passed at the end of military action against Iraq in April 1991, justifies the renewed use of force. But, like resolution 1441, resolution 687 did not itself authorise the use of force. As it was, the only security council resolution expressly authorizing the use of force against Iraq was 678, which was passed at the start of the Gulf War in November 1990, and the only action it authorised was such force as was necessary to restore Kuwait's sovereignty. This was not the case in 2003.

'Against that background, it is no surprise that the government has been coy about its advice so far. But on the eve of war that is not good enough. If the attorney general's advice is that force can be used against Iraq without a further UN resolution, he must explain fully how the legal difficulties set out above are to be overcome. Simply to argue that the interpretation of resolution 1441 accepted by all the other security council members except the US and the UK should be abandoned in favour of military action won't convince anybody. Flawed advice does not make the unlawful use of force lawful.'

This could not have been easy reading for Tony Blair who took the country to war three days later.

Even though his words had not landed, Starmer was not one to sit-back. In February 2005, Starmer attacked the government again when it refused to release the advice the attorney general Lord Goldsmith had given Tony Blair about the legality of the Iraq War. The government argued that the Freedom of Information Act, which the Labour government itself had passed, did not apply as confidentiality was needed to allow ministers and their advisers to discuss sensitive issues frankly.

On the *Guardian*'s website, Starmer said that Lord Goldsmith's advice was not legally protected by professional privilege as the government had waived it by 'cherry-picking'—that is, publishing in parliament what ministers said was a summary, claiming the war to be legal. This destroyed the basis of the government's claim to secrecy.

'If a party voluntarily seeks to put part of a privileged document or part of a sequence of privileged documents before a court, they must also put before the court the rest... to ensure fairness to their adversary,' he said.

He quoted a judgement in 1999 where Lord Bingham ruled that 'a party cannot deliberately subject a relationship to scrutiny and at the same time seek to preserve its confidentiality. He cannot pick and choose'.

Starmer said: 'There is in my view a very strong argument that the government has waived any privilege... by putting into the public domain what is in essence at least a summary of part of that advice'.

It was irrelevant, he said, that the government did not intend to waive privilege by sending a memo to MPs on the foreign affairs committee and by giving a written answer to parliament in Lord Goldsmith's name. Once more, he was attacking a party which he would one day lead.

Furthermore, still capable of finding a sense of victory in smaller successes, Starmer searched for solutions to individual frustrations with the Iraq war. As part of his opposition to the Iraq war, Starmer took on the case former SAS soldier Ben Griffin who had been served with an injunction preventing him making further disclosures about the work of Special Forces in Iraq. Griffin maintained that Prime Minister Gordon Brown, Tony Blair and other senior UK government officials should be charged with breaches of international conventions protecting individuals from torture over the alleged involvement of British forces in detaining people in Iraq. He told the press conference in March 2008 that British Special Forces were being used to detain suspects for extraordinary rendition and he claimed that the UK/US task force had broken international law. Extraordinary rendition was the process where US forces have transported terror suspects around the world for inter-rogation that would not be subject to the normal constraints.

Starmer's commitment to the Human Rights Act soon became a point of contention between him and Blairites, as it called into question the use of torture in British interrogation tactics in Iraq. Tony Blair and other Labour ministers were among those openly expressing doubts about the Human Rights Act which they had hailed when they passed it just five years earlier as 'bringing rights home'. They feared that, when judges were asked to decide whether to accept no-torture deals between Britain and countries with dubious human rights records, they would follow a Strasbourg judgment which said they should not balance state security against an absolute right of the individual not to be tortured.

But the necessity of the Human Rights Act was ground which Starmer would not relinquish. Working-class background or not he was ready to take Labour to task for questioning its validity.

To prove his point Starmer, representing fourteen human rights organisations, argued before law lords that international agreements impose absolute obligations on states to prevent torture. The case involved ten suspected foreign terrorists—mostly Algerians previously detained under anti-terrorism legislation rushed through in the wake of the 9/11 attacks in the US—who were appealing the decision of the Special Immigration Appeals Commission to deport them. They argued that some of the evidence against them had been extracted under torture from third parties in Algeria and other countries.

The law lords then ruled that evidence obtained by torture was not admissible in a British court. It barred evidence obtained by 'extraordinary rendition' of suspects—that is, flying suspects to a third countries for interrogation—and ruled that evidence extracted by torture could only be used against the torturers. Starmer hailed this as 'the leading judgment in the world on torture'. Though once again fighting against the party he would one day run-for, there was something about the Human Rights Act that transcended partisan divides. Not just the final word 'on torture' it was the final word dictating where Starmer drew lines in the sand.

In addition to his growing affinity for international debates Starmer was also demanding structural change on a national level. Starmer was part of a panel set up by the *Times* newspaper that called for a written constitution and changing the way that people bought and sold house, as well as updating the laws on divorce and privacy in a way that would transform people's lives. He also looked into constitutional reform, the disestablishment of the Church of England, scaling back the monarchy and rewriting of social contract between government and citizens to ensure the correct balance of freedoms and protection against terrorism. He also worked for the organisation Justice, making submissions in a 2007 terrorism where it was argued that British anti-terrorism laws protected foreign tyrants and dictators. And he fought the use of control orders that imposed an eighteen-hour curfew and restricted social contacts.

But despite the inclination towards structural change, and big moves against government, Starmer continued to take on more parochial cases at home, especially those involving police negligence or abuse of power. In the early 2000s Starmer was representing Christine Hurst whose son Troy had been murdered by neighbour Albert Reid in Stroud Green, north London.

Arguing in front of the High Court, he said that, at the time of the killing that both the Barnet Council and the Metropolitan Police knew Mr Hurst's killer was 'capable of carrying out threats of violence up to the level of death'.

'Had the Metropolitan Police and the London Borough of Barnet acted differently, the death may have been avoided,' he said. 'Both the police and the council knew Reid had violent tendencies and had attacked his neighbours.'

Though at face value the case seemed narrower in scope compared to the huge successes of his career, Starmer did not hesitate to bring it into the nexus of Human Rights law. He pointed out that Article 2 of the European Convention on Human Rights 'requires public authorities to take reasonable steps to safeguard the lives of individuals'. The judge agreed and re-opened the inquest. The coroner appealed on the grounds that the death occurred before the Human Rights Act incorporating the European Convention on Human Rights into UK law had come into force. The court of appeal dismissed the appeal and order the inquest to be re-opened. The case went all the way to the House of Lords.

Starmer again took on the police in 2005 when he defended a Mr R. Mondelly in his case against the Commissioner of the Metropolitan Police after he had been cautioned for the possession of cannabis. At 9.30pm on 16 February 2005, two policemen were investigating a burglary but had gone to the wrong address. They knocked on the front door of Mondelly's flat. He answered and invited them inside. The police officers said that they could smell cannabis. Mondelly responded: 'It's just a spliff, man.'

One of the officers noticed a joint, a grinder, one small cube of cannabis and some marijuana. They took his keys and tried them in the front door to check that he lived there. He did, so they arrested him for allowing his premises to be used for the smoking of cannabis.

Mondelly was handcuffed and taken to the police station where he was cautioned. However, this happened on the same day that cannabis was reclassified as a class C drug. A notice had been issued by the Metropolitan police that, if the officers were satisfied that the cannabis was solely for the possessor's own use and there were no aggravating circumstances, the drug should be seized and no further action taken. Mondelly contested the caution on those grounds and demanded a judicial review. However the Queen's bench decided that, although the Metropolitan Police had changed their policy, that had not been sanction by parliament so the police had every right to arrest and caution him.

In his push to curb unmitigated police power a spark of the same Starmer who had defended acid house parties in the 1980s shone through. Once again defending the right to assembly in the face of assertions of public disorder, Starmer represented anti-globalization protesters in 2001. These protesters had been corralled by police in 'May Day Riots' through a tactic called 'kettling.' Three thousand people in Oxford Circus had been corralled without food or water for over seven hours.

He took up the case of breastfeeding mother Lois Austin and businessman Geoffrey Saxby who were suing the Metropolitan Police for false imprisonment in breach of their right to liberty under the European Convention on Human Rights.

Louis Austin, who had been attending the peaceful protest, was not allowed to leave to pick up her eleven-month-old daughter from a crèche, while Saxby claimed that the police ignored him when he told them he was not involved in the demonstration. He was caught up in it when he got off a slow-moving bus, he said.

Starmer told the court that the lack of lavatories in particular led to 'inconvenience and distress'. Many people had to urinate in front of others in the crowd and police officers. That was relevant to the reasonableness of the action taken by the Metropolitan Police and the question of damages, Starmer maintained.

'Our broad position is that there is no power to detain those who are not presenting any danger to the peace,' he said. But in the end, the Court of Appeal dismissed their claim for damages. Starmer's frustration with the damages done by the Metropolitan Police were incentive to eventually take on the position of Director of Public Prosecutions, climbing inside the machine to create change.

For a man soon to become Director of Public Prosecutions Starmer had a great deal to say about the management of police, and the role of police in ensuring fair trial. In *Miscarriages of Justice* Starmer writes in his concluding remarks 'every year, hundreds of litigants obtain substantial damages as compensation for serious police misconduct.'

However, Starmer did not see this as solely the fault of the police but rather an issue with complacency of the prosecutors meant to oversee them. He cites the 1997 decision by the Crown Prosecution Service to not prosecute any police officers following two deaths in policy custody and a High Court finding that police officers had tortured a suspect during interrogation as evidence of CPS negligence. 'For its part, the Crown Prosecution Service has failed to live up to expectations.'

It was not only Starmer's dislike for the Metropolitan Police that made him an odd candidate for the position of DPP. The media specifically picked up on Starmer's tolerance regarding those facing allegations of terrorism in order to question the validity of his appointment. In 2004, Starmer had led a team appealing the internment of Hilal Abdul-Razzaq Ali Al-Jedda. Al-Jedda had made a successful claim for asylum in the United Kingdom in the 1990s and held dual British and Iraqi nationality. In October 2004 he visited Iraq, where he was arrested by British troops and taken to a detention centre operated by British forces in Basra. He had remained there ever since. The Court of Appeal found that the reason for his arrest and detention was that he was suspected of membership of a terrorist group involved in weapons smuggling and explosive attacks in Iraq. He was therefore detained on the basis that his internment was necessary for imperative reasons of security in Iraq. He had not been charged with any offence as there was not enough admissible evidence against him to support the bringing of criminal charges in a court of law. So he was being detained on a purely preventative basis.

Starmer also represented an anonymous complainant, known only as MB, against a control order made by the Home Secretary under the Prevention of Terrorism Act because the secretary of state believed that he intended to go to Iraq to fight against coalition forces. However, the order interfered with the respondent's rights to respect for his private and family life under Article 8.1 of the Human Rights Convention. The court found the MB had not been given the fair hearing to which he was entitled. However, this was overturned by the Court of Appeal on the grounds that the relevant UN resolution had the effect of qualifying rights to liberty and took precedence over the European Convention on Human Rights.

When Starmer was offered the job of DPP in 2008 the *Daily Telegraph* expressed surprise on 26 July 2008 that the human rights barrister who had won a House of Lords case that resulted in terrorist control orders being declared illegal has been appointed as the country's top prosecutor.

Questioning his suitability for the position, the newspaper said: 'Mr Starmer, 45, has acted as a prosecutor and CPS adviser in the past but he is best known for his work challenging Government decisions in the fields of human rights and criminal law.

'Last year he acted for two terror suspects in front of law lords, who declared the control order system for terror suspects unlawful under human rights law.

'In 2005 he led a team representing 14 human rights organisations in a critical Lords case that ruled that intelligence extracted by torture is not admissible in any British court.

'In April this year the barrister represented the family of James Ashley, who was shot dead by police when naked and unarmed in 1998, in their successful Lords case for the right to bring a civil misconduct action against Sussex Police.

'He also conducted an independent review of the coach licensing system at the Lawn Tennis Association.'

It was, the *Telegraph* said, a case of 'poacher turning gamekeeper'.

But perhaps that was exactly what was needed. 'Keir has always subscribed to the view that you have to get into the system and not stand outside it' says Millar. 'He would want to be on the inside, not out on the barricades.'

The question was whether in the face of heavy scrutiny could Starmer maintain the commitment to structural change he felt the CPS so desperately needed.

27. Director of Public Prosecutions

To many Keir Starmer did not seem like the obvious choice for Director of Public Prosecutions. the *Sun* was outraged, saying that 'his appointment as Director of Public Prosecutions for England and Wales raised concerns last night. As well as defending a paedophile's right to remain anonymous, Mr Starmer QC has:

BATTLED for the rights of asylum seekers to claim benefits.
HELPED two terror suspects overturn control orders.
QUESTIONED the legality of British forces fighting in the Iraq War.
He has also spoken out against the death penalty and worked for nothing to save brutal killers from being executed in the Caribbean.

The newspaper said that senior police officers were 'dismayed' by the appointment. It quoted former Flying Squad commander John O'Connor saying that the criminal justice system needed positive action—not 'a human rights lawyer going on the offensive for defendants. The public have a right to be protected and we need a robust and determined Director of Public Prosecutions. We do not need a barrister putting human rights top of the agenda. The primary objective of policing is protecting life and property and punishment of the guilty. It has to be questioned if appointing a lawyer who has spent his career in human rights is appropriate.'

At the same time others appreciated that Starmer would not be another government lackey, and had the potential to transform the CPS. Attorney General Baroness Scotland said: 'Keir brings with him a breadth of experience in human rights, international law, police and criminal law. He has previously prosecuted for the Crown and advised the CPS, and has also acted against the Government on various issues. That is in the nature of his present role as an independent barrister.'

The *Guardian*, too, was more enthusiastic, saying that the move was 'described in legal circles as bold, exciting and encouraging' as he had 'challenged the government over the reach of its anti-terror legislation and taken on the British military over the abuse of prisoners held in Iraq'.

Attorney General Baroness Scotland appointed Starmer as DPP in 2008, following in the tradition of his predecessors in appointing a defence attorney to the position. While Brown and Starmer did not see eye to eye on foreign policy decisions such as the war in Iraq on other topics they were similar. Brown was committed to public services such as the NHS and was a fierce advocate for closing the gap of economic inequality in Britain. It was not then completely unfounded that he would choose a man unafraid of reform.

However, at first glance, for a man so committed to structural change during the latter part of his legal career, Starmer, upon first becoming DPP, seemed to take a while to find his footing.

As a younger lawyer Starmer had advocated in his writing and in his case-work to curb police power and abuse but once in charge of the CPS, the inclination to make big moves without having air-tight evidence faded. In February 2009, Starmer ran into controversy when he approved a decision not to prosecute any police officers over the death of Jean Charles de Menezes, the Brazilian shot dead by mistake by officers of Metropolitan Police Service at Stockwell tube station after the 2007 London bombings.

Jean Charles's cousin Vivian Figuierdo said the decision was 'deeply upsetting'. 'We are in shock and cannot understand how the deliberate killing of an innocent man and an attempt by the Metropolitan police to cover it up does not result in a criminal offence,' she said. 'We condemn the CPS decision and reject the logic of their argument.' This decision seemed like a far cry from the man who had taken on Mondelly's case in 2005.

He also approved the decision not to prosecute seven officers who fired eleven bullets at Mark Saunders after he had shot at neighbours from a window of his £2.2-million house in Markham Square in Chelsea. It had been decided that murder, attempted murder and manslaughter charges against the officers could not succeed as it could not be proved beyond reasonable doubt that the officers did not genuinely believe that either they or others were in immediate danger. Gross negligence, misconduct, and health and safety charges were considered against those in charge of the operation.

Starmer seemed hung-up on evidence. The image of the young boy on the 401 bus to Reigate poring over books to prove Cooper wrong comes to mind. A Labour man back in a Conservative environment Starmer had returned to the formula he knew: go by the rules, go by the evidence, and before you make a decision make sure it is so right no one can prove you wrong.

Starmer's focus on irrefutable evidence seemed to dampen the spirit of the man who had once taken such pride in exploiting the assumptions of the law to overturn convictions on absurd cases. The appointment of Keir Starmer as DPP had given hope to Gary McKinnon, who faced extradition to the US. A sufferer from Asperger's Syndrome, McKinnon admitted hacking into computers in the Pentagon from the bedroom of his north London flat, but said he was only looking for evidence of UFOs. However, he had been indicted by a federal grand jury in the Eastern District of Virginia. Rather than being sent to America, he hoped that the CPS would prosecute him in the UK instead. He was out of luck. Starmer found that the CPS could not prosecute him because the evidence against him was in the US. Eventually the then-Home Secretary Theresa May blocked extradition to the United States.

A family man whose wife had just given birth to their first son, Toby, in 2008, he was increasingly becoming the stoic man known in Labour party politics today. While as a young lawyer he had joined picket-lines and defended the right of assembly, he was increasingly concerned with the 'image' of the cases brought before him. From the off, Starmer decided that eleven members of an anarchist group called the Space Hijackers would face prosecution. One woman was dressed provocatively in a black bra. Another wore red high heels and stockings. Their long-haired male companions were dressed in boiler suits and the occasional riot helmet. They were pictured en route to last April's G20 protests with a dilapidated Saracen personnel carrier, plastic machine guns and speakers blaring out the Ride of the Valkyries. Bizarrely they were charged with impersonating police officers, an offence that carries a maximum sentence of three months.

'If I'm guilty of anything it's of impersonating a stripper, not a police officer,' said thirty-year-old Leah Borromeo whose boiler suit was rolled down to her waist. 'Our lawyers never thought anyone would be charged because it is so ridiculous. It is a farcical case.'

The case had already cost the taxpayer tens of thousands of pounds and occupied detectives and prosecutors for hundreds of hours. MPs, senior legal experts and the group's lawyers this weekend said the prosecution should be withdrawn as it was likely to backfire—as indeed it did. It was also described as 'a terrible abuse of power'. They claimed that it was obvious they were taking part in an April Fool's Day joke as world leaders were meeting in London on 1 April.

'It was a parody and a spoof,' said their leader. 'This case is a complete overreaction. We think this case is a complete waste of taxpayers' money. We wore blue boiler suits and helmets we had bought from eBay and we had all saved up and bought the armoured personnel carrier between us. We did everything entirely lawfully and there was nothing sinister about any of it. It is a very serious charge. The charge exists to stop people dressing up as police officers and robbing old women, it's not for people legitimately protesting.'

After four court appearances the CPS dropped the case against them and they were paid £100,000 compensation. Their solicitor Raj Chada said: 'This was always a ridiculous case. The CPS's time and effort could have been better spent looking at bringing prosecutions for potential police misconduct.'

This bait and switch on Starmer's approach to public disorder also materialize in his decision to not take action over the death of newsvendor Ian Tomlinson who had been knocked to the ground by a Scotland Yard riot squad officer Simon Harwood during the G20 protests in London in 2009. Starmer said: 'After a thorough and careful review of the evidence, the Crown Prosecution Service has decided that there is no realistic prospects of a conviction against the police officer in question for any offence arising from the matter investigated and that no charges should be brought against him.'

Forty-seven-year-old Tomlinson had died from internal bleeding a short distance away from the original incident. However, medical experts could not agree whether the two events were related.

'In the face of this fundamental disagreement between the experts about the cause of Mr Tomlinson's death, the CPS embarked on a detailed and careful examination of all the medical evidence and held a series of meetings with experts in an attempt to resolve, or at least narrow, the areas of disagreement,' said Starmer. 'This inevitably took some considerable time.'

Again, he considered there was 'no realistic prospect' of a conviction, because of a conflict between the post-mortem examinations.

Commenting on Starmer's decision, Tomlinson's stepson Paul King said: 'He has just admitted on TV that a copper assaulted our dad. But he hasn't done anything. He's the man in charge... why hasn't he charged him? They knew that if they dragged this out long enough, they would avoid charges. They knew just what they were doing. They've pulled us through a hedge backwards—now we have to go on living our lives.'

Tomlinson's death became global news after amateur video evidence emerged that challenged the original official version of events. Police had told his widow and nine children he died of a heart attack after being caught up in the crowd movements in the busy streets around the protests, rather the action of a single officer. This led to accusations by Tomlinson's family of a police cover-up. After a subsequent inquest found that Tomlinson had been unlawfully killed, Starmer announced that Harwood would be prosecuted for manslaughter. The officer was acquitted in July 2012, but dismissed from the police that September.

The question left in the minds of many was whether Starmer was becoming complicit in the CPS oversight he had spent years of his life criticising. He had promised reform—but when would that happen?

Even when it came to critiquing government Starmer seemed less keen to go toe-to-toe with the Brown government than he had been with Labour's Tony Blair. In 2008 Starmer was immediately thrown into controversy over the arrest of Tory MP Damian Green after the Metropolitan Police had raid his constituency home and office in the House of Commons on suspicion of 'aiding and abetting misconduct in public office' and 'conspiring to commit misconduct in a public office'. Four documents that were potentially embarrassing to the then Labour government had been leaked to him by a junior civil servant. The Home Office who told the police: 'We are in no doubt that there has been considerable damage to national security already as a result of some of these leaks.'

It turned out that the police did not have a search warrant nor had Starmer, as DPP, given his approval for the raids. A spokesman for the Crown Prosecution Service, which would decide whether Green should face criminal charges, said that Starmer had been told about the arrest only ten minutes before detectives moved in. He was said to be privately aghast that the Met took the decision to arrest Green and search his Commons office without taking proper legal advice.

Some months after the raids, Starmer made his first statement on the case.

'Some material has now arrived here and we are considering it,' he said. 'We will reach a decision as soon as is reasonably practicable... we will not be hurried.'

In the end, the CPS announced that it was not going to bring a case against either Green as there was 'insufficient evidence'. In another statement, Starmer said: 'I have concluded that there is evidence upon which a jury might find that there was damage to the proper functioning of the Home Office.

'Such damage should not be underestimated. However, it has to be recognised that some damage to the proper functioning of public institutions is almost inevitable in every case where restricted and/or confidential information is leaked.

'I have concluded that the information leaked was not secret information or information affecting national security: It did not relate to military, policing or intelligence matters. It did not expose anyone to a risk of injury or death. Nor, in many respects, was it highly confidential.

'Much of it was known to others outside the civil service, for example, in the security industry or the Labour Party or Parliament.

'Moreover, some of the information leaked undoubtedly touched on matters of legitimate public interest, which were reported in the press.'

Starmer's relationship with government was increasingly one of compromise and negotiation. While the Human Rights Act had previously appeared to be a hill he would die on throughout the late 2000s Starmer took on an approach increasingly made of compromise and negotiation.

In office he took a more conciliatory approach to counterterrorism legislation, insisting it would be for the courts to decide whether new measures eroded the rights of defendants. Nevertheless, he did not completely reverse his former position. In some ways Starmer was much more anti-terror than he had been in the past.

In September 2009, Starmer issued a statement saying that it was in the public interest to have a retrial of three British Muslims though two earlier cases had ended without a verdict. He said he believed that there was a realistic chance of convicting each man on conspiracy to murder charges in a retrial. The men were accused of plotting to down seven airliners in August 2006 with liquid explosives smuggled onto the planes disguised as soft drinks as they headed to the US and Canada. The plotters planned to assemble the bombs in airplane toilets using hydrogen peroxide-based explosives injected into soda bottles. If it had been successful, two-thousand passengers would have died, along with many more on the ground if the bombs had been detonated over North American cities.

'Having regard to the very serious nature of the charge and the very considerable public interest in having the allegation determined by a jury one way or the other, I have concluded that, in this exceptional case, it is in the public interest to seek a further retrial,' he said, admitting that it was unusual for prosecutors to seek a third trial. Three other British Muslims had been found guilty of conspiracy to murder by detonating explosives on aircraft while they were in-flight. It was thought that the plotters had close ties to al-Qaeda.

However, he was not quite ready to relinquish the relevance of the Human Rights Act when it came to anti-terror measures: 'The European convention on human rights,' he said, 'that is the yardstick.'

Starmer's continued support for Human Rights Act provoked critics who were still calling for it to be repealed.

'The Human Rights Act is a constitutional instrument of the first importance,' Starmer said. 'It is often overlooked that a lot of the thinking about the rights of victims comes from human rights—under the common law it was much more difficult to argue that victims had a right to an effective investigation.'

But, yet, Starmer's commitment to the Human Rights Act seemed less rigid in January 2009, when he gave his tacit support for a 'super database' tracking all phone and internet communications, provided certain safeguards were in place.

'There has always been a tension between the retention of private information necessary for the investigation of crime and privacy,' he said. 'Any invasion of privacy will have to have a clearly defined purpose, be necessary and proportionate, and have effective safeguards. If those features are in place it is obviously legitimate to collect data.' This was an interesting stance for a man who had written chapters in textbooks dedicated to the right of individuals to privacy, staring that correspondences included 'telephone calls, faxes and (presumably) other forms of communication such as email.'

Starmer's support for the plans marked a stark contrast to his predecessor, Sir Ken Macdonald QC, who warned that any such database would prove a 'hell house' of personal private information. It also surprised critics of the plans, who were expecting a similarly critical line from the new DPP who was well known for his work as a leading human rights barrister.

Starmer was also increasingly involved in cases involving not the underdog, but quite high-profile athletes and actors. While Starmer seemed willing to be lenient with the right to privacy in parliament he took a much firmer line when it came to the phone-hacking scandal in 2006. Starmer ordered an 'urgent examination' of material provided by the police in the newspaper phone-hacking scandal first exposed in 2006, where government ministers, actors, singers, football stars, models and novelists were among those targeted by top-selling *News of the World*. Three years on, the *Guardian* said that publishers News Group Newspapers had paid more than one million pounds out of court to suppress legal cases that would have revealed evidence about the scale of phone tapping.

Starmer said he wanted reassurances that 'appropriate actions' were taken over the evidence originally supplied by the police, and would make a statement within days.

'In the light of the fresh allegations that have been made, some preliminary inquiries have been undertaken and I have now ordered an urgent examination of the material,' he said, although he added: 'I have no reason to consider that there was anything inappropriate in the prosecutions that were undertaken in this case.'

Unlike in the cases of Saunders and Tomlinson, Starmer was more willing to question the Metropolitan Police, who refused to re-open the case. However, it wasn't just the status of the victims which had changed but also the solidity of the evidence involved. This seemed like a case Starmer might be able to win. Starmer was particularly interested in the evidence relating to phone hacking gathered in the investigation of *News of the World* reporter Clive Goodman and private investigator Glenn Mulcaire, who were jailed for obtaining information illegally.

Solicitor Mark Stephens, Starmer's friend and close collaborator, told the BBC: 'I think Keir Starmer, the director of public prosecutions, will force the police to reopen this investigation.'

Former deputy prime minister John Prescott urged Keir Starmer to go to the high court to challenge the sealing of the case file of Gordon Taylor, chief executive of the Professional Footballers Association. Taylor sued the *News of the World* for hacking his phone and was paid more than £700,000 in damages and costs on condition that he kept silent and that the whole file was sealed from public view. However, Starmer said that the CPS would have to limit the number of charges they followed up.

'Any other approach would have made the case unmanageable and potentially much more difficult to prove,' he said. 'This is an approach that is adopted routinely in cases where there is a large number of potential offences.'

He also confirmed that when police raided Mulcaire's office they found further evidence of interception and invoices for payments the private investigator had received from the *News of the World* for 'research' into individuals who had no connection with the royal family, including politicians, sports personalities and other celebrities.

Coming to the conclusion that the CPS and the police properly handled the prosecution of Goodman and Mulcaire—both imprisoned at the Old Bailey in January 2007—he said it would not be appropriate to reopen the cases of the two men. But he added: 'I am not in a position to say whether the police had any information on any other victims or suspects that was not passed to the CPS.'

The CPS then discovered that detectives did not give them a key email naming the tabloid's chief reporter, Neville Thurlbeck. In the email, a junior *News of the World reporter* had copied a transcript of more than thirty messages hacked from the phones of Gordon Taylor, and his legal adviser, Jo Armstrong. The email noted that the transcript had been prepared 'for Neville'. The *News of the World* had consistently claimed that the hacking of voicemail by a private investigator involved only one rogue journalist, their royal reporter, Clive Goodman, acting alone.

In a new statement, the CPS said: 'The email was not in the possession of the CPS and so did not form part of the examination that the DPP carried out earlier this week.' It added: 'The DPP is now considering whether any further action is necessary.'

Yet, at times, Starmer did seem like he might stick to his commitment to pursue structural change within the CPS. 'Now is the time for some radical rethinking about criminal justice. Not everyone who plays a part in the criminal justice system considers themselves to be part of a service at the moment... That needs to change,' he added.

Starmer was a strong advocate for increased transparency in prosecutions, supporting televised trials. He told an audience at London Metropolitan University: 'The more the public knows about the way the criminal justice system works, the better for everyone. Subject to appropriate safeguards, there's no reason why there shouldn't be televising of very many cases.'

He said he was not advocating open season for all trials, but 'in common with the principle of transparency I would not stand in principle against the televising of court proceedings'.

Despite a successful pilot project in the Court of Appeal, ministers took no action and senior judges continued to have reservations.

'My vision,' he said, 'is of a modern transparent prosecution service that engages in an open and honest way with the communities it services, which prosecutes cases firmly and effectively, but also fairly and which is publicly renowned both for the quality of its casework and high ethical standards it adheres to.'

Starmer was also focused on reducing the community bias of the CPS. He said that CPS prosecutors were becoming community prosecutors. Based firmly within their communities, they would get to know the types of crime causing local concern and be able to take the public's views into account in the decisions they take and in the information they place before the courts. It was their duty to ensure that there is no bias in criminal justice.

'The CPS was originally a service squeezed between the police and the courts. The police were responsible for deciding on the charge and preparing the case file for the prosecutor; the prosecutor reviewed these cases, largely behind the scenes, and handed them over to the self-employed Bar to present at court.

'Today things could hardly be more different. Modern prosecutors work upstream with the police and other investigating agencies, advising on the evidence pre-charge. They determine the charges in all but minor cases—a service that is now available 24 hours a day, seven days a week through CPS Direct. And they increasingly present their own cases in court using a growing team of specially trained in-house advocates.

'They engage with their communities, using innovative means such as the highly regarded community involvement panels and hate-crime scrutiny panels. The latter actually involve members of the community examining our files to help to improve our handling of future cases.'

'A criminal justice service must not favour, or be thought to favour, one section of the community over another,' he said. 'Equality before the law lies at the heart of the criminal justice service and at the core of the public prosecution service. At the same time, visibility and account-ability are no longer optional extras; they are the duty of the prosecution service. The norm must be to tell people what we do, explain our decisions clearly and, wherever possible, be willing to provide as much information about them as possible.'

But while many had hopes that Starmer's structural changes within the CPS would mean a curbing back of police power, and end of police abuse in smaller communities Starmer's efforts to modernize the system and bring the CPS out of communities looked like it might have the opposite effect. In July 2009, Starmer decided that the CPS needed an overhaul. He said that the role of modern prosecutors had become unrecognisable from that envisioned by the CPS's founders in 1986.

'A modern public prosecution service is emerging, which requires a modern framework. The blueprint, created in 1986, no longer describes what we do,' he said. And he identified several key areas for change.

In future, the CPS would work towards a coherent scheme to deal with low-level 'volume' offending, such as criminal damage. As prosecutors, the police and local authorities should make continued use of out-of-court penalties such as fines and cautions.

In his structural changes, he desire for increased conversation and dialogue between different branches of state came through, especially in his oversight of the merger of the CPS with the Revenue and Customs Prosecutions Office. For the first time there will be one prosecution service for the police, the Serious and Organised Crime Agency, the UK Border Agency and HM Revenue and Customs.

Increased dialogue and collaboration between branches of the state did allow Starmer to somewhat keep to his promise of questioning government. The enquiry into MPs expenses became a joint venture between the CPS and the Metropolitan Police. In May 2009 the *Daily Telegraph* began publishing the records of MPs expenses. These revealed all sorts of abuses often involving second homes and the misuse of allowances. This put a man who would later become an MP in a difficult position but, as Director of Public Prosecutions, Starmer had no choice. He set up a panel to assess the allegations of misuse of expenses after several days of speculation as to whether any criminal inquiries would be launched. Even before it was convened, ministers were being forced to quit their posts.

Discussions between Starmer and the Metropolitan Police Commissioner Sir Paul Stephenson rendered the decision to put a timescale on the enquiry into MPs expenses. By then, more than 180 MPs paid back a total of almost £500,000 with £23,000 coming from the cabinet. One of the key issues Starmer and Stephenson discussed was whether home 'flipping'—where for expenses purposes MPs swapped the address they claimed was their second home—was a crime. But they decided it was not against the rules laid down by the Commons Fees Office.

However, despite pressure to decide whether charges would be brought forward, and the timescale set jointly with the Metropolitan Police Starmer declined to set a precise time for a charging decision but he promised that rapid action would be taken as soon as all the material had been submitted to him.

'There must be no delay. We must go as speedily as we can,' he said. 'The investigation has to be careful and detailed. Inevitably the best way of achieving that is through focusing on the few cases that warrant the investigation that is going on.' In his newly Conservative position Starmer seemed less sure of how to proceed. As one of his biggest, and potentially most political decisions, it was clear that Starmer wanted to make sure that he was sticking to his proven course of air-tight evidence.

Starmer's more tentative approach to decision-making in his new role as DPP was also seen in his case-by-case approach to assisted suicide. A relatively moral issue it was more difficult for a man like Starmer, who liked to play by concrete rules and keep morals out of the law, to take a firm stance. When a twenty-three-year-old rugby player Daniel James killed himself in the Dignitas clinic in Switzerland, after being left paralysed from the chest down after a scrum collapsed on him during a practice session, the CPS decided not to prosecute his parents who had accompanied him. Starmer said that would not be in the public interest and no further action would be taken.

'I don't underestimate the anxiety many individuals go through,' he said. 'In the case of Daniel James I made our approach as open and honest as possible.'

However, the position of the Crown Prosecution Service was the same with assisted suicide as for every other offence, he said: 'It never has nor can it indicate in advance whether it will prosecute for specific conduct.'

It was clear to Starmer that there needed to be stricter, clearer guidelines around the offence. He said he believed a law on assisted suicide was 'workable' and that it was for parliament to provide clarification. If parliament changed the law and clarified the categories of offence then 'that obviously means everyone is in a better position, but that is not in my gift, that is for parliament'.

Starmer's unwillingness to take a sturdy stance on assisted suicide without guidance from Parliament soon got him into hot water. In a case before the Court of Appeal, Debbie Purdy, who suffered progressive multiple sclerosis, wanted to know if her husband, Cuban violinist Omar

Puente, will be prosecuted if he helps her travel abroad to die in a country where assisted suicide was legal. In England and Wales, aiding and abetting suicide was a criminal offence, punishable by up to fourteen years in prison.

Mrs Purdy and her husband listened in court as her counsel Lord Pannick argued that the Director of Public Prosecutions, Keir Starmer QC, should be required to issue specific policy guidelines. Such guidelines already exist for crimes of domestic violence, bad driving and football-related offences.

Lord Pannick told the judges the appeal concerned 'whether the Director has a legal duty to adopt and publish a policy as to the criteria to be applied by him, and by Crown prosecutors on his behalf, in deciding whether to bring a prosecution for aiding and abetting suicide, contrary to the Suicide Act'.

Lord Pannick even used Starmer's beloved Human Rights Act against him: Lack of proper guidance infringed Mrs Purdy's Article 8 right to private and family life under the European Convention on Human Rights, he argued. She then took the issue to the Law Lords in a two-day appeal hearing opposed by Keir Starmer, who argued that the general code of practice was sufficient and he should not be required to issue specific policy guidelines. Mrs Purdy won her case and Starmer said he accepted the judgment and would publish an interim policy on assisted suicide. Thought it was seemingly abnormal for Starmer to take a decisive position on issues of morality it was perhaps the kick he needed to become more assertive in his role as DPP. Starmer had spent a long time playing by the rules, but now it was time for him to make some.

28. Guiding the Rule of Law

The creation of the guidelines on assisted suicide seemed to trigger a new decisiveness in Starmer. On 23 September 2009, Keir Starmer published his guidelines on assisted suicide. He stressed that his new policy did not mean that helping someone to commit suicide was now legal.

'There are no guarantees against prosecution, and it is my job to ensure that the most vulnerable people are protected, while at the same time giving enough information to those people like Debbie Purdy who want to be able to make informed decisions about what actions they may choose to take,' he said. 'Assisting suicide has been a criminal offence for nearly fifty years, and my interim policy does nothing to change that.'

While it remained illegal to help someone kill themselves, nobody has so far been prosecuted for helping a person travel abroad to end their life. The new guidelines issued outlined sixteen factors likely to result in prosecution and thirteen that would help prevent legal action.

Prosecution would be more likely if the person who had died was under eighteen, had a mental illness or was not acting on their own initiative. If they were maliciously encouraged to commit suicide, did not have an incurable illness or physical disability, or had previously demonstrated indecision about wanting to commit suicide, their helper would be libel to face prosecution.

Prosecutors would also have to be satisfied that the person aiding the suicide was wholly motivated by compassion, and that they, or anyone close to them, had nothing to gain from the death. Cases less likely to be prosecuted include those where the person had a clear and expressed wish to commit suicide, was suffering from an incurable disease, and where the helper was a partner, family member or close friend.

It remained illegal to help someone to die, but the new guidelines stated that if the help given were minor, it would help to protect against prosecution. Starmer insisted that each case must be considered on its facts and merits.

'I also want to make it perfectly clear that this policy does not, in any way, permit euthanasia,' he said. 'The taking of life by another person is murder or manslaughter, which are among the most serious criminal offences. I recognise how sensitive this area of law is and I respect the fact that there are many people who hold strong views on assisted suicide. I want to hear those views and that is why I have also launched a public consultation… by considering as many views as possible, I can produce a final policy which is faithful to both the law and public feeling.'

He acknowledged that there may be a rise in the number of suicides. 'Only time will tell,' he said.

Starmer's new decisiveness continued as he finally began making decisions involving the scandal regarding MP expenses. While he had been meticulous and slow in collecting evidence, seemingly scared to rock the boat of Parliament too hard, in 2010 he came-out hard. Keir Starmer announced that Elliot Morley, a former minister, David Chaytor, the MP for Bury North, Jim Devine, the MP for Livingston, and Lord Hanningfield, a former Conservative business spokesman, would be charged under the Theft Act on 5 February 2010 for false accounting. Morley, Chaytor and Devine are Labour MPs; Hanningfield is a Conservative peer and was leader of Essex county council until he resigned after the statement from the DPP.

Starmer said the four were being charged following a 'careful and detailed' police investigation. The CPS had then reviewed the files carefully before deciding there was sufficient evidence to bring criminal charges. He said the CPS had decided not to prosecute the Labour peer Lord Clarke of Hampstead because there was 'insufficient evidence to provide a realistic prospect of prosecution'. Another parliamentarian was still under investigation, but he did not say who.

As Starmer found surer footing as DPP, a bit of his old self-assurance came back. For a man who had so long left making rules to Parliament he seemed to enjoy the newfound power of creating guidelines, especially when he could use them to bring to the fore his precious Human Rights Act.

This was the case especially for his new set of guidelines regarding the consideration of whether court hearings were 'proportionate to the offence'. In October 2009, Starmer published another new set of guidelines allowing offenders to escape prosecution in cases where it is deemed that a charge and the court hearing that would follow would not be 'proportionate' to the offence they committed. Any prosecution should take the cost of a trial into consideration.

Under the code, offenders could be let off even when there was sufficient evidence to bring a prosecution and when a charge would be in the public interest. However, charges would be more likely to be brought if the offence had led to complaints from a community who either live in the same geographical area or share common 'characteristics' or interests. This was an attempt to ensure that prosecutors respond effectively to problems such as anti-social behaviour which is disturbing local residents. The likelihood of action would also be increased if the offender's inflammatory conduct antagonised other groups of people.

The *Daily Telegraph* said the new rules 'will let criminals off the hook' and David Davies MP called the guidelines a 'criminals' charter'.

'This is another blow for those who believe that criminals should be punished,' he said.

But in some ways this new set of guidelines seemed like an appeal back to the Human Rights Act which walked a fine line between supporting the collective versus the individual.

Starmer's vocal support for the Human Rights Act seemed back in full-swing, and he wasn't afraid to be political about them. Making a speech to mark his first twelve months as DPP, Starmer stepped outside his official role to attack a key Conservative policy by insisting that scrapping the Human Rights Act would bring shame on Britain. Tory leader David Cameron repeatedly pledged to abolish the controversial law, which he said 'flew in the face of common sense'.

'I find myself in difficulty when I hear talk of the need to 're-engineer' or 'rebalance' the criminal justice system,' Starmer said. 'Such talk usually emerges after a particularly questionable decision which receives undue notoriety. Usually this has a thread back to the Human Rights Act of how a victim's rights have been trampled on by an almost Orwellian spectre of European-inspired legislation.

'It would be to this country's shame if we lost the clear and basic statement of our citizens' human rights provided by the Human Rights Act on the basis of a fundamentally flawed analysis of their origin and relevance to our society.' He added that it was a 'lie' to describe the legislation as a 'criminals' charter'.

In fact, Starmer's increasing politicalness was a major topic of criticism. Starmer's comments on the Human Rights Act invited heavy judgement, especially from the Conservative sector. The London *Evening Standard* said: 'He has already given a recent newspaper interview which was seen by critics as barely masking his left-wing views and is certain to attract further Tory hostility if he seeks to make more direct political interventions after the election.'

The Tories called for him to resign. David Davies added: 'We should tear up the Human Rights Act—and Starmer's contract as well.'

BBC interviewer Martha Kearney dug deep into his past, harkening back to his more radical left-wing hey days. You have published magazines called *Socialist Alternatives*. You have had a political background.'

But Starmer's response was measured rather than defensive, he was the young man who'd written *Socialist Alternatives* articles, but he was also the much older man who had refused to prosecute without hard evidence: 'These are things of twenty-five, thirty years ago now. They're not relevant to the work I do now,' he said. 'I hope that since I've been in office I've made it absolutely clear that every single decision is made absolutely independently.'

And despite the criticism Starmer did not back down from his political objectives—perhaps already seeing a platform for himself within Labour. While he had been responsible for encouraging a renewed attack on 'low-level-volume' crime, he now raged against the 'post-code lottery' of justice. In a speech to the Howard League for Penal Reform, he said young offenders are being 'inconsistencies of approach which mean that similar criminal behaviour is sometimes dealt with in different ways' based on location.

In one example 'a youth caught stealing could receive a reprimand or a warning or penalty notice or youth restorative disposal'. Starmer added: 'There needs to be a clear and structured approach so that there is greater consistency and therefore fairness in application.'

Starmer also took an unapologetically non-Conservative stance when it came to Tory proposals to give greater legal protection to householders who tackled burglars. The law as it stood worked well, he said. He told the BBC that it was often the case that prosecutions were not brought when a householder had used force because it was considered that a jury would not convict.

'There are many cases, some involving death, where no prosecutions are brought,' Starmer said. 'We would only ever bring a prosecution where we thought that the degree of force was unreasonable in such a way that the jury would realistically convict. So these are very rare cases and history tells us that the current test works very well.'

And within this new decisive and political DPP there was also a hint of the old humour. Starmer's response to the 'King Con' case seemingly winks at the British public, as if to say I'm still good for a laugh. Paul Bint—aka 'King Con'—claimed to be Britain's top prosecutor while wining and dining women he'd met through lonely hearts ads in the *Sunday Times*. The forty-seven-year-old charmer said he owned a fleet of luxury cars, including one used in the James Bond film *Goldeneye*. Bint boasted he had socialised with former 007 star Pierce Brosnan, and had once been married to British actress Sarah Alexander.

In 2003, Bint had been jailed for four years for impersonating Orlando Powell, the QC who prosecuted in the Jill Dando murder trial. Previously he had been a ballet dancer, a doctor and a property magnate. He had also been jailed for stealing a £55,000 Aston Martin during a test drive in Glasgow.

Asked about the deception, Starmer said: 'He started an affair with two women saying: 'I'm Keir Starmer and I'm the DPP.' 'I know Tony Blair' was one of his chat up lines. And these two women fell in love with him but Paul didn't have a lot of money but thought, I know what makes relationship work you have to give jewellery. So he's hit upon the idea of nicking the jewellery of one of them and giving it to the other, and vice versa. So these two women swapped their jewellery sets unbeknownst to them. Eventually he did all sorts of other things. He took long taxi rides in my name. He tried to buy a house in Buckinghamshire for three million quid in my name and then a piece of art for £80,000 in my name, which is when I first got to know of him because the art dealer phoned up to see whether I was going to complete on the deal.

'Eventually he was arrested and prosecuted but, of course, the Crown Prosecution Service had to take the decision whether to prosecute him. So the team said to me well since you're the victim you can't be involved.

I said fine just tell me the answer to three questions: is he pleading not guilty, is his defence that he is Keir Starmer and where do I stand if the jury acquits him? You should never wish for conviction, you really shouldn't, because its a genuinely independent post, but I was quite relieved when in the end the jury said you're not Keir Starmer, bad luck.'

Asked whether either of the women had every got in touch with him, Starmer said: 'No, they haven't but of course at trial they had to give evidence and they were asked: 'When you saw poor Bint, did you not think this doesn't look anything like Keir Starmer?' And one said; 'I had my suspicions, but everybody can have a bad day."

However, even with these hints of the old Starmer it was true that something about him had grown and changed in an irretrievable way. Starmer's rediscovered commitment to the Human Rights Act and sense of humour became a grey-area when it came to anti-terror campaigns. The same man who represented the anonymous MB, and vehemently opposed UK involvement in Iraq was now dedicated to surveillance, and collecting evidence on would-be terrorists.

While before, Starmer may have seen the joke in the Twitter Joke Trial, as DPP Starmer was compelled to take the case seriously. Starmer made the controversial decision to prosecute Paul Chambers. In the January 2010 bad weather led Robin Hood Airport in South Yorkshire to cancel flights. Chambers was planning to fly to Northern Ireland to meet his girlfriend. Exasperated by the cancellation, he went on Twitter and tweeted: 'Crap! Robin Hood airport is closed. You've got a week and a bit to get your shit together otherwise I'm blowing the airport sky high!!'

Although the airport manager who came across the tweet did not consider this a credible threat, the management contacted the police anyway. Chambers was arrested by anti-terror police and charged with 'sending a public electronic message that was grossly offensive or of an indecent, obscene or menacing character contrary to the Communications Act 2003'. He was found guilty at Doncaster Magistrates' Court, fined £385 and ordered to pay £600 costs. He also lost his job as a result.

A younger Starmer may have enjoyed a battle for free speech, especially in a case which had garnered so much media attention. However, over the past few decades Starmer had clearly aged and now his goal was not to demonstrate how assumptions in the law could be exploited for good fun but to close those very holes he'd manipulated in his youth.

Journalist Nick Cohen drew comparison with Milan Kundera's anti-communist novel *The Joke*, while Stephen Fry offered to pay Chambers' fine and subsequent legal bills. Chambers lost his appeal, prompting thousands of Twitter users to re-post Chambers' Tweet using the hashtag #iamspartacus.

In second appeal, John Cooper QC, wrote that if the tweet was 'menacing' so was John Betjeman's poem, 'Slough' with its line: 'Come, friendly bombs, and fall on Slough!' Then he asked whether Shakespeare would have been prosecuted if he had tweeted his line from Henry VI, Part 2: 'The first thing we do, let's kill all the lawyers'. This drew laughter in court. The comedy continued when Chambers was accompanied to court by Stephen Fry and Al Murray, who defended Chambers' right to make bad jokes.

After two years, the conviction was quashed. the *Observer* reported that lawyers at the CPS had wanted to drop the case against Chambers, even sending him and his solicitor, free-speech campaigner David Allen Green, papers stating that it was agreed that the case should be brought to an end. However, at the last minute Starmer had overruled them.

Chambers said: 'Mr Starmer was prepared to put me through the worry of yet another hearing, waste yet more taxpayers' money and waste the time of the lord chief justice.' The case went ahead until the high court found in Chambers' favour.

A CPS spokesperson denied Starmer was the decision-maker in the case and insisted he did not overrule his subordinates. The spokesperson said that conceding the appeal had been a consideration at one stage, but this was not possible because only the high court could overturn a crown court finding.

The CPS confirmed that it spent £18,000 fighting the case that had provoked protests worldwide. Friends of Chambers said Starmer was trying to save face by refusing to admit he was in the wrong. Louise Mensch, Chambers' MP, has called on the Commons home affairs or justice committees to investigate the DPP's behaviour.

Starmer's commitment to anti-terrorism came through in his

continued support for surveillance schemes. In a submission to the Home Office in November 2009, Starmer asked for new powers to track the email, text message, phone and computer activity of every citizen as these were vital for law enforcement.

'Communications data is often a vital tool in establishing the necessary connections between suspects and it can place suspects at specific locations,' he said. 'The CPS works closely with police to build evidentially strong cases. Many of our prosecutions for serious offences are based on strands of circumstantial evidence which often include communications data.'

He insisted that he struck an 'appropriate balance' between individuals' right to privacy and the needs of national security—and that proposed safeguards to prevent misuse of the power to access data were 'sufficient at present'. Critics argued that the planned powers would be an unjustified extension of government 'snooping'.

The CPS came under fire quite frequently during Starmer's time as DPP with regards to surveillance methods. The CPS again had egg on its face when the case against six people accused of trying to shut down the coal-fired power station at Ratcliffe-on-Soar in Nottingham collapsed on 10 January 2011 after an undercover policeman who had infiltrated the environmental group offered to testify on behalf of the defence. The CPS said the case had been dropped because new information had come to light, 'not the existence of an undercover officer'.

The revelation of the use of undercover cops for surveillance was always a somewhat blurry part of the Human Rights Act. Starmer wrote in 1999 about the role of undercover police officers when it came to issues of entrapment, fair trial and privacy. While 'the use of undercover agents in the investigation of crime is not incompatible with article 6… actions of undercover agents must not exceed passive surveillance.' As such, Starmer took these cases seriously. Rather than being outwardly defensive Starmer appeared ready to hold the CPS responsible when he asked retired high-court judge Sir Christopher Rose to carry out an inquiry. His dedication to improvement showed he'd definitely grown from the cockier young man he'd been.

He found that crown prosecutor Ian Cunningham should have discovered more about the extent of PC Mark Kennedy's undercover involvement in the investigation before building the prosecution case on his evidence. Starmer said that he took the findings 'very seriously indeed' as he ordered disciplinary proceedings against Cunningham.

In a letter to the attorney general, Starmer said: 'To avoid any recurrence of similar issues, I propose that a police/CPS memorandum of understanding be prepared that makes it absolutely clear that in any future cases, the full extent of any authorisation and activity of an undercover officer must be shared between the police and the CPS as soon as a criminal prosecution is contemplated.'

Asked by Channel 4 News if there were other similar cases that should be investigated, Starmer said: 'If Sir Christopher Rose had found systemic problems, then I would quite accept perhaps a retrospective look at all the cases. But he didn't, he found individual failings.'

Individual failings, however, clearly went past the passive surveillance allowed by the Human Rights Act. Twenty people had their convictions quashed after previously being found guilty of conspiracy to commit aggravated trespass. Disclosures about the use of undercover officers had not been made because of 'failures, over many months and at more than one level, by the police and the CPS,' Sir Christopher said. 'The general picture of what occurred is that, at several stages, there was a failure between police officers and between the police and CPS to pass on such information.'

It turned out that, under the pseudonym Mark Stone, Mark Kennedy had infiltrated several protest groups for the National Public Order Intelligence Unit between 2003 and 2010, before being unmasked by political activists as an undercover policeman. He later sued the Metropolitan Police for failing to 'protect' him from falling in love with one of the environmental activists whose movement he infiltrated.

'I worked undercover for eight years,' he told the *Mail on Sunday*. 'My superiors knew who I was sleeping with but chose to turn a blind eye because I was getting such valuable information. They did nothing to prevent me falling in love.'

His wife, Edel, filed for divorce, and he was seeking compensation for 'emotional trauma'.

'When my cover was blown it destroyed my life. I lost my job, my girlfriend and my reputation,' he said. 'I started self-harming and went to a shrink who diagnosed me with post-traumatic stress syndrome. The blame rests firmly at the feet of my superiors at the Met, who had a duty to protect me.'

Ten women and a man also sued the Met for emotional trauma, saying they were duped into having sex with undercover officers. Three of the women were former lovers of Kennedy. An enquiry into the abuses of undercover policing was set up in 2015. It was supposed to have reported by 2018 but was embroiled in deciding how it should hear and publicise evidence. It's first hearing were set for 2010 and it is unlikely to report before 2023. Only then with the CPS's involvement be known.

Issues of sexual harassment became a huge part of Starmer's reform campaign within the CPS, and not just because of the accusations brought forth by the women suing the Met, but largely because of Jimmy Savile revelations and the successful Rochdale Abuse prosecutions. These revelations came around the same time as the birth of Starmer's daughter. As a young man Starmer had defended paedophiles right to privacy but when it came to reforming the CPS' approach to sexual harassment the desire to protect young victims certainly gave Starmer a family-man quality.

Starmer introduced other reforming guidelines in the wake of the Jimmy Savile revelations and the successful Rochdale abuse prosecutions which he had belatedly authorised. He said that men who groomed teenagers for sex had escaped justice for decades because police, prosecutors and the courts failed to understand the nature of the abuse. After an in-depth review of the CPS's initial reluctance to charge men involved in a notorious sex-grooming network in Greater Manchester, he ordered a comprehensive restructuring of the Crown Prosecution Service's response to sex grooming, designed to raise the number of convictions. The new approach would apply to the handling of all current and historic cases of sexual exploitation involving girls and boys, including reviews of the crimes allegedly committed by Jimmy Savile and some of his associates.

The guidelines stipulated that witnesses should be assessed on the credibility of their evidence rather than whether they would look like 'model victims' in court, a proposal caricatured as suggesting witnesses claiming abuse should automatically be believed.

He said, Rochdale, police and prosecutors had in 'good faith' previously decided not to prosecute members of grooming gangs because their very young girl victims were abusing drink and drugs, and in some cases had not gone straight to the police and had continued a relationship with their abusers. This meant that 'the more vulnerable you were, the less likely the criminal justice system was to be able to provide you any protection… The idea that the guidelines simply said 'believe the victims' is just mythical nonsense'.

The broadcaster Paul Gambaccini, who was wrongfully arrested, was among others who claimed the new guidelines later led to overzealous pursuit by the police of false sexual abuse claims against public figures.

Ever committed to evidence Starmer created a report which dispelled the myth that false claims of sexual abuse were proliferate. False allegations of rape are rare, but they can, and do, devastate the lives of those falsely accused and must be treated seriously. My guidance to prosecutors highlights the fact that these cases must be informed by wider circumstances, for example, a prosecution would be highly unlikely where a woman may have retracted a true allegation of rape in the context of an abusive relationship.' While perhaps there is the potential to criticize this view as a particularly leftist interest the report reveals a certain balance that would come to characterize Starmer's later career. While acknowledging that false abuse claims should not act as a reason for not taking sexual harassment claims to court, the report still did acknowledge that false abuse claims exist, and had to acknowledged as such in the law.

Although Starmer was increasingly political just as in the report on false abuses, and in his proactive rather than defensive response to the undercover police officer scandals, Starmer approached criticism with a stoic response which acknowledged the possibility for improvement. When Starmer fell foul of the BBC's *Panorama* program, he took a conciliatory approach, careful to acknowledge the justification of the accusation made. BBC's Panorama program, which used Freedom of Information requests to discover that in 2008 the police handed out nearly 39,000 cautions to people accused of actual bodily harm. In response, Starmer called for an overhaul of the way cautions are used to punish violent offenders.

'I accept that what is needed is a coherent system across the board with one overarching scheme,' he said. 'There is now a case to be made for a review. My view is that there should be a structured tiered approach which specifies what case will be dealt with at what level and will be transparent.'

He said that while there was a proper place for trivial offences to be dealt with outside the courts, the system had developed in an 'incoherent way' and needed to be looked at again. But extending the use of cautions brought the accusation of 'instant justice' by Judge Keith Cutler, a senior circuit judge on the Council of Circuit Judges, who said: 'It is only a matter of time where we will have a domestic murder and we will find on the offender's antecedent sheet that they were cautioned for an earlier assault on the murder victim. It is getting that serious.'

Starmer was no longer the young lawyer who took on cases guns-a-blazing. His idealism had faded when faced with the practicalities of prosecuting cases based only on hard evidence. While he was still loyal to the rule of law there was a part of him that was beginning to see both the defendants and victims as more human; he took their cases seriously, less able to see the joke in defending paedophiles. Though his beliefs were hardening, he was more open to negotiation and discussion—the foundations of politics.

After standing down as DPP Starmer was appointed a Knight Commander of the Order of the Bath (KCB) in the 2014 New Year Honours for 'services to law and criminal justice'. This entitled him to use the honorific 'Sir'—something he avoided. The knighthood led some on the left to regard him as a sell-out.

According to Lord Falconer, after leaving the Crown Prosecution Service in 2013, Starmer could have followed his predecessors by becoming a Labour peer, but he had no interest in that. Instead, the weekly meetings of permanent secretaries and his regular contact with ministers had whetted his appetite for government. 'He could see the importance of elected politicians,' said Falconer.

Starmer had spent the past few years creating guidelines, now he was ready to create policy.

29. MP

Before heading into politics Starmer took the time to return to how he started, Doughty Street. 'I'm back in private practice,' he told the BBC. 'I'm rather enjoying having some free time, and I'm considering a number of options'.

But though Starmer was stepping back in some ways, now that he'd had a taste of making guidelines, he wasn't quite ready to relinquish the power to create structural change. Starmer was ready to be a political advisor, and as a man with practical experience he certainly had something unique to bring to the benches of professional-politicians in Westminster. Starmer especially, was keen on bringing what he'd learned about vulnerable victims in the CPS to the Labour party. If Labour won the 2015 election, he said, he would advise the new government on introducing legislation to give greater protection to vulnerable witnesses in court.

'The more vulnerable you are as a victim or witness, the less able our criminal justice system is to protect you,' he said. 'Most victims, particularly vulnerable victims, don't have the confidence to come forward. Most of them have a pretty awful journey through the court process and nearly all of them, at the end of it, say they will never do it again.'

Starmer was soon given the opportunity to shape policy instead of guidelines, finally letting his red strip shine. The Labour Party announced that Starmer would lead a legal task force looking into the issue of vulnerable victims. 'I think particularly of the child sexual abuse cases and so-called grooming cases. In those cases victims were put through a very great ordeal and so were witnesses so it is troubling,' he said. 'Our criminal justice system has been set up as a straight fight between the prosecution and defendant and victims and witnesses have had a walk on part. We need to rethink that and make sure that we do have a system fit for victims and witnesses, and we don't at the moment.'

His task force included Labour peer Baroness Lawrence of Clarendon, whose son Stephen Lawrence was murdered in a racist attack in 1993.

But the 2015 general election brought opportunities for Starmer to go beyond giving advice, and perhaps most importantly, to begin to shape the nature of the Britain he was building his family in. In December 2014, former Health Minister Frank Dobson announced his retirement as MP for the safe Labour seat of Holborn and St Pancras and Starmer was selected as the new Labour candidate.

The constituency was quite similar to East Surrey where Starmer had grown up. While encompassing the village-like area of Primrose Hill and the affluent Highgate and Hampstead, the majority of the housing was social and there was a large Bangladeshi Muslim community. Starmer's experience living the line between the vastly different demographics within the community would be key to helping him win their votes.

There was certainly something appealing about Starmer, he was good-looking in a polished way, with a full-head of hair and a square jaw, but at 5ft 9 not so disarmingly attractive as to not feel human. The local newspaper, the *Ham & High*, pointed out that he had an advantage over the bearded septuagenarian Dobson. Keir was 'something of a housewives' pin-up,' the paper said.

Living in the constituency, with his wife and their five-year-old son and three-year-old daughter, Starmer epitomized family-values. He was not some rogue young politician out to smirk at your wives, he was a regular guy, raising kids—and with the grey hair to prove it—who had simply aged well. Even his style was local and attainable. His barber was just round the corner from Ed Miliband's house, which was also in his constituency. According to Starmer, the barber said: 'You're great. You're the MP who's going to be prime minister.'

Starmer was duly elected at the 2015 general election with an increased majority of 17,048, though Labour lost in the country.

Winning the election meant closing the chapter of his life involving Doughty Street Chambers. 'I'm winding down my cases which is why I'm so busy. I will no longer take on cases as a lawyer,' he said. 'I gave up Doughty Street Chambers completely when I became DPP and I'm ready to give it up again. It's sad in the sense I will be giving it up for good.' After years of fighting highly intellectualized battles regarding Human Rights it seemed humbling to watch Starmer step back into community work.

The end of Starmer's time at Doughty Street was not the only bittersweet accompaniment to the start of his political career. Two weeks before he won the election, his mother, Jo, had died. But though she did not live long enough to see her son take on the Labour Party, Starmer's future commitment to defending the NHS and public funding would carry the weight of her memory.

After having been a part of such high-profile cases and controversy for so long Starmer's recommitment to community and especially to family presented a humble persona. As one generation of his family passed on and his own, new generation continued to grow up Starmer focused on his roots to keep him grounded, even as many begged him to run for the leadership of the party. 'I'm grounded by my kids we've got a girl who's eight and a boy who's ten and a couple of weeks ago my eight-year-old girl said: 'Are you going to be in tonight?' 'No.' 'What are you doing?' 'A fundraiser.' This was like a slow-motion cross-examination that's always going to be a disaster. 'What's a fundraiser?' 'It's when people pay money to come to dinner or to hear someone speak.' The next question is, of course: 'Who's speaking?' 'Me.' 'Why would anybody pay money to hear you speak?' I couldn't think of an answer.'

Starmer, still figuring out the rules of what being a politician meant in comparison to a lawyer, tactfully acknowledged his own lack of experience. Following the resignation of Ed Miliband as party leader, Starmer was encouraged to stand in the leadership election. Supporters set up a Facebook page called 'Sir Keir Starmer QC KCB for Labour leader', which attracted more than two hundred members on its first day, and soared to 1,275 by the weekend. Followers planned to launch a Twitter storm under the hashtag #keirforleader with the aim of encouraging senior figures in the party to back a Starmer leadership bid.

Narice Bernard, one of the campaign founders, said: 'I just have a belief that he wants the job but isn't prepared to say so.'

He and others had sent a series of tweets and emails to Starmer but heard nothing back.

'Silence speaks volumes,' Bernard said. 'He hasn't said he will stand, but he hasn't said he won't. It's clear that when someone goes into politics at his stage of life they do so for very good reason—they want to make a difference.'

But Starmer refused to join the campaign, citing his lack of parliamentary experience.

Keir eventually tweeted: 'V flattered by #keirforleader initiative and thanks for so many supportive messages but Labour needs s/one with more political experience.'

'Could a party consider a leadership candidate somebody who has only just joined the party and only just become an MP?' he asked. 'Many people would say no. But goodness me wouldn't that electrify the campaign?'

But, despite Starmer's silence he represented a newness in the Labour Party. As he had yet to firmly establish himself in the political sphere, those disenchanted with Labour's defeat could pin to him any hopes they wanted. He was a blank canvas. Bernard said he was disillusioned with the other candidates because they were associated with Labour's defeat.

'I just don't think that on the back of such an election failure, the people instrumental in that failure are the right choice to move us forward,' he said. 'We need something so dynamic, so fresh, so strong that we need a born leader.'

'What's obvious about Keir Starmer is that he is fresh and new and experienced,' he said. 'People have a vision of a person of that calibre, without baggage, really being able to take on the Tories. We can't put up some little fish to take on David Cameron when he is on a massive bounce. We have got to match that bounce and Starmer is the man that can revive that bounce.'

And Bernard wasn't the only one to pin their radical hopes on Starmer. Former City minister Lord Myners, who funded Gordon Brown's leadership campaign, was also a fan. He told LBC: 'I wouldn't be surprised to see other names come forward. I would like to see someone really quite radical. I would like to see Keir Starmer, who has only been a member of parliament for a week, but he's got a real background, he's done a proper job—he's been director of public prosecutions, he's an extremely thoughtful person, he's an able communicator.'

But Starmer, still inexperienced as a politician, was not ready to be Labour's radical poster boy and threw his support instead behind Andy Burnham, who had a strong history in fighting for healthcare, but who finished a distant second to the socialist Jeremy Corbyn.

With the party now in the hands of Momentum, there seemed little room for Starmer. With his relative youth and good looks Starmer seemed more of a Blairite, ironic considering his pointed criticism of Blair throughout his early law career. And his distinguished career in the law, his role as DPP and his knighthood made him appear to be an establishment figure. Corbyn was a life-long leftist who had spent his entire career in radical politics, so the two did not appear to be natural bedfellows. But there was still a little bit of Starmer ready to 'stick-it' to Cameron's Conservative government, albeit in a more polite way than he might have in his youth and with that in mind he joined Corbyn's shadow Home Office ministerial team.

As ever vocal about international affairs Starmer made sense in the role of Shadow Minister of State for Immigration. There was a critical vote on whether to take military action in the civil war in Syria. The debate harkened back to the controversial decision to invade Iraq which Starmer had spent years picking apart in relation to the Human Rights Act. Though he was new to politics examining war in the context of human rights was something he knew how to do.

Writing in the *Guardian* Starmer said that airstrikes undertaken in Syria were lawful, but that he would be voting against them.

'I would back military action,' he said, 'however, the prime minister's strategy to defeat Isis is flawed without an effective ground force.'

He pointed out that Britain was already involved in military action in Iraq and providing surveillance and logistical support in Syria. The prime minister wanted to go further and outlined his strategy in the House of Commons. Donning his lawyer's hat once again, Starmer said that the test that should be applied to his strategy was whether it was lawful, coherent and compelling.

'In my view, the military action taken in Iraq in 2003 was not lawful under international law because there was no UN resolution expressly authorising it,' he said. 'The situation now in Syria is different, but calls for great clarity.'

While the US resolution passed by the UN Security Council did not provide legal basis for military action, he said, 'the collective self-defence of Iraq is, in my view, a sufficient legal basis for the action he proposes'.

But that was not enough.

'The question whether the prime minister's strategy, while lawful, is also coherent and compelling is much more difficult to answer,' he said. 'The argument that there is no logic in taking military action in Iraq but not in Syria because Isis does not recognise the border between them is seductive. But it soon unravels. The situation in Syria is very different to the situation in Iraq. The civil war has a different dynamic; the opposition forces are differently constituted; and, of course, Russia has a heavy involvement in support of the Assad government.'

Britain should put its weight behind new political talks to secure a transition to an inclusive government in Syria capable of restoring peace and stability, he said. Britain should also use its aid budget to alleviate the immediate humanitarian suffering; improve its contribution to alleviating the refugee crisis; and step up its efforts to counter radicalism in the UK.

'I am not a pacifist and I would back a lawful, coherent and compelling case for the use of military force by the UK against Isis,' he said. 'In my view, airstrikes without an effective ground force are unlikely to make any meaningful contribution to defeating Isis. And there is no effective ground force.... I accept that Isis must be defeated and I would be happy to consider a revised strategy. But the current plan is flawed.'

Parliament voted for airstrikes by 397 to 223, but no ground force was sanctioned.

The role of Shadow Minister of State for Immigration, a job Starmer was to hold for a year, seemed fitting given his life-long passion for international law and human rights. Here was an opportunity for Starmer to expand on the work he'd started as a QC in the early 2000s.

Immigration was a particularly pressing issue especially given the coming EU referendum. Starmer's approach to the topic was that of a man who had spent the majority of his life perfecting rules, and learning how to argue and counter-argue. Starmer maintained that the party had reached 'a balanced position' on immigration in its 2015 manifesto, but admitted it needed to be willing to talk to voters.

'The party needs to be talking to people all of the time and that is going to involve uncomfortable conversations,' he said.

His strategy was not rabble-rousing but tedious and bureaucratic. He undertook a three-month review of Labour's immigration policy, taking views from the public, trade unions, businesses and universities. His consultation would take into account changes since the election affecting immigration policy, including the EU referendum and Europe's refugee crisis.

Of course, Starmer's approach to immigration was much more moderate than his younger self would've appreciated. Setting a course at odds with his leader, Starmer argued that immigration had been too high and said Labour must support 'some change to the way freedom of movement rules operate' as part of the Brexit negotiations. He was also open to the UK leaving the jurisdiction of the European Court of Justice—the prime minister's core demand—as long as another body was established to settle disputes between Britain and the EU. However, he remained a staunch Remainer.

Starmer's position as a Remainer was not only shaped by his passion for immigration and the rights of asylum seekers which he'd worked on as a younger man. It was also shaped by the practical benefits of European cooperation he had experienced as DPP in the more conservative context of anti-terrorism. As DPP, he had worked with European counterparts to tackle cross-border issues such as trafficking, cyber crime and terror.

'We rely very heavily on the EU criminal justice measures and when I say very heavily, I mean 24/7,' he said. 'I'm talking here about terrorism, people trafficking, cyber crime, sexual exploitation, trafficking of children and paedophilia: they all go across the borders into Europe.

'To give you a practical example, if you have a number of [criminals] operating in different jurisdictions, you absolutely have to arrest them on the same day at precisely the same time. It requires a huge amount of co-ordination. If you arrest one person in Paris, ten minutes before you intend to arrest someone in London on the same allegation, the person in London will be gone by the time you get there.'

Though, Starmer remained a convinced Remainer, while a majority of the British people voted to leave the EU in the referendum on 23 June 2016.

Starmer's response to the Referendum results was that of an academic trained to consider a counter-argument. He employed his classic tactic of acknowledging the motivations of the other-side, and with a great deal of empathy said: 'If the referendum tells us anything it ought to be that millions of people who voted to leave were voting because they were telling us the political and economic system isn't working for them,' he said. 'And they're right about that without going into any report on an equality has been published in last five years and they all tell you the same thing, which is that equality in every way is getting worse not better. That's not just wealth and income but you know health, regional inequality, inequality of influence over politics.'

Perhaps this empathy was because Starmer had grown-up and formed his opinions in both a council house in Oxted and the spires of Oxford. Starmer certainly observed the drastic inequality in his own constituency. 'In Holborn and St Pancras, which is basically most of Camden, the life expectancy difference between Primrose Hill, which is obviously very well-off, and Somers Town, which sits between Euston and Kings Cross, which is very deprived, is ten years. Can you believe that. Ten years? Honestly, I couldn't believe it. I expected that kind of life expectancy difference to be across a continent, not within any constituency. That's got to change and actually that's quite a unifying thing. I obviously campaigned and voted to remain, but I've not met many people who voted to remain that are not up for fundamental change.'

Somehow, while still acknowledging the plight of the Leave campaign, Starmer still came-out looking like a devout leftist, focused on reducing economic inequality.

Frustrated by the lacklustre referendum campaign, two days after the referendum several Labour Party shadow cabinet ministers quit in protest of Jeremy Corbyn's leadership. It is in keeping with Starmer's vocal position on the necessity of international cooperation that he would first bring a plight against Corbyn over international relations. Tendering his resignation, Starmer said: 'It is simply untenable now to suggest we can offer an effective opposition without a change of leader.'

Corbyn lost a vote of no confidence by 172 to 40, with 4 abstentions. There followed a new leadership election. Starmer nominated Owen Smith, but the Labour Party re-elected Jeremy Corbyn September 2016. For whatever their differences, Corbyn again brought Starmer into the shadow cabinet. Though at first seemingly a case of 'hold your friends close and your enemies closer,' in reality Corbyn quite cleverly brought into the fold a committed internationalist, with extensive legal experience to advocate for a Brexit deal that would keep the UK in decent relations with the rest of Europe. What the deal needed was not an idealist, but a man capable of navigating rules and practicalities.

The website politicalbetting.com said: 'Whilst the focus might be on the appointment of Diane Abbott as Shadow Home Secretary I think Jeremy Corbyn has pulled off a master stroke by appointing former Director of Public Prosecutions, Sir Keir Starmer, as Shadow Brexit Secretary.

'David Davis doesn't exude confidence as Brexit Secretary, and he has been very publicly slapped down by Mrs May a few weeks ago, and the complexity of Brexit, Sir Keir's agile legal and forensic mind, coupled with his experience as a barrister, it won't be tears for Keir's supporters, but tears for David Davis' supporters. Jeremy Corbyn might have just brought a bazooka to a water pistol fight. With Brexit going to dominate for a least the rest of this Parliament Corbyn is right to bring in the very best to cover this important role as the government introduces the 'great' repeal bill.'

While in 2015 Starmer hadn't been ready for Labour supporters to pin their radical hopes on him, this was a task which he could undertake with certainty and with commitment. He was not the man to front the Momentum agenda but taking on Brexit was a job true to his beliefs. Starmer's dedication came through and he was increasingly seen as the unofficial leader of the party.

The Politico website asked whether Keir Starmer was 'Britain's last Remaining hope', in an article in November 2016. The piece was subtitled 'Meet the real leader of the opposition'. Following Miller's high-court victory that forced prime minister Theresa May to get parliamentary approval before taking Britain out of the EU, the website said, Labour's Brexit spokesman Keir Starmer 'is suddenly one of the most important figures in British politics' as Jeremy Corbyn was increasingly absent or ignored.

'In his stead, MPs are turning to the UK's forensic former chief prosecutor as their last hope of serious resistance to a hard Brexit,' the article continued. 'Despite only being elected in 2015, what Starmer thinks about Brexit now matters. His ability to build and cajole parliamentary opposition to the government will shape Britain's relationship with

Europe for decades to come.'

Uniquely, Starmer did not want to be only the hope of the Labour Remainers but also those who had voted Leave. Where Corbyn would perhaps have faltered in reaching across the divide Starmer was not one to write off the benefits of comprise and conciliation. 'We've got to have both sides represented in this,' he said. 'I think one of the big things that happened after the referendum was that when the prime minister set out her redlines, they were so extreme that lots of people who voted to remain felt they've been pencilled out of the future of the country, so it was really important, I think, to give if we're going to give voice. We've got to give voice to both sides but we have genuinely actually tried to represent both sides in this. It's not been easy.' But by walking the middle line Starmer would face what would be a continuous issue through out his career: difficulty sparking passion in one side against the other. In an article in *Prospect* one legal adviser who wanted to stay anonymous said: 'There's something slightly missing where the rousing stuff might need to be... Keir's real speciality is getting it right. He can unpick an argument brilliantly, but he's not such a natural at the passion behind the argument.'

In 2017, Theresa May called an ill-judged snap election which overturned her overall majority of twelve, making the Conservatives dependent on the Democratic Unionist Party to govern. Labour's gain of thirty seats, though not giving the party power, secured Jeremy Corbyn's position as leader.

Not one to take the spotlight for himself, despite his significant involvement in the Labour policy on Brexit leading up to the election, Starmer gave the credit for Labour's success to Corbyn. 'When Jeremy ran the 2017 election campaign he did really well and he really cut through to people,' he said. 'In places like York he got six-thousand people out. He does have an ability to reach people that other politicians don't have. There's no doubt about that. I mean that's probably the frustration that people had with the EU referendum campaign. I think it's wrong to say that he doesn't have that ability the reach people, but also to be contrasted with someone like Boris because the personality couldn't be more different.

However, despite the small victory for Labour the work on Brexit was not made easier. The best he could do was ask the government to lay out its strategic plans before formal talks. He went on to warn that if Britain left without a deal it risked being plunged into an 'unsustainable legal vacuum'.

At the Labour Party Conference in Liverpool in September 2018, Starmer laid his cards on the table when it came to Brexit.

'Like many of you, I was devastated by the referendum result,' he said. 'Like many of you, I'd campaigned passionately to stay in the EU. Not for the technical benefits—important though they are. But because I'm an internationalist. Because I believe that nations achieve more together than they do alone. I believe that the greatest challenges facing our nation—armed conflict, terrorism, climate change or unchecked globalisation—can best be met together with our EU partners. And the greatest opportunities—medical research, scientific advancement, art and culture—can only be realised together with our EU partners. Those values did not die on 23 June 2016.'

The Conservative government under Theresa May, he said, was tearing itself apart. What Labour wanted was clear: 'We want a general election that can sweep away this failed Tory Government and usher in a radical Labour Government that would put jobs and living standards first. But if a General Election is not possible then other options must be kept open. That includes campaigning for a public vote. It is right for Parliament to have the first say, but if we need to break the impasse, Labour campaigning for a public vote must be an option.'

During the middle of a series of key Brexit votes, Keir's father Rod died just as the media was beginning to posit Keir as the next leader of Labour. 'I wouldn't say we were close. I understood who he was and what he was but we weren't close and I regret that,' Starmer told the BBC of his father, but his dedication to the left went deep. Both his parents, Starmer says were 'Labour through and through'. The Left was a passion that he shared with his parents, his commitment to Leftist policy was their memory living on in him. And with that reminder came increased pressure to stay the perfect, balanced, sturdy son, capable of fulfilling not only his dreams but also theirs.

In February 2019, Starmer was arguing that there should be a second referendum. While Corbyn was more equivocal, he was forced to promise a second referendum if Labour won the next general election. The manifesto would promise to reach a better Brexit deal, but would not commit to leave or remain. This indecision brought fresh disaster for the Labour Party in the European elections in May 2019, where it polled less than fourteen per cent.

'You look at the Europe election results and you have to accept that there's going to be a change in our position frankly,' said Starmer. 'You can't on the one hand have the Labour Party getting less than ten per cent in Scotland, coming fifth for the first time in our history and coming third in Wales behind Plaid [Cymru] and pretend that your Brexit policy doesn't need some adjusting. You know I went around the country. When you campaign, we have this list—a very efficient list—in the Labour Party where you've got how people voted last time and whether you think they're sympathetic. Then you've got the really good ones are marked up as a Labour member. Normally when you go to these doors you're not so much persuading them to vote Labour, because that's kind of taken is read, but you might say 'will you put a poster up for us in your window?' This time people open up the door of a Labour member saying; 'I'm not voting for you', which was a bit of a shock to the system.'

When it came to Brexit, the young MP, unafraid to go against the party if it meant sticking to his guns, continued to come through. Keir, diverged from Corbyn when he pushed for an extension to Article 50 to try to stop a no-deal Brexit being put into law. 'We are not going to be deflected from that. Having got control from Boris Johnson last night we are not going to hand it back to him in what is very obviously a trap,' he said. 'No one in parliament trusts this man. We are not going to dance to Boris Johnson's tune. What we want to ensure is we've got the insurance policy of taking no deal off the table and we will have a general election on our terms, not Boris Johnson's terms.'

In contrast, Corbyn had told a rally in Salford that the opposition was always ready for a general election, suggesting he would back an election in all circumstances.

Labour's muddled Brexit strategy became a key issue in the 2019 election campaign after the TV leadership debates and Starmer, as shadow Brexit secretary, was picked out as a target by the Conservatives. A doctored video of him showing him unable to speak after being asked about the issue was posted on social media, when in fact he had given a lengthy answer to the question as was his wont.

But Keir Starmer was no stranger to media and controversy and his response was one of a man unphased. However, instead of sparking rage in Labour over the dissemination of misinformation, Starmer chose to take it like a lawyer trained to see all sides of the argument. His stoic response: 'I actually saw it as an act of desperation. It is only when you think things are not going well that you get involved in those sorts of activities,' he told the *Guardian*.

Rishi Sunak, then chief secretary at the Treasury, apologised for the doctored video, but the attacks on Starmer continued from another quarter.

It was not only Starmer's firm guiding hands on the Brexit deal which made him a natural candidate for Labour leadership, but also his intense and public dislike for the new Conservative Prime Minister, a staunch Leaver, Boris Johnson. The two were immediately at odds, especially as result of their darkly contrasting personalities.

Theresa May had stepped down and Boris Johnson took over as prime minister in 2019. Despite Starmer's normal willingness to reach across the aisle he had little time for Boris Johnson. When it came to Boris Johnson, cool-collected Starmer allowed the British publish to see beneath his calm veneer:

'I shudder. I mean where do you start with him? I think it may be this whole bit where he ruffles his hair and pretends he doesn't know what's going on—people say it's brilliant because underneath he's so clever and think it's actually a double bluff. I think he wants you to think he's really clever because he's not really clever, so the double bluff is that was what you get.' Boris' somewhat unkempt appearance drastically opposed Starmer's carefully pieced together presentation.

Starmer drew attention to an interview Boris had done with the BBC's political editor Laura Kuenssberg.

Starmer, a believer in hard-facts, would have none of Johnson 'ummm's and 'errrr's and beating around the bush: 'I mean everything is just guff, everything he said on the serious questions she was asking him. He was just coming out with complete and utter nonsense and so you know do you want that as your prime minister. Preferably not,' Starmer said. 'When dealing with difficult questions with the EU, you want a really good diplomat who knows how to handle the country's interests. What are you getting? Boris Johnson. His reputation when he was foreign secretary was absolutely awful.'

The interview had taken place after Boris had allegedly fallen out with his girlfriend Carrie Symonds. Then they were pictured together in the countryside, apparently reconciled and they later got married.

'The thing that really gets me about him is this casualness with the truth,' said Starmer, who had spent his life dedicated to proving the truth. 'Even that picture that came up this weekend about him in Sussex. I don't care what he does in his private life, I really don't. But the fact that picture came out—obviously faked and that he couldn't care less that it's out there that it doesn't even matter that its fake. This sort of 'beyond bothering' to care whether you're telling the truth or not. I mean it all started in the referendum with him standing in front of the bus with £350 million on the side. This casualness with the truth... You've got to accept that there's going to be at least a truthful premise for what you're saying. Once you abandon that where are you? In the interview yesterday he was asked twenty-six times when was it taken and he just wouldn't answer the question.'

Despite offering to back Boris's Brexit bill if it included a second referendum and the option of remaining in the EU, Starmer warned that Johnson's deal had a 'trapdoor to no deal' contained within it.

Speaking to BBC One's The Andrew Marr Show, he said: 'We will see what that looks like but it makes sense to say that by whatever means we get that referendum. The spirit of this is clear. We offered this to Theresa May. We said: we don't think your deal is very good but if it's up against the safeguard of being able to remain then we will allow it to proceed in that way.'

He added: 'The position we have adopted is whatever the outcome, whether it's Boris Johnson's bad deal or a better one which could be secured, it has got to go to a referendum up against remain.'

Starmer opposed Johnson's call for a snap general election in 2019 despite having called for an election for the past two years and would vote against it.

'We are not going to be voting with Johnson today,' he told BBC Radio 4's Today programme.

By 2019, though still relatively new to politics, Starmer was beginning to come into the centre of Labour party spotlight and was ready to make his bid for leadership. Starmer carefully kept intact the image of the humble, family man who even as DPP had never enjoyed people calling him director. However, it was clear that Starmer saw Brexit as territory which needed rules and guidelines, and he as the man to write them.

'I feel young in the sense inside only been there five minutes. I was only elected in four-and-a-bit years ago. So you know whatever you've done before you go into politics, however much you think you know, when you get there it's a completely different ball game and you just got to learn the ropes, and the rules—and the rules are all unwritten. So there's a lot of learning to do in that and you do that with the group of people you're elected in with.'

'I was the 2015 intake. But you know what's happened in my four years has been incredible. When I was standing to be the MP for Holborn-St Pancras, Ed Miliband was leader of our party. David Cameron was prime minister. Nick Clegg was deputy prime minister. Barack Obama was president of America and the EU was the eleventh most important subject to people. It wasn't even in the top ten. Somebody shoved about forty years worth of change into my first four years, so I feel young in the sense I'm learning the ropes. I feel old in the sense that so much has happened in that four years wherever you are in politics.'

Starmer presented a more mainstream alternative to 'the party's current brand of unrefined, corduroy-wearing Marxism.' Many criticized his attempt to be the 'more acceptable face of Corbynism.' In the *Daily Telegraph* Hector Birchwood, the Brexit Party candidate for Holborn and St Pancras, called him 'dubious' and 'ruthless.' And while it was easy to see Starmer's more moderate approach to politics as weak or untrue to the party, in the choppy waters of Brexit perhaps what was needed was man firm in his conviction of building bridges rather than parting the Red Sea.

30. Leader of the Opposition

Starmer threw his hat into the ring for Labour leadership in 2019. On 12 December 2019 the deadlock over Brexit was broken when Johnson won a majority of eighty in the general election. The following day Jeremy Corbyn said he would step down as leader of the Labour Party early the following year, following a 'period of reflection.'

In response, Starmer tweeted: 'There is no hiding from the overall result. It is devastating. It will hurt the millions of people who so desperately need a Labour government. They have suffered so much under ten years of Tory austerity and will suffer more because of this result. We must now reflect; but we must also rebuild.'

Though Starmer had often portrayed himself as a man who had never wanted leadership, he certainly had created a solid foundation for a campaign, leading the race.

Starmer announced he was standing for leadership with the same message of community orientation as when he first ran for his seat as MP. Posting a video to social media on 4 January followed by a launch in Stevenage he told the *Sunday Mirror:* 'Over the coming weeks, I'm looking forward to getting back on the campaign trail and talking to people from across the country about how Labour can rebuild and win. Britain desperately needs a Labour government. We need a Labour government that will offer people hope of a better future. However, that is only going to happen if Labour listens to people about what needs to change and how we can restore trust in our party as a force for good.' As always, Starmer was keen for discussion and debate. Eager to prove his worth by pleasing.

Labour's National Executive Committee set out the timetable for the election of the new leader. Nominations from the Parliamentary Labour Party and European Parliamentary Labour Party would open on 7 January and close on 13 January. Between 15 January and 15 February, constituency parties and affiliate organisations could then nominate their preferred candidate. Applications to become a registered supporter opened on 14 January and closed on 16 January.

Voting in the membership ballot opened on 24 February and closed at midday on 2 April. The result of the leadership election would be announced at a special conference on 4 April, but this was scaled-back due to the Coronavirus pandemic.

Throughout the electoral process Starmer came out on top. Immediately, Keir Starmer was odds-on favourite to win the leadership election with Betfair offering 13/8. Rebecca Long-Bailey followed at some distance at 5/1. Angela Rayner and Jess Philips were at 8/1, with Emily Thornberry at 13/1 and Yvette Cooper at 16/1.

He was the fifth Labour MP to announce their candidacy. Both Jess Phillips and Lisa Nandy had launched their campaigns, while Shadow Foreign Secretary Emily Thornberry and Shadow Economics Minister Clive Lewis had already officially declared. Then Shadow Business Secretary Rebecca Long-Bailey, a Jeremy Corbyn ally favoured on the left of the party, announced she would stand in an article for *Tribune* magazine on 6 January.

Candidates had to be nominated by at least ten per cent of the combined membership of the Parliamentary Labour Party and European Parliamentary Labour Party—that is, twenty-two MPs and MEPs at the time. Starmer won the support of enough MPs and MEPs to progress to the next round of nominations on 8 January, when he was also endorsed by the trade union Unison. The following day, Long-Bailey, Nandy and Phillips got the necessary nominations. Lewis only got five nominations, including his own, and withdrew. Some of his supporters switched to Thornberry getting her across the line with ten minutes to go.

Starmer was way ahead of the field with eighty-eight nominations. Long-Bailey had thirty-three and Nandy thirty-one, while Phillips and Thornberry both had twenty-three.

The next hurdle was to win at least five per cent of the Constituency Labour Parties—that is, thirty-three of them—or at least three party affiliates that consist of at least five per cent of affiliate members including at least two trades unions. Starmer led the pack there too, leading the nominations from the Constituency Labour Parties and winning the support of the Union of Shop, Distributive and Allied Workers. He qualified for the ballot on 20 January. Phillips pulled out the following day, saying she could not unite the party. Nandy crossed the line on 22 January with the support of the GMB, the National Union of Mineworkers unions and the Jewish Labour Movement. Long-Bailey also qualified with trade union support, notably the backing of Unite the Union whose general secretary Len McCluskey said she had the 'brains and brilliance' to take on Boris Johnson. She won this endorsement even though Nandy was a member of Unite the Union. Thornberry failed to rally enough support by the 15 February deadline and was eliminated.

Starmer, with his history as the DPP, and his appearance as a straight, white middle-aged man with the perfect nuclear family in Holborn and St Pancras, barely even needed the media to render him as the moderate candidate. This was especially the case in comparison to his competitors, who made even young Starmer seem like a 'centrist.'

Starmer, Long-Bailey and Nandy went forward to the hustings with debates being held at eleven places around Great Britain, one of which had to be postponed when Starmer's mother-in-law died. He missed two others while she was critically ill and had to cancel a number of campaign events, though it made little difference.

Like Starmer, Long-Bailey wanted to take energy, water, rail and mail back into public ownership. However, she also wanted to abolish the House of Lords and stir up a democratic revolution to break the hold Westminster and the City had over British politics. She then aimed to spark a Green Industrial Revolution to unite Labour's heartlands while advocating a universal basic income for all people in the UK regardless of wealth. She also gave Corbyn 'ten out of ten' as a politician, even though many party members held him responsible for the devastating defeat in the 2019 election.

Nandy accused the Blair and Brown governments of continuing the 'consensus that Thatcher built', saying that New Labour was 'as tight as the Tories'. One issue she took head-on was anti-Semitism, acknowledging in the *Jewish Chronicle* that Labour had lost the trust of the British Jewish community.

But while Starmer's competition would have him thought of as a 'c**trist,' the truth was that Starmer was neither Blairite or Corbynite.

He was still committed to furthering some of Corbyn's more radical goals but he was also capable of walking the middle line in order to ensure party unity.

When asked who was the Labour leader he most admired over the last fifty years Starmer picked Harold Wilson, 'because he got the party to unite behind him.' Starmer also procured support from individuals left right and centre. He was endorsed by former prime minister Gordon Brown, Lord Adonis, Doreen, Baroness Lawrence, mayor of London Sadiq Khan and the London *Evening Standard.* But the truth was that while party unity was an admirable goal, diplomacy tends not to light fires in the hearts of voters

Even in his most radical days Starmer had refused to be pulled along in the leftist tide; he made up his mind for himself, building a campaign based on anti-austerity and party unity. 'Our party has moved to a more radical position in the last few years. And we were right to do it,' he said. 'We are now the party of anti-austerity and rightly so. We're not going back.

'We're the party of common ownership, of investing in our public services, and we're not going back.

'We're the party that believes something cannot be good for the economy but bad for the environment. So there's no going back.

'And we're the party that welcomes everybody wherever they come from, including all migrants. And we're never going back.'

Labour's policy of scrapping tuition fees would continue, along with the renationalisation of the railways, Royal Mail, water companies and the energy companies. The outsourcing in the NHS, local government and the justice system had to stop.

Starmer supported former shadow Chancellor John McDonnell's policy to raise taxes on the top five per cent of earners with incomes of more than £80,000.

And as always Starmer was capable of rethinking his decisions, reflecting and changing his mind. This was the case with his earlier position on immigration—where previously he had opposed Corbyn he now argued that the party should propose the reintroduction of free movement within the European Union.

But the most jarring change in Starmer's political stance is also perhaps the one that may have appealed the most to Conservative voters and anger the most supporters of Labour. Though Starmer had pushed for a second Brexit referendum and been a staunch supporter of remain and the need for a carefully crafted Brexit deal he now sees the Brexit debate as a thing of yester-year. 'Leave-Remain is over,' *Politico* quotes a senior aide. 'We're out, no chance of us going back in so we've got to focus on what the future looks like.'

Though this may seem too many like Starmer selling-out, it falls into a familiar pattern of presenting a conciliatory stance until he's mastered the rules of the game. As a lawyer he wanted solutions tied up with neat strings, which was impossible while arguments were still raging across the country around family dinner tables. His attempt to move on from the debate in the hopes of unity was not quite true to British citizens who felt the divisions caused by Brexit too deeply to begin letting them scab.

Quite predictably Keir Starmer won the leadership election. He beat out Long-Bailey and Nandy handily, collecting 56.2 percent of the vote. Though he would go on to incorporate Long-Bailey and Nandy into his shadow cabinet Starmer did not hesitate to reenforce the idea that Labour was rebuilding anew. 'First and foremost, the public need to see that Labour is changing and that's what we're trying to demonstrate,' said one senior Starmer aide. 'But people also need to understand that Labour is trying to build people's trust again. There's no point having a policy if people don't trust you to implement it—or believe that you're ever going to be in power to do it.'

The hard part certainly was not over though, no one had predicted what 2020 would hold.

On 12 March 2020 Prime Minister Boris Johnson made a statement regarding Coronavirus. While the new Brexit deal had been the main headline throughout the end of 2019 Corona was now at the forefront of everybody's mind: 'I've got to be clear,' said Johnson, 'we've all got to be clear, that this is the worst public health crisis for a generation.'

Although a terrible hit for not just Britain but the world, Coronavirus fed well into Starmer's campaign for unity. In his acceptance speech, Keir Starmer immediately addressed the issue of the moment—'a moment like none other in our lifetime'. Starmer appealed to a sentiment which had become quite strong throughout his political career, the individual relationships within communities: 'Coronavirus has brought normal life to a halt. Our cities, our towns and our villages are silent, our roads deserted. Public life has all but come to a standstill and we're missing each other,' he said. 'People are frightened by the strangeness, anxious about what will happen next. And we have to remember that every number is a family shaken to its foundation.

'Unable even to carry out the most poignant of ceremonies, a funeral, in the way that they would like. It reminds us of how precious life is, but also how fragile. It reminds us of what really matters, our family, our friends, our relationships. The love we have for one another. Our health.

'Our connections with those that we don't know. A greeting from a stranger, a kind word from a neighbour. These make up society. They remind us that we share our lives together. We have to trust one another and look after one another. And I can see this happening, people coming together to help the isolated and the vulnerable, checking on their neighbours.'

Coronavirus also acted as a moment to reach across the aisle. Though Starmer assured Labour voters that he would not be selling out or succumbing to Tory pressure in the long-term, he did advocate for a conciliatory approach to solving the crisis. 'It's a huge responsibility and whether we voted for this government or not, we all rely on it to get this right. That's why in the national interest the Labour Party will play its full part. Under my leadership we will engage constructively with the government, not opposition for opposition's sake. Not scoring party political points or making impossible demands, but with the courage to support where that's the right thing to do.'

'That is not the only task for the Labour Party. The weeks ahead are going to be really difficult. I fear there are going to be some awful moments for many of us. But we will get through this. The curve will flatten, the wards will empty, the immediate threat will subside. And we have scientists working on vaccines.'

Starmer positioned himself as the perfect man for creating links between Labour and Tory parties, highlighting that working on the

Brexit deal he quite frequently had to work with MPs from the other side. 'I tend to get on with people across the House because I don't have that sort of tribal stuff so much as other people do,' he said. 'Quite frankly in the last two to three years we've had to work across the House to get any of the victories we had on Brexit. Dominic Greave was attorney general when I was director of public prosecutions, so I actually worked with Dominic in that capacity before I got to the House of Commons. So the whole meaningful vote thing was something he and I worked very hard on together.'

Yet, even when reaching out to shake hands with the opposition Starmer did not fail to take an opportunity to further his image in contrast to Johnson.

Advocating on behalf of the NHS became a key part of Starmer's first year in office. The NHS had been a cause close to Starmer's heart since he was a child, as his mother was a nurse before she fell ill. His support of Andy Burnham in the 2015 Labour leadership election demonstrated a profound care for the national healthcare system. The connection between Coronavirus and the NHS gave Starmer a chance to highlight the part of himself that had fought on the side of unions and workers as a young lawyer. 'When we get through this it'll be because of our NHS staff, our care workers, our ambulance drivers, our emergency services, our cleaners, our porters. It will be because of the hard work and bravery of every key worker as they took on this virus and kept our country going. For too long they've been taken for granted and poorly paid. They were last and now they should be first. In their courage and their sacrifice and their bravery, we can see a better future.

In 2021 Starmer drew lines in the sand when it came to Johnson's threat of NHS pay-cuts. Starmer tore Johnson apart for 'breaking promise after promise' after he said a 1% boost for NHS staff was all he could afford. Headlines in the *Daily Mirror* read 'Keir Starmer savages Boris Johnson over NHS 'pay cut' as nurses '841 pounds a year' worse off". It of course helped that the NHS held a certain national reverence, only by Coronavirus and campaigns to 'clap for the NHS'. Going to town on Boris Johnson over paycuts did minimal harm in terms of rebuilding national unity and gaining back the 'red wall'.

Starmer appealed to national unity while acknowledging that the virus would hit different communities differently, perhaps a fact he witnessed in his own constituency of Holborn and St Pancras in which a variety of demographics with drastically different socio-economic backgrounds resided. 'We should know what that exit strategy is, when the restrictions might be lifted and what the plan is for economic recovery to protect those who have been hardest hit.' Pushing for the UK to build vaccination centres in towns and cities across the country Starmer said 'the minute a vaccine becomes available, we can begin to *protect the entire population.'*

It helped that it didn't take too much political leadership experience to unite people against an inhuman villain. It was easy to hate Corona.

Starmer knew COVID was a time for him to prove his leadership qualities. As a lawyer Starmer fell into the trap of thinking that the best way to prove he could lead was to find a solution to the case; more than that though he had to show that he was the only one who could.

And so Starmer immediately brought Boris Johnson's government to task over their handling of the pandemic, declaring that Johnson had 'lost control.' And indeed, it did appear that Jonson's government had lost control in many respects. At the beginning of the pandemic Johnson said that he was shaking hands with COVID-19 patients and not to long after he found himself in emergency care after contracting the virus himself. And then during the pandemic there was confusion over lockdown rules in different parts of the country and there were successive U-turns on a number of government policies, from policies concerning A-Level grades to free school meals.

Prime Minister Material?

Starmer's 'forensic' analysis of Johnson's government's various open weaknesses was perceived to be effective during the successive Prime Minister's Questions. Where Johnson had allowed the promise of 'herd immunity' to plunge the UK into mayhem, Starmer followed all the proper procedure. He self-isolated three times over the past year, updating Twitter to confirm to the public that he had no symptoms. He followed stay at home orders, and received his Corona jab alongside the rest of his age group. His clarity and concision attempted to establish some type of certainty in the face of the public's anxiety over 'what will happen next.'

However, Starmer's 'forensic' nature did not lead to the Labour Party's increased popularity with the British public. The Conservative party rarely polled below the Labour party throughout the pandemic, and this may be because whilst Starmer's analysis was 'forensic' and perceptive his personality was still not deemed dynamic enough to be taken seriously as a Leader of the Opposition. The result of the May 2021 Hartlepool by-election was disastrous and so was his misshuffle of Angela Rayner in his Shadow Cabinet. There were only gains in the South-England Tory belt.

Starmer's measured approach to Coronavirus might have been what was needed to find a solution, but it did not seem to be the key to sparking the fire in the Labour party. While Corona was certainly the issue of the moment, when case counts began to fall it would not be the great universalizing force Starmer was banking on. The government's decision to apply the vaccine stock to giving as many in the population a single jab—instead of two per person spread over several weeks—as quickly as possible before the May 2021 local elections and Hartlepool by-election was to dramatically change the picture in Johnson's favour. Rather, other big-picture issues regarding regional disparities in socio-economic prosperity, and the big 'isms' of race and sex were key to creating the force Labour needed.

Starmer was falling short when it came to securing that public appeal. In fact, many in the press and social media started calling 23-year-old footballer Marcus Rashford the Leader of the Opposition, because through energetic campaigning—that later won him an MBE—Rashford was able to force the government to reverse their free school meal policy in days. If not for him, the government would likely not have extended their free school meal voucher scheme, which provided children from poorer families with free meals, into the summer of 2020. Starmer, in contrast, struggled to become popular in the eyes of the general public and indeed amongst members of his own Party.

Starmer's habits of compromise and conciliation also lost him support within the party, who found it hard to rally around his more centrist policies. For instance, he asked Labour MPs to abstain voting on the controversial 'spy cops' bill, or the Covert Human Intelligence Source bill, which allowed for police officers to undertake criminal actions whilst undercover. Despite the fact that, when he was DPP, Starmer had critiqued the activities of spy cop Mark Kennedy, who was alleged to have committed criminal offences and entered sexual relationships with several women who did not know he was an undercover police officer, Starmer argued that the 'spy cops' bill at least had 'a clear requirement that says nothing can be authorised if it conflicts with or breaches the Human Rights Act.'

But this did not stop fury from those on the Labour left, including former leader Jeremy Corbyn who seemed to invoked the memory of the Mark Kennedy scandal when he pointed out that this proposed 'spy cops' bill would provide no protection to women duped into sexual relations with undercover officers. As Corbyn said in the House of Commons, 'Does this bill protect women from that in the future? I think we all know the answer to that.'

Baroness Shami Chakrabarti also condemned the bill, arguing that 'Blanket licence for crime without limit, is completely alien to equality before the law.' And Shadow Treasury minister Dan Carden resigned, stating in his resignation letter to Starmer that:

'You will understand that as a Liverpool MP and trade unionist, I share the deep concerns about this legislation from across the labour movement, human rights organisations, and so many who have suffered the abuse of state power, from blacklisted workers to the Hillsborough families and survivors.'

Indeed, when it came time to vote on the bill, 18 Labour MPs defied Starmer and voted against it, including young MPs Zarah Sultana and

Nadia Whittome, as well as veteran MP Diane Abbott who has since suggested that Starmer is a 'suspicious' opportunist, who does not have strong political convictions but acts in whatever way will make him look good.

Especially in the face of Corona where it was difficult to feel in control, the idea of abstaining as opposed to taking action against an enemy you can see had minimal appeal.

In some ways dealing with Coronavirus offered a distraction from Starmer's role in the Brexit negotiation, acting as the perfect vehicle to push forward a plan of national unity. But in other ways his plan for unity in the party did not see the success that he hoped. Although he had incorporated both Nandy and Long-Bailey into his shadow cabinet his firing of Long-Bailey in June 2020 stoked controversy, with many accusing him of purging progressives from the party.

The situation arose when Long-Bailey retweeted an article including the insinuation that police tactics used on the Black Lives Matter protestors in the United Stated were being taught by Israelite soldiers. In response Starmer said: 'The article Rebecca shared earlier today contained an antisemitic conspiracy theory…Antisemitism takes many different forms and it is important that we are all vigilant against it.'

Perhaps this was Starmer's attempt at learning the new rules of the political game which involve letting your emotions and morals shine through. However, if so, it was a read on the rules of a man still learning and many felt that this sacking was unfair. Long-Bailey hadn't meant to endorse every aspect of the article. John McDonnell, who was a member of the shadow cabinet under Corbyn tweeted: 'Throughout discussion of antisemitism it's always been said criticism of practices of Israeli state is not antisemitic. I don't believe therefore that this article is or @RLong_Bailey should've been sacked. I stand in solidarity with her.'

But others applauded Starmer's decisive action and commitment to the goal of eradicating anti-Semitism outlined in his campaign plans. A letter published in the *Guardian* written by Matthew Franks reads, 'In common, I suspect, with other Jews, I was both pleased to see Keir Starmer take swift action after Rebecca Long-Bailey failed to disclaim the antisemitic conspiracy theory she had appeared to condone, and discomfited to see Jewish people thrust carelessly into the public spotlight once again.'

The fight against anti-Semitism was one of Starmer's ways of breaking his cultivated exterior and showing the public his heart. Eradicating anti-Semitism had been a part of Starmer's campaign from the beginning. While historically Starmer had tended to be a man who made decisions based around clear rules and not emotions or morality, in this case the campaign was heavily driven by familial motivations.

Starmer's wife Victoria was Jewish and both of their children had been brought up in the faith. After losing his mother and father in the past five years, while at the same time building his own family it's clear that familial tradition and the connection it created had a strong place in Starmer's heart. Starmer said he cherishes his Friday nights 'which we actually do as a family.'

'It's about being a bit more disciplined, about being home with our children and the family—they are growing up fast…When you're an MP or running to be leader of the Labour Party there is a heavy pull on your diary all of the time and it's the easiest thing in the world just to fill it all up.'

The family-man that began burgeoning in Starmer in 2015 materialised in his commitment to his family's history. Victoria's father is a Polish immigrant of Jewish heritage: 'It's very important that [my children] understand the history of their granddad.' In an interview with the *New Statesman* Starmer argues that although many may say he hasn't done enough to fight anti-Semitism in the party there were large rows in the shadow cabinet that though public didn't see mean something to those that were there.

Starmer, the young QC and DPP, argued hardily for the separation of morality and law, highly intellectualized and placing the rational of the law above that of emotions. Though perhaps in some ways seemingly less fierce, there was something appealing about this family-oriented man coming back down to the ground.

It was clear that there was still a lot of work to do on anti-Semitism in the party. While Starmer's moves were well-meaning they often came across as awkward. Labour's anti-Semitism scandal rocked the nation throughout Jeremy Corbyn's leadership of the party, from 2015-2020. Under Corbyn's leadership the Labour Party became the second national political party, after the avowedly racist British National Party, to be investigated for racism by the Equality and Human Rights Commission. Indeed, in 2018 it was reported that nearly 40 per cent of British Jews would 'seriously consider' leaving Britain if Corbyn became Prime Minister.

In October 2020 the Equality and Human Rights Commission published their report which concluded that there were 'serious failings in leadership and an inadequate process for handling antisemitism complaints across the Labour Party' and that there were 'unlawful acts of harassment and discrimination for which the Labour Party is responsible'.

To show his commitment to the cause Starmer's Labour Party also suspended Corbyn from the Party in October 2020, in a move that some described as a strong disavowal of anti-Semitism and others described as a move to attenuate the political power of the former Labour leader. Although Corbyn has been a member of the Labour Party since he was 16, he was suspended, at the age of 71, after releasing a response to the Equality and Human Rights Committee's report in which he claimed that 'the scale of the problem [with anti-Semitism] was also dramatically overstated for political reasons by our opponents inside and outside the party, as well as by much of the media.'

Starmer said that he was 'disappointed' with this response and after Corbyn later confirmed to a reporter that he believed that complaints of anti-Semitism within the Labour Party were 'exaggerated' Corbyn was expelled from the Labour Party, with Labour Party stating that: 'In light of his comments made today and his failure to retract them subsequently, the Labour Party has suspended Jeremy Corbyn pending investigation.'

Starmer advised that while he was not directly behind the decision to suspend Corbyn, Labour general secretary David Evans was, he did support it. Corbyn was later reinstated in the Labour Party in November 2020. However, despite this effort to stamp out anti-Semitism within the Party, there were still concerns about anti-Semitism within the Labour Party and it remained to be seen how Starmer would regain the support of Jewish and other minority communities in Britain. Starmer was still finding his sea-legs when it came to addressing the many 'isms' easily caught in the attention of the media.

However, while Starmer's commitment to the traditions of his family may resonate with older voters, younger voters were certainly frustrated by what they saw as an attack on progressive Labour politics. In contrast, to Jeremy Corbyn Starmer had not been as successful in appealing to young people. Corbyn's team shrewdly utilised social media to appeal to those under 25. Colourful videos and infographics easily shareable online helped to create a larger audience. The protest-culture of Corbynism had a neat appeal to young Marxists reading the *Communist Manifesto* in their Introduction to Politics classes for the first time.

The new generation which lived their political lives on Twitter and Instagram wanted full access to politicians at all times in the name of 'authenticity.' The desire for insider understanding of representatives did not fit with Starmer's protection of his private life. Although Starmer allowed for his family traditions to be slowly brought into the spotlight he still refused to name his children in the media, keeping them out of press releases and pictures.

As well, quite significantly, Starmer seemed to misstep on the issues close to the hearts of young people. Not insignificantly Starmer's dismissal of Long-Bailey came on the back of quite dismissive comments regarding the Black Lives Matter protests. The Labour leader called the movement a 'moment' to the chagrin of many, especially young people, and made what were deemed dismissive comments regarding the defunding of the police. 'Nobody should be saying anything about defunding the police. I was director of public prosecutions for five years. My support for the police is very, very strong, and evidenced in the joint actions I've done with the police,' Starmer told BBC Breakfast.

Whilst the Labour Party's response to the Black Lives Matter protests was generally perceived better by Black communities than the Conservative Party's—due to, inter alia, Priti Patel condemning protestors and Dominic Raab mocking those taking the knee in solidarity with the deceased—some Labour members took issue with Keir Starmer describing Black Lives Matter as a 'moment', an odd Freudian slip for a man who as a young barrister instinctively stood up for the tiniest of minorities. Some felt that comment minimised the importance of Black Lives Matter movement—a movement set up in 2013—with Florence Eshalomi tweeting in response to Starmer's statement that:

'For the year 12 students I spoke to last Friday at Lilian Baylis School, where a number of the boys (and one girl) mentioned they had been stopped and searched, Black Lives Matter isn't a moment. '[The] choice of words in the interview was wrong. I will continue to relay constituents' views to Keir.'

It seemed almost ironic that Starmer was losing supporters over a debate to curb police powers when for many years Starmer was the young idealistic socialist taking the police to task over abuse and misconduct. Perhaps that was why young people felt a connection to him despite their dislike. Underlying it all was a fear that they were like him. That they were only radical because they were young. That when the practicalities of true legislation come their way they would be forced to relinquish their anti-government articles in student magazines in exchange for a suit, tie and close-cropped hair cut from the barber around the corner from Ed Miliband's house.

Classically, when Starmer saw the response to his comments he readily admitted he was in the wrong. He later expressed regrets for this statement and, to be fair, the Labour Party has seen continued support from the vast majority of black people in Britain. Whilst the Runnymede Trust indicates that increasing numbers of black people vote Conservative the reality was that when black people vote they were more likely to vote Labour than Conservative. This was likely because many within Labour Party often advocate for anti-racism, including Keir Starmer who had, for example, supported campaigns to increase Black British representation in the National Curriculum, a campaign that, polls indicated, most Black British people would get on board with. In a statement released during Black History Month in 2020 Starmer said that: 'Black British history should be taught all year round, as part of a truly diverse school curriculum that includes and inspires all young people and aids a full understanding of the struggle for equality. While some schools are already doing this, the government should ensure all students benefit from a diverse curriculum.'

But while some may applaud his lack of defensiveness and ability to admit he was wrong, the comment also indicated that Starmer was 'reacting' more than he was 'acting.' He was still learning the ropes of appealing to a wide public in Britain rather than laser-beam a single issue as a lawyer might.

Moreover, Starmer's outward professional and polished appearance made it difficult to feel connected to the motives stirring beneath the surface. On some level, it was understandable that Abbott found Starmer suspicious, especially because of the indefinite delay of the Forde inquiry, an inquiry into Labour's handling of anti-Semitism complaints. The inquiry was reported to include discussion of anti-black racism within the party, and how some Labour members allegedly expressed racist sentiment towards black Labour MPs, including Diane Abbott. Nine black Labour MPs, including Abbott, wrote a statement lamenting this delay in early 2021, stressing that:

'Delaying the Forde inquiry and failing to provide a future date by which its findings will be published risks further doubling down on the impression that the party does not take issues of anti-black racism seriously. The abuse contained within the report and the issues it seeks to address are incredibly serious and must be part of our attempts to ensure the Labour party is an inclusive and tolerant place. The fact that members who contributed to anti-black racism have been readmitted to the party is a cause of concern and this delay only adds to the anxiety.'

Though no longer the young radical living in a ramshackle flat in North London, Starmer was also no longer the career-only, no-nonsense DPP, so intensely focused on proving himself incapable of making mistakes. Instead, he was attempting to find a middle-ground. Uniting not only the party but two sides of himself. The analytic, fact-driven DPP capable of constructing a bullet-point plan that will get the nation out of Corona. And the voracious young man willing to make public bold claims against the government without the fear of displeasing people.

Now in his fifties Starmer faced controversies, has had to renege on promises, and apologise for misassumptions. He watched his children grow and lost both his parents. If anything, Starmer can see multiple sides to every issue because he has lived those opinions himself. But despite his legal training and experience navigating the nitty-gritty details of practically applying laws he had work to do on becoming a big-picture thinker. For instance, getting stuck on his commitment to the police rather than understanding that it is an 'ism' like 'racism' that created a sense of unity. And it seemed that whilst Starmer has the unenviable task of trying to repair the reputation of the Labour Party, and win back the many voters that Corbyn lost, he was still very much a man finding his feet. It was not clear whether the man who throughout his life used to move in a close-knitted football formation, spending five hours on his constituency surgery of two hours, was also as good as Harold Wilson at herding cats in Parliament.

Index